At the Syntax–Pragmatics

Oxford Studies in Theoretical Linguistics

This series provides a new forum for cutting-edge work in theoretical linguistics. Its focus will be on the interfaces between the subcomponents of grammar and between grammar and other components of the mind. The books will be accessible at postgraduate level, and will be published simultaneously in hardback and paperback editions.

At the Syntax–Pragmatics Interface

Verbal Underspecification and Concept Formation in Dynamic Syntax

LUTZ MARTEN

OXFORD

UNIVERSITY PRESS

OXFORD

UNIVERSITY PRESS

Great Clarendon Street, Oxford OX2 6DP

Oxford University Press is a department of the University of Oxford.
It furthers the University's objective of excellence in research, scholarship,
and education by publishing worldwide in

Oxford New York

Auckland Bangkok Buenos Aires Cape Town Chennai
Dar es Salaam Delhi Hong Kong Istanbul Karachi Kolkata
Kuala Lumpur Madrid Melbourne Mexico City Mumbai Nairobi
São Paulo Shanghai Taipei Tokyo Toronto

Oxford is a registered trade mark of Oxford University Press
in the UK and in certain other countries

Published in the United States
by Oxford University Press Inc., New York

British Library Cataloguing in Publication Data

Data available

Library of Congress Cataloging-in-Publication Data
Marten, Lutz.
At the syntax-pragmatics interface: verbal underspecification and concept formation in
dynamic syntax / Lutz Marten.
p.   cm. — (Oxford studies in theoretical linguistics)
Includes bibliographical references and index.
1. Grammar, Comparative and general—Verb phrase. 2. Grammar, Comparative and
general—Syntax. 3. Pragmatics. 4. Semantics. I. Title. II. Series.
P281 .M268 2002
415—dc21   2002074273
ISBN 0-19-925063-4
0-19-925064-2 (pbk.)

1 3 5 7 9 10 8 6 4 2

Typeset in A Garamond
by SNP Best-set Typesetter Ltd., Hong Kong
Printed in Great Britain
on acid-free paper by
T.J. International Ltd. Padstow, Cornwall

Contents

Oxford Studies in Theoretical Linguistics

General Preface

The theoretical focus of this series is on the interfaces between subcomponents of the human grammatical system and the closely related area of the interfaces between the different subdisciplines of linguistics. The notion of 'interface' has become central in grammatical theory (for instance, in Chomsky's recent Minimalist Program) and in linguistic practice: work on the interfaces between syntax and semantics, syntax and morphology, phonology and phonetics, etc. has led to a deeper understanding of particular linguistic phenomena and of the architecture of the linguistic component of the mind/brain.

The series will cover interfaces between core components of grammar, including syntax/morphology, syntax/semantics, syntax/phonology, syntax/pragmatics, morphology/phonology, phonology/phonetics, phonetics/speech processing, semantics/pragmatics, intonation/discourse structure as well as issues in the way that the systems of grammar involving these interface areas are acquired and deployed in use (including language acquisition, language dysfunction, and language processing). It will demonstrate, we hope, that proper understandings of particular linguistic phenomena, languages, language groups, or inter-language variations all require reference to interfaces.

The series is open to work by linguists of all theoretical persuasions and schools of thought. A main requirement is that authors should write so as to be understood by colleagues in related subfields of linguistics and by scholars in cognate disciplines.

We are pleased to present the fourth volume in the the series. Lutz Marten examines the relationship between language rules and linguistic behaviour so as to distinguish between language-specific syntactic knowledge and the general reasoning people need in order to understand and to make themselves understood.

David Adger
Hagit Borer

Preface

This study is concerned with the relation between verbs and their complements, and the interpretation of verb phrases in context, and addresses questions such as: Which elements in the verb phrase are licensed by the verb, and how? What is the difference, if any, between optional and obligatory elements of the verb phrase? What are the respective contributions of lexical, syntactic, and pragmatic knowledge in the construction and interpretation of verb phrases? It approaches these questions from the perspective of the hearer, who is faced with the task of ascribing a specific communicative intent to the speaker on the basis of a linear string of words, and is embedded in the overall research programme of Dynamic Syntax on the one hand and relevance theory on the other. Two key notions explored in this book are syntactic underspecification and conceptual enrichment, since it is argued that verbal subcategorization is thoroughly underspecified, and that it is thus only with recourse to pragmatic processes such as enrichment that verb phrases, including their predicate–argument structure, are established in context. In other words, the study provides an essentially pragmatic analysis of a phenomenon which is more commonly thought of in syntactic or semantic terms.

The book is a development of my 1999 University of London doctoral dissertation, and I would like first and foremost to thank my thesis supervisor, Ruth Kempson, for her support, encouragement, and guidance throughout my graduate study and beyond. Both the thesis and the book were written at the School of Oriental and African Studies in London, and I am happy to record my gratitude to my teachers, colleagues, and friends here, in particular in the Linguistics Department. For comments on earlier versions and aspects of the material presented here, I wish to thank Ronnie Cann, Robyn Carston, David Adger, Thea Bynon, Antony Hunter, Nancy Chongo Kula, Wilfried Meyer-Viol, Victoria Rebori, Thilo Schadeberg, David Swinburne, and audiences in London, Leiden, and Lomé, as well as the students in my Advanced Syntax class in the spring of 2001.

Parts of the research reported here have in various ways been supported by grants from SOAS, the University of London, and the German Academic Exchange Service (DAAD). In 2000, I had the fortune to be appointed a Millennium Research Fellow at the School of Oriental and African Studies, which gave me the time and space to prepare the present version of the material. I would like to express my gratitude for this institutional and financial support.

The study originated partly from my interest in the Swahili language, in particular (at the time) applicative constructions in that language. I wish to thank everybody who shared this interest with me and helped me to better understand both language and culture, in particular Sauda Barwani, Ridder Samsom, Abdulla Othman Ahmed and his family, Lewis Lukindo, Haroub Nassor Hamoud, and Donovan McGrath, as well as the Taasisi ya Kiswahili, Zanzibar.

L.M.

School of Oriental and African Studies, London
July 2001

In memory of my grandmother Erna Dalkowski (1905–1998)

I

Introduction

I.I OVERVIEW

This study is concerned with aspects of the syntax, semantics, and pragmatics of the verb phrase. It shows how verbal subcategorization systematically under-specifies its associated syntactic information and how verb phrase interpretation is built on-line, with the aid of pragmatic processes of enrichment, in particular processes of ad hoc concept formation. The central empirical question investigated is how nominal constituents of the verb phrase, taken here to include noun phrases and prepositional phrases, are licensed and interpreted, and how they interact with information provided by the verb. The discussion thus turns around the question of verbal subcategorization, optional and ob-ligatory constituents, the argument–adjunct distinction, and the function of prepositions, as illustrated in the following examples:

(1a)   Fran was baking a cake for Mary in the oven.

(1b)   Sally put the flowers on the table with a vengeance.

(1c)   The McDonalds live with their two cats in a house by the seaside.

What all these examples have in common is that the verb is combined with more constituents than seem to be required in syntactic terms. The sentences also show that although prepositional phrases (PPs) are usually optional, some PPs are required by the verb's subcategorization information, e.g. *on the table* in (1b). The analysis of sentences like those in (1) is the main topic of this work.

The theoretical perspective adopted combines Dynamic Syntax (DS, Kempson et al. 2001) with relevance theory (Sperber and Wilson 1995). Dynamic Syntax is a formal model of natural language syntax which provides an explicit characterization of the process by which hearers access words in the order in which they appear in the utterance and use the information provided to build structured semantic representations in a step-by-step fashion. This dynamic perspective on structure building places restrictions on the analysis of how verbs and their complements combine, since the process has to be modelled as proceeding strictly incrementally, as well as in a goal-driven fashion, guided by the overall requirement that hearers establish propositional structures to derive inferential effects from the words encountered. A range of syntactic facts show that, from this perspective, verbal subcategorization information is systematically underspecified, and that the establishment of predicate–argument structure is part of the overall task of the hearer to assign an interpretation to the incoming utterance. This analysis of adjunction has consequences for the characterization of the syntax–pragmatics interface which, since syntactic structures are built only with recourse to pragmatic reasoning, cannot be structurally defined as a syntactic output level. Rather, the argument presented here shows that pragmatic processes of enrichment, which enable hearers to construct occasion specific conceptual representations, play a central role not only in the interpretation of natural language verbs but also, as part of the interpretation process, in the establishment of the syntactic structure of verb phrases.

The overall aim of this study is thus threefold. It offers a new approach to verbal subcategorization and the status of arguments and adjuncts from the perspective of a dynamic, hearer-based syntactic model, incorporating notions of syntactic underspecification. Secondly, it develops an analysis of verb phrase adjunction in Dynamic Syntax. Thirdly, it shows that the analysis entails a redrawing of the syntax–pragmatics interface, since the interplay of lexical verbal information, syntactic structure, and pragmatic processes of concept formation conspire to produce the interpretation of verb–complement arrays in context.

1.2 VERBAL SUBCATEGORIZATION, ARGUMENTS, AND ADJUNCTS

As a somewhat idealized historical starting point of the study of lexical verbal information and subcategorization, we can take the lexical entry in (2):

(2)   *murder*, transitive

The lexical information associated with the verb in (2) is that it is a transitive verb, which means that it combines with a (nominative) subject and an (accusative) object to form a clause. In more modern linguistics, within both generative and formal approaches, verbal subcategorization is traditionally analysed in a more fine-grained fashion by identifying the arguments of the verb, for example with the aid of variables:

(3)   *murder* (x, y)

The information in (3) identifies *murder* as taking exactly two arguments, to form, for example, a sentence like (4), where *Donald* and *Roger Ackroyd* fill the two argument slots indicated by 'x' and 'y':

(4)   Donald murdered Roger Ackroyd.

The entry in (3) not only identifies two nominal expressions as the arguments of the verb, but also implies that any nominal expression found with the predicate other than the subject and object, such as *out of jealousy*, *in his garden*, and *at noon* in (5), are not arguments of the verb:

(5)   Donald murdered Roger Ackroyd out of jealousy in his garden at noon.

The static, fully specified subcategorization information in (3) thus entails a strict division between arguments, those elements identified by the lexical information of the verb, and non-arguments or adjuncts, i.e. those elements which are not so identified. The aim of the present study is to improve on this format of lexical representation of argument structure, not in detail, with respect to individual constructions or verbs, but in general, reflecting the very general character of adjunction and valency variation. The lexical entries which will be introduced in Chapter 4 are underspecified, so that a given predicate may occur with any number of arguments, in addition to the fully specified, obligatory ones. The verb *murder* in (5), for example, can from this perspective be regarded as quinary, that is, as having five arguments. After the formal nature of such underspecification has been established, the major part of this investigation is devoted to understanding why natural language should have such widespread underspecification at a central place in the grammar, namely predicate–argument relations. Note the contrast to formal languages, where a given predicate has a particular arity, and if there are too many or too few nominal expressions, the whole expression is ill-formed. The answer, I propose, is that underspecified predicates are an extremely useful tool for expressing infinite occasion-specific meanings with finite resources.[1] The resolution of underspecified verbs is consequently analysed at the pragmatic level; in particular, it is aligned with other cognitive processes of ad hoc concept formation such as metaphor which are subject to considerations of relevance. The direction of explanation taken here is thus from discourse via syntax to the lexicon, in reverse to the more customary order from conceptual-semantic structure via lexical structure to syntax, as is the direction taken in, for example, Grimshaw's (1990) approach to argument structure.

The view that lexical subcategorization is static and strict underlies the majority of linguistic work on verbal lexical information. However, several variants and improvements of the general format of the lexical entry in (3) have been proposed in the literature, including thematic and aspectual roles to identify different arguments, the identification of specific (e.g. the external), and the order of all arguments. More relevant to the present discussion are proposals which, like the view explored here, blur the strict division between arguments and adjuncts. This idea has been discussed, but never, as far as I am aware, as a general theory of VP adjuncts, being instead always restricted to a particular application. McConnell-Ginet (1982), for example, introduces a category Ad-Verb, intermediate between arguments and adverbs, to account for the fact that some predicates subcategorize for adverbs, and that those adverbs function more as arguments than as modifiers of the predicate:

(6)   Liz resides in Kalamazoo.

(7)   Sophie behaved badly in court.

The verbs *reside* and *behave* subcategorize, according to McConnell-Ginet, for an adverbial phrase, *in Kalamazoo* in (6) and *badly* in (7).[2] From examples like these, McConnell-Ginet develops a notion of natural augmentation, which allows predicates to take non-arguments as arguments, thus weakening the argument–adjunct distinction, since now lexical subcategorization information can be overridden, subject to semantic parameters. I will argue below (in Chapter 5) that semantic parameters are not useful for the resolution of underspecified subcategorization, and in this context discuss McConnell-Ginet's proposal in more detail. The idea that some nominal expressions are Ad-Verbs is, however, a clear predecessor to the argument developed here.

---

[1] Verbal underspecification is in this respect similar to other forms of underspecification; cf. Kempson et al. (2001).

[2] The status of *in court* is less clear from McConnell-Ginet's perspective—within the present study, it is analysed as an optionally introduced argument.

McConnell-Ginet's notion of augmented predicates has been extended to the analysis of purpose clauses by Chierchia (1989). Chierchia argues that the Control properties in purpose clauses, i.e. the interpretation of their unsaturated argument slots, can best be analysed with recourse to (some formalized version of) thematic roles.

(8a)   John$_j$ bought it$_i$ [___ $_j$ to read ___ $_i$].

(8b)   John gave it$_i$ to Mary$_j$ [___ $_j$ to read ___ $_i$].

From examples such as (8), Chierchia shows that, for example, the obligatory gap in object purpose clauses is controlled by the matrix theme (*it* in both (8a) and (8b)), while the non-obligatory subject gap is controlled by the matrix goal, if there is one (*Mary* in (8b)), and, in the absence of a goal, by the matrix agent (*John* in (8a)). Given Chierchia's notion of control, the details of which are of no concern in the present context, the purpose clause has to be an argument of the predicate in order to state this generalization more formally. So Chierchia employs McConnell-Ginet's idea and argues that not only Ad-Verbs but also purpose clauses can become arguments of an augmented predicate (purpose clauses are—in contrast to adverbs—never subcategorized for). A further advantage of this treatment is that the idiosyncratic behaviour of predicates as to which purpose clause they accept is to be expected, since augmentation is a lexical property.

(9a)   Mary built that board for the children to play with.

(9b)   *Mary destroyed that board for the children to play with.

The difference between (9a) and (9b) results from the different augmentation licensed by the two predicates. Thus Chierchia proposes that not only nominal expressions but also propositional (or eventual) expressions can be introduced as arguments to augmented verbs, and thus significantly broadens the empirical range for the valency-changing operation proposed by McConnell-Ginet. The present study, although not concerned with purpose clauses or control, can be seen as continuing this research direction by assuming variable subcategorization throughout, without specific lexical rules. Chierchia's approach to purpose clauses is of course highly compatible with this proposal, and it is interesting to note that applied verbs such as those discussed in Chapter 6 encode a nominal argument to express purpose or motivation in many languages.

In related research, Grimshaw (1990) has defined an intermediate category similar to the Ad-Verb category proposed by McConnell-Ginet (1982) as argument-adjunct, or a-adjunct. Grimshaw argues that suppressed arguments in passives and nominalizations are licensed differently both from real, non-suppressed arguments and from adjuncts, i.e. elements which may be part of the lexical-conceptual structure of a predicate but not of its syntactic argument structure. Suppressed arguments in passives are characteristically expressed by a prepositional phrase introduced by *by*:

(10)   Roger Ackroyd was murdered by his nephew Donald.

The phrase *by his nephew Donald* is, according to Grimshaw, different from other adjuncts since it invariably expresses the external argument of the verb's subcategorization frame and thus directly relates to argument structure. Yet, like adjuncts and unlike arguments, the *by*-phrase is not theta-marked, and hence optional. In order to provide an analysis for the unique status of the *by*-phrase, Grimshaw introduces the category of a-adjunct. However, a-adjuncts are strictly reserved for the expression of suppressed arguments. Thus, while the theory of a-adjuncts is germane to the present proposal in that it explores an alternative to the argument/adjunct dichotomy, it aims at a very different problem, one which is in fact not addressed in the present study, namely passives and operations where arguments are suppressed.[3] In contrast, the problem which is at the centre of discussion here, the representation of adjuncts in general, is not explicitly addressed by Grimshaw (1990), where it is assumed that '(at least some) participants' (p. 54) of lexical-conceptual structure are mapped onto argument structure, but where the details of this process are not discussed. In the absence of a different analysis of passives and *by*-phrases, I assume that a-adjuncts are different from the underspecified verbs discussed here, and are subject to stricter licensing than ordinary adjuncts. Note that the availability of further arguments is not diminished for passive verbs:

(11)   Roger Ackroyd was murdered (by his nephew Donald) out of jealousy in his garden at noon.

Both the active verb (cf. (5) above) and the passive form, with or without the *by*-phrase, can be used with a number of PPs, indicating that the general underspecified nature of the predicate is independent of grammatical voice.

A more general approach to argument structure variability has been proposed more recently within Head-Driven Phrase Structure Grammar (HPSG) terms. The starting point for this work is the observation that arguments and

---

[3] By providing an analysis of applicative verbs in Swahili, the case study in Ch. 6 addresses a different valency-changing operation.

adjuncts behave alike under extraction, as can be observed in particular in languages which overtly mark extraction paths (Hukari and Levine 1995). The evidence will be discussed in more detail below (in Chapter 3), so that one example is sufficient to illustrate the point here. In Duala, a Bantu language spoken in Cameroon, the particle *no* is cliticized to the verb when a constituent has been extracted (Biloa 1993: 68):

(12) nja o   bodi no   moni?
      who you give *no* money
      'Who did you give the money to?'

The particle marks the verb whenever a constituent has been extracted, including adjuncts, as can be seen in (13):

(13) njika wuma   w-en   no   mo?
      wh-   place you-see *no* it
      'Where did you see it?'

Evidence like that provided by Duala can be found in many languages, and it points to the fact that arguments and adjuncts are alike at some level of representation. Work in HPSG (e.g. Bouma et al. 1997, Copestake 1996, Przepiórkowski 1999) tends to emphasize that adjuncts can be treated as arguments at the level of syntactic argument structure, but that they receive a more conservative modifier semantics at some other, semantic, level of representation.[4] This approach differs from McConnell-Ginet's original work, which sought a semantic solution for adjuncts functioning as arguments. As will be discussed below (in Chapter 5), the present proposal treats adjuncts as arguments on all levels of analysis and can thus be seen to be closer to McConnell-Ginet's than to the HPSG approach. However, in contrast to previous work, the approach to subcategorization here is essentially pragmatic in nature.

There seems, then, to be some agreement across frameworks that on occasion the argument/adjunct distinction needs to be blurred, and that optional elements of the clause may nevertheless be treated as arguments. However, there is no general theory of this blurring which abstracts away from specific constructions on the one hand and provides a principled account of the interpretation of verbs with blurred subcategorization on the other. The present study aims to provide just that. The particular argument developed reflects the assumptions underlying the study, in particular a dynamic perspective on

---

[4] Bouma and van Noord (1994) propose a related analysis, couched in Categorial Grammar, which equally treats adjuncts syntactically as arguments and semantically as modifiers.

clause structure with an attendant notion of structural underspecification, and a relevance-theoretic view of conceptualization which assumes that there are many more mental concepts than lexical items, including many unstable, ad hoc concepts.

The questions of verbal subcategorization and the blurring of the argument/adjunct distinction are taken as the starting point for a more general inquiry into what verbs and verb-complement arrays mean and how they come to have this meaning. In the course of this inquiry, we will see that at this central place in the interpretation of natural language, the interpretation of predicate–argument structure, model-theoretic semantics does not provide the necessary flexibility to accommodate the facts. In lieu of a semantic treatment, the proper frame for understanding the role and importance of verbal underspecification developed here is a pragmatic one, based on relevance theory, in particular work on contextual concept formation (Carston 1996, Sperber and Wilson 1997). According to this analysis, verbal complements function as an aid to the establishment of the occasion-specific concept addressed by the verb, which encodes only an incomplete concept, in need of pragmatic enrichment in order to play a role in the derivation of inferential effects. From this perspective, the underspecification of verbs as developed in this study can be viewed as being simply an overt syntactic reflex of this much more general phenomenon of context dependency. Verbs encode their incomplete conceptual meaning by being syntactically underspecified with respect to the number of complement expressions with which they combine on a given occasion. Complementarily, the role of adjuncts can be regarded as an aid in concept formation. The form and interpretation of underspecified verbs and optional constituents in the verb phrase is thus determined by syntactic rules of structure-building on the one hand and by general cognitive principles—the calculation of inferential effects over cognitive effort—on the other. Underspecified verbs and their interpretation are thus prime examples of how different cognitive abilities interact in natural language understanding and are used here to chart a stretch of the syntax–pragmatics interface.

1.3 OUTLOOK

The foregoing introductory discussion has touched on the topics which will be discussed in more detail in the following chapters. The next chapter provides the background to the study, and introduces key notions of relevance theory and Dynamic Syntax, which are synthesized into a model of utterance interpretation. The empirical evidence—the relation between arguments and adjuncts and their parallel behaviour in a number of contexts—will be reviewed in Chapter 3. The chapter delimits the data to be discussed in the study, which include NPs and PPs, but only marginally lexical adverbs, and furthermore only those PPs and NPs which function as (possibly optional) arguments of the verb, to the exclusion of sentence and NP adverbials. In Chapter 4, a formal account of verb phrase adjunction in DS is developed, and underspecified verbs are introduced. Chapter 5 turns to the interpretation of underspecified verbs, argues that model-theoretic approaches are too static to provide an appropriate model for understanding verbal underspecification, and develops a pragmatic approach instead, by providing an explicit link between processes of enrichment and the establishment of argument structure in context. Chapter 6 presents an analysis of applied verbs in Swahili. In contrast to standard analyses, which assume that applied verbs encode a syntactic operation of valency-changing, the argument developed here is that applied verbs encode an instruction for concept formation, so that the hearer is entitled to derive additional contextual effects, thus providing an explicit link between valency and concept formation. Finally, Chapter 7 provides the conclusion of the study, summarizes its results, and offers a brief evaluation.

This study brings together ideas and results from syntax, formal semantics, and pragmatics, and assumes a particular perspective on linguistic knowledge, namely a hearer-based perspective, as has been developed by (among others) workers in relevance theory and Dynamic Syntax. It thus addresses readers interested in such disparate topics as adjunct extraction and unbounded dependencies, the pragmatics of Swahili applied verbs, ad hoc concept formation, and the use of logical trees in the analysis of natural language syntax. Because of this heterogeneous mix, but also because I argue that all these things belong together and can be moulded into a coherent whole, I have provided introductory discussions to most points, as well as a more detailed discussion of the novel framework of Dynamic Syntax which is in many ways simpler than the full exposition found in Kempson et al. (2001).

2

A Formal Model of
Utterance Interpretation

2.1 INTRODUCTION

This study is written from the perspective of Dynamic Syntax (DS) on the
one hand and relevance theory on the other. Both these approaches are
discussed here and worked into a more comprehensive model of utterance
interpretation. It is against this background that the problem of verb phrase
underspecification becomes more acute (as discussed in Chapter 4), and
that the pragmatic analysis of verb phrase interpretation is developed in
Chapter 5.

2.2 A MODEL OF UTTERANCE INTERPRETATION

The main concern of DS is to model the syntactic aspects of the process
of utterance interpretation. In the broadest sense, utterance interpretation
involves an incoming signal, prototypically a continuous undivided input
stream of sound on the one end and a completely interpretable enriched
mental representation on the other. A preliminary sketch might look like (1):

(1)   *Utterance Interpretation (first version)*
       sound → (phonology, syntax, semantics, pragmatics) → interpretation

The sketch in (1) shows that the mapping from sound to meaning involves as intermediate steps the application of phonological, syntactic, semantic, and pragmatic knowledge, in that all of them contribute to the processing of some input. However, from the perspective of utterance interpretation, the interesting question with respect to this knowledge is not so much the independent characterization of each kind of knowledge, but the contribution to deriving an interpretation for the signal; a dynamic perspective highlights the relationship between different kinds of linguistic knowledge in fulfilling an overall task. If, and to what extent, different kinds of knowledge can be characterized as being distinct components or modules can then be characterized with reference to their particular contribution to the building of interpretations.

Before looking further at the components postulated in (1), a preliminary assumption has to be addressed, namely the underlying claim in the sketch in (1) that it is possible to study linguistic knowledge from the point of view of the hearer, without looking at production or competence.

2.2.1 Competence and performance

The study of utterance interpretation is related to the study performance, since it is concerned with how language is used and thus puts language into a functional perspective. On the other hand, the question of what enables hearers to perform the task of deriving interpretations is a question about knowledge, or competence. Competence and performance are concepts most closely associated with Chomsky (e.g. 1957, 1964). In Chomsky's conception competence is characterized as the mental ability to produce and understand a potentially infinite number of novel sentences, and is contrasted with performance, i.e. language use, which involves competence, but also non-linguistic factors such as limitations of memory, distortion in the speech channel, or questions of sentence planning. In order to find out about linguistic knowledge on which speakers draw, the linguist has to abstract away from performance factors, and postulate a body of mental principles or rules which determine the set of all possible ('well-formed') sentences. The well-formedness of sentences is checked against grammaticality judgements of speakers. In addition, Chomsky assumes that syntactic knowledge is encapsulated, that is to say, it constitutes a distinct mental module which operates independently of other modules. In recent writings, Chomsky (1995) points out that the analysis of syntactic competence should only postulate components which are 'virtually conceptually necessary', namely (1) an interface with the auditory–perceptual system, (2) an interface with the conceptual–intentional level, and (3) an interface with the lexicon.

Competence in the Chomskian sense, then, is the innate, abstract knowledge, e.g. a body of principles and fixed parameters, of speakers of a given language, which enables them to understand and produce an infinite number of novel sentences. This knowledge is autonomous, i.e. not determined by, or similar to, any other mental facilities, but its design is constrained by the virtual conceptual necessities of three interfaces; sound, meaning, and the lexicon. This conception gives rise to the 'T-model', which has in its basic form (i.e. with or without 'deep' and 'surface' structure) been assumed at all phases in generative linguistics. The interface to the conceptual–intentional system is the level of logical form (LF), the interface to the auditory–perceptual module is the level of phonetic form (PF), and the interface to the lexicon is at the bottom, without its own level:

(2)   *T-model*

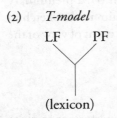

(lexicon)

The point where the paths to PF and LF branch corresponds traditionally to surface structure (S-structure), but in the more recent Minimalist Program to a point of 'spell-out', since no level of representation is assumed.

Compared to the interpretation model (1) above, it seems that both PF and LF are part of interpretation. The interface levels could thus be just taken over and connected with, say, a line:

(3)   *Utterance Interpretation (rejected version)*
       sound → phonology → PF–LF → (semantics, pragmatics) →
       interpretation

In (3) 'syntax' is replaced with 'PF–LF'. However, the immediate problem is that there would be no words in the interpretations derived—there is no interface to the lexicon.[1] This is not a mere technical problem. Rather, it follows

---

[1] There is also no room for 'movement', or purely syntactic derivations, i.e. from deep structure to surface structure, or from a 'numeration' to spell-out. However, despite the importance of movement in most analyses within Chomskian linguistics, it is not conceptually necessary. That is, the 'PF–LF' notation might work even if most of Chomsky's assumptions are maintained, by shifting from derivation to representation, and from movement to chains (as proposed e.g. by Brody 1995).

from the competence/performance distinction: the T-model represents competence only—it is not intended to be related, or even relatable to language use (see Jackendoff 1998: 8). The relation between competence and performance is achieved by different, additional knowledge, for example parsers. A parser might make use of competence, but functions independently of it. However, there is no need under the Chomskian conception for the (theoretical) characterization of knowledge of language to be influenced by (psycholinguistic) evidence of language use.[2] There is also no need to incorporate the model of grammar into 'the model of the mind'; that is, since grammar, and syntax in particular, is encapsulated, the relation of these systems to other cognitive systems (e.g. vision, general reasoning) is irrelevant, except for the rather weak characterization of the interface levels.[3]

Of course, there is nothing wrong per se in assuming that humans have linguistic competence in the sense that we can classify sentences as right or wrong (as grammatical and ungrammatical), but it is not something which we do often, nor something which is a (functionally, evolutionarily, . . .) sensible activity. It is, in this sense, not a virtual conceptual necessity for our cognitive makeup. On the other hand, we do use language to communicate: we act as speakers and hearers, and in order to do so we employ knowledge. The shift in perspective advocated in DS is to devise a theory which starts from the fact that in utterance interpretation, a physical structure (sound) is mapped onto a mental structure (a representation of meaning), so that the explanation can, or at least could, be measured against psycholinguistic data and is embedded, or at least potentially embeddable, into a larger theory of cognition. But from this perspective, utterance interpretation is not performance, at least not in the sense of limitations resulting from (lack of) concentration, or memory limitations. Rather, competence can be viewed, in contrast to the Chomskian conception, as the underlying ability of two distinct activities—speaking and understanding. Since these are two distinct activities, the respective underlying knowledge might in fact be different, although, of course, it would be somewhat surprising if it turned out to be two completely distinct systems of knowledge. Competence in the Chomskian sense can probably be reconstructed from the conception(s) of competence assumed here, but it is, cognitively, epiphenomenal. Throughout this study, I will thus assume that the knowledge modelled by linguistic theory is the knowledge which mediates between sound and meaning, in particular as used in building interpretations.

---

[2] See e.g. Jackendoff (1998) for discussion. Models of grammar which incorporate psycholinguistic evidence tend to depart from the respective classic generative model (e.g. Bresnan 1978, Berwick and Weinberg 1984, Gorrell 1995).

[3] This is one of the main problems identified and discussed by Jackendoff (1998).

In the next section, I look more closely at the difference between interpretation and production, and try to show why it makes sense to restrict attention to interpretation.

2.2.2 Interpretation and production

At the beginning of this section, I introduced the DS assumption that a theory of linguistic knowledge should start from the fact that language is used in communication, and that it involves, in utterance interpretation, a process, possibly involving several subsystems, of mapping sound structures to interpretation. There are reasons for assuming that understanding is cognitively prior to production, and thus for focusing on utterance interpretation rather than utterance production. First, there is the (pre-theoretic) consideration that in language acquisition, perception appears to precede production. Children universally undergo a number of stages in production, using increasingly complex structures. However, it seems plausible to assume that children are able to understand at any given stage utterances which are at least as complex as the ones they produce. This is also implied in theories of language acquisition—whether one says that structures are bootstrapped from recurrent patterns or that parameters are set from appropriate input, one is thereby committed to saying that children are able to parse some relevant input before it is acquired. From the primacy of understanding, a theory of production can be developed by assuming that production presupposes perception in the sense that the sentence builder checks structures against its own processor—in relevance terms, the speaker produces structures which he can reasonably assume the hearer is able to parse. In that way, perception and production work with similar knowledge not because they result from, or are employing, a common source neutral between production and perception ('the grammar' in the traditional sense), but rather because they are in an asymmetrical relation; as a producer we make decisions measured against our own ability to parse. I assume in the following that a perception model of grammar is both workable and reasonable to explore, and continue to flesh out more details of such a model.

2.2.3 Phonology as a parsing device

From the performance perspective developed here, the role of phonology is best viewed as a parsing device. Under this view, phonological knowledge serves to divide a continuous input stream into phonological units which provide access to lexical entries.[4] The functional view of phonology as being essentially a tool for identifying phonological domains to give lexical access is motivated empirically by a number of cross-linguistic phonological phenomena which serve to indicate domains, either by marking edges (such as final obstruent devoicing in German or Russian, final gemination in Gamo, or the interpretation of domain final vocalic positions (see Charette 1991)) or by marking members of a domain internally (e.g. vowel harmony such as found in Turkish or Swahili (see Marten 1997)). Theoretically, this view of phonology offers two interesting points. First, to characterize phonology as a tool for parsing and lexical access entails, in line with the argument presented in this section, that interpretation is cognitively prior to utterance production. The nature of phonology is such that it enables hearers to decode information, so that a speaker, in order to encode, has to be able to decode.

Secondly, this view is compatible with the interpretation analysis of linguistic knowledge, as expressed in the following:

(4)   *Utterance Interpretation (second version)*

sound → phonology → lexicon (syntax, semantics, pragmatics) → interpretation

That is, phonology is a mapping from incoming sound to the lexicon; phonological knowledge under this view provides access to lexical information. As can be seen from (4), the view overcomes the problem with the T-model noted above, since it is the interface to the lexicon which makes the T-model difficult to integrate into the model of utterance interpretation. In (4), the lexical entries identified by phonological domains can be seen as input to further processing. It is this process of structure-building from the lexicon which is modelled in DS. Before turning to DS, however, I discuss how the primacy of interpretation (as opposed to production) is motivated from relevance theory.

2.2.4 Relevance theory

The DS model is closely linked to relevance theory (Sperber and Wilson 1986, 1995). DS provides a model of syntactic knowledge based on the relevance-theoretic assumption that utterance interpretation is a goal-directed process. In the present study, in particular the discussion of concepts and concept

---

[4] This view has recently most consistently been argued for in Government Phonology (see e.g. Kaye 1989, 1995, Kaye et al. 1990, Charette 1991).

formation in Chapter 5 is based on results from research in relevance theory. In the section here, I am mainly concerned with the overall cognitive model proposed in relevance theory, and how it relates to the DS perspective.

Relevance theory is a cognitive theory, where pragmatic aspects of natural language interpretation are explained by principles of cognition. It takes the work of Grice (1967, 1989) as its historic antecedent, which is worth spelling out in more detail. Grice proposes that some aspects of communication involve inference on the part of the hearer, so that, in addition to decoding the meaning of sentences, hearers derive implicatures in interpretation to establish the full meaning of an utterance. The inferential aspects of interpretation follow, according to Grice, from the assumption that certain conversational rules are being obeyed by speakers and hearers. In particular, Grice proposes that communication is governed by a co-operative principle, which instructs speakers as follows: 'Make your conversational contribution such as is required, at the stage at which it occurs, by the accepted purpose or direction of the talk exchange in which you are engaged' (Grice 1989: 26). The principle can be further specified by a number of rules, grouped under four 'maxims'. Grice proposes the following rules (Grice 1989, quoted from Sperber and Wilson 1995: 33–4):

(5)   *Grice's Maxims of Conversation*
      Maxims of quantity
      1.   Make your contribution as informative as is required (for the current purpose of the exchange).
      2.   Do not make your contribution more informative than is required.
      Maxims of quality
      Supermaxim: Try to make your contribution one that is true.
      1.   Do not say what you believe to be false.
      2.   Do not say that for which you lack adequate evidence.
      Maxim of relation
      Be relevant.
      Maxims of manner
      Supermaxim: Be perspicuous.
      1.   Avoid obscurity of expression.
      2.   Avoid ambiguity.
      3.   Be brief (avoid unnecessary prolixity).
      4.   Be orderly.

While Sperber and Wilson agree with Grice that communication involves inference, they do not adopt the co-operative principle and maxims, for three reasons. First, it is not clear which status they have in linguistic or cognitive theory—are they learnt or innate, universal or culture-specific, part of our linguistic or our social knowledge? While the maxims of quality, for example, have an almost moral flavour, the maxims of manner sound rather more stylistic. Secondly, the maxims are comparatively vague. Thus, it is not clear how, for example, the maxims of manner can be made more precise. Furthermore, there seems to be a certain amount of overlap—the maxim of relation, 'be relevant', for example, probably involves some consideration of the quality in relation to the quantity of the utterance—but these aspects are expressed by different maxims. Lastly, and most importantly, Sperber and Wilson argue that inference plays a role not only in finding out what has been implied but also in establishing what has been said in the first place, i.e. inference is required even for the establishment of linguistic meaning, in addition to the establishment of inferences drawn from it. The role of non-demonstrative inferential reasoning in the establishment of what has been said, as opposed to what has been implied, includes cases of ambiguity resolution, reference assignment—where notably pronominal elements underdetermine their encoded, truth-theoretic content—and the enrichment of encoded meaning, a process which will be discussed more extensively in Chapter 5.

The consideration of these questions leads Sperber and Wilson to propose a different view of pragmatics. They argue that inferential activities are all-pervasive not only in communication but also in the way we interact with our environment in general. The inferential abilities hearers use in establishing meaning in communication result, according to Sperber and Wilson, from the general cognitive abilities which are operative in information processing. Thus Sperber and Wilson propose that the inferential aspects of communication can be regarded as a reflex of principles of cognition. The argument is summarized below.

Humans are information-processing animals. Input modules (in the Fodorian (1981) sense) constantly extract information from the environment, largely automatically—we don't choose to see the things in front of us (unless we close our eyes), to smell a smell in the air, and we don't choose to process incoming natural language. This processing of incoming information results in a situation where at any given moment there is more sensory information than can be processed by central reasoning processes, where incoming information is projected. One of the central challenges for the human cognitive architecture is to make relatively fast and relatively reliable choices as to which incoming information is worth attending to, to distribute cognitive resources so as to improve our information state as efficiently as possible. In other words, we process maximally relevant information—our reasoning is goal-directed (Sperber and Wilson 1995: 49):

Our claim is that all human beings automatically aim at the most efficient information processing possible. This is so whether they are conscious of it or not; in fact, the very diverse and shifting conscious interests of individuals result from the pursuit of this permanent aim in changing conditions. In other words, an individual's particular cognitive goal at a given moment is always an instance of a more general goal: maximising the relevance of the information processed.

With this observation in mind, Sperber and Wilson propose the Cognitive Principle of Relevance (1995: 260):

(6)   *Cognitive Principle of Relevance*
        Human cognition tends to be geared to the maximisation of relevance.

The relevance of a particular piece of information, where information can be characterized as a set of contextual assumptions, can be measured against the information state of the processor without these assumptions, i.e. before they are processed. If nothing changes, the gain in information is zero, and hence processing the information is not relevant. On the other hand, if the new information changes the initial information state drastically, the information is very relevant. This change of information state can have a number of instantiations, depending on how exactly the new information interacts with old information—beliefs might be strengthened or contradicted, or the new information might provide a premise to derive a conclusion which would not have followed from the initial information state. That is, relevance involves the maximization of contextual effects. But maximization on its own cannot explain how choices about which information to attend to can be made. Somehow or other, most information probably interacts with what we believe already in some way or other, so that it is inefficient to process all incoming information and check for potential contextual effects. Sperber and Wilson propose that maximization of contextual effects is counter-balanced by processing cost. Mental activity involves 'cost'—thinking, information retrieval from long-term memory, deriving conclusions are activities which need cognitive resources. These resources have to be allocated so as to derive maximally relevant information (in the maximal effect sense) with justified cognitive effort. This is expressed in the definition of relevance (Sperber and Wilson 1995: 125):

(7)   *Relevance*
        Extent Condition 1: an assumption is relevant in a context to the extent
        that its contextual effects in this context are large.
        Extent Condition 2: an assumption is relevant in a context to the extent
        that the effort required to process it in this context is small.

The definition in (7) includes the two conditions on relevant information in a given context in two clauses: relevant information derives maximal contextual effects with minimal cognitive effort. The cognitive principle of relevance governs the relation between incoming data from the perceptual system (the input modules) and the central reasoning system. Note that the activity regulated by relevance is inferential, that is, contextual effects can be characterized as inferential potential of an assumption, while cognitive effort is the cost associated with inferential activity. From this characterization of cognitive activity, Sperber and Wilson then develop a characterization of communication.

Communication involves cognitive activity. Sperber and Wilson's approach to characterize cognition as a basis for communication makes this relation more precise. In particular, since communication involves the processing of information, and since processing of information in general is geared towards maximization of relevance, as expressed in the cognitive principle of relevance, the very same principle can serve to explain the inferential-cognitive processes in communication. This approach answers those questions which were left open by Grice: what for Grice are a number of rather loose cooperative conventions is for relevance theory cognitively mandatory. Our ability to handle communication (more or less successfully) results from our ability to handle information (more or less successfully). Both abilities result from our cognitive makeup, not from social convention; both abilities are ultimately grounded in general reasoning—they are not part of linguistic knowledge or knowledge about language use.

One of Sperber and Wilson's basic assumptions about cognition is that there is always more information coming from the perceptual modules which could be processed than the amount of information which can actually be processed by the central reasoning system. Since incoming utterances are part of the incoming information, they compete with other data for the attention of the processor—the specialized, 'narrow' linguistic module is, after all, only another input module. However, there is a difference between just information and information communicated (or, more precisely, ostensively communicated): by addressing someone, we claim their attention. For the hearer, this means that an ostensively communicated message (linguistic or otherwise) not only carries the content of that message but also, and 'prior' to that content, expresses the informative intention of the speaker. The hearer is justified in assuming that the speaker, by addressing the hearer, implicitly claims that the content of the message will be relevant to the hearer (of course, it might turn out to be not as relevant to the hearer as the speaker had thought, but that is a different problem). This is expressed in the Communicative Principle of Relevance (Sperber and Wilson 1995: 260):

(8)   *Communicative Principle of Relevance*
        Every act of ostensive communication communicates the presumption of
        its own optimal relevance.

The phrase 'presumption of optimal relevance' is defined as follows (1995: 270):

(9)   *Presumption of Optimal Relevance*
        (a)   The ostensive stimulus is relevant enough for it to be worth the
                addressee's effort to process it.
        (b)   The ostensive stimulus is the most relevant one compatible with the
                communicator's abilities and preferences.

That is, the hearer is justified in spending cognitive effort on processing a
communicated message because she can assume that there are enough contextual effects to be derived to make the processing worthwhile. By the presumption of optimal relevance, hearers can expect to derive maximally relevant
inferential effects with no more than necessary cognitive cost, since they can
expect that the ostensive stimulus (i.e. in verbal communication, the utterance) used is the most relevant one possible in the given situation. The two
principles of relevance thus highlight the relation between cognition and
communication, since inferential reasoning in communication can be seen
as a subcase of the more general cognitive constraint to process information
efficiently.

Although the outline of relevance theory given so far is very brief, one
important point for the present discussion can be noted: in relevance theory,
inferential abilities in communication are explained as resulting from cognitive abilities relevant for processing information, that is, from interpretation
rather than from production. Sperber and Wilson derive communicative
behaviour—as expressed in the communicative principle of relevance in (8)—
from general cognitive behaviour, namely from our relevance-driven processing as embodied in the cognitive principle of relevance and definition of
relevance. In other words, our ability to assess and choose information in
linguistic communication is a reflex of our ability to handle information in
general, but this latter ability does not presuppose ostensive stimuli—
understanding is prior to informing.

There is another point worth raising here, although the details will be
more extensively discussed in Chapter 5—the relation between linguistic
knowledge and pragmatics which is advocated in relevance theory. In their
formulation of relevance, Sperber and Wilson are very careful to retain the
Gricean conception of the role of inference in utterance interpretation. The
pragmatic aspects of utterance interpretation are inferential, and involve

the central reasoning system. However, other aspects of utterance interpretation are handled in the specialized linguistic module. These are automatic, algorithmic processes which crucially do not involve general reasoning, but the decoding of an arbitrarily defined code. The specialized linguistic module then provides input to the general cognitive system. Sperber and Wilson propose that the distinction between general reasoning and the linguistic system involves the distinction between non-demonstrative inference, the working mode of the general reasoning system, and decoding in the linguistic module. In view of the boundary between the two systems, Sperber and Wilson (1995: 185) argue that there are three aspects of utterance interpretation which require general reasoning, but which need to be resolved *before* a proposition can be established (where a proposition is a structure which can be evaluated for its truth value against a semantic model): disambiguation, reference assignment, and enrichment. That is, in contrast to Grice, Sperber and Wilson argue that non-demonstrative inference plays a role not only in recovering what has been implied by an utterance but also in discovering what has been said. The output of the linguistic module is a semantic representation, but 'semantic representations are incomplete logical forms, i.e. at best fragmentary representations of thoughts' (1995: 193). The first task of the central reasoning system is thus to derive a propositional form to which (model-theoretic) content can be assigned, and only after that any implied meaning. On the other hand, the output of the linguistic system is not a proposition, but an underspecified logical form (LF), in need of disambiguation, reference assignment, and enrichment.

For utterance interpretation, this conception means that there is no full semantic representation for linguistic expressions without the contribution of pragmatic inferencing:

(10)   *Utterance Interpretation (third version)*
         sound $\rightarrow$ phonology $\rightarrow$ lexicon (syntax, pragmatics) $\rightarrow$ {interpretation, semantics}

The sketch of information flow in (10) shows that the establishment of semantic representations is part of the interpretation process, to which all components before this process contribute.

2.2.5 Dynamic Syntax

Against this background, the DS model is designed to provide an explicit characterization of the structure-building processes required to use lexical information for the derivation of inferential effects. Hearers take information provided by lexical entries and use this information to build interpretations. This process is modelled as the incremental building of structured representations, reflecting the step-by-step contribution of lexical items to the establishment of the eventual representation. In accordance with relevance-theoretic assumptions about the nature of pragmatic inference, DS structures do not represent a direct mapping from linguistic form to model-theoretic interpretation. However, in contrast to relevance theory, DS does not employ a notion of interface level such as LF. Rather, the assumption is that pragmatic inferencing may apply to lexical items directly, as well as at each step of the process of structure building. This view implies that syntax and pragmatics derive propositional forms in tandem, so that pragmatic inferences may determine the well-formedness of a DS tree. In line with this general thought, I argue in Chapter 5 that even basic predicate-argument structure is only established with recourse to general pragmatic processes such as enrichment and strengthening.[5]

The sketch of the information flow in utterance interpretation can thus be completed as given in (11):

(11)   *Utterance Interpretation (final version)*

      sound $\rightarrow$ phonology $\rightarrow$ lexicon $\rightarrow$ {syntax, pragmatics} $\rightarrow$ {interpretation, semantics}

The final diagram in (11) is meant to describe the process of utterance interpretation as follows. Hearers receive a physical signal, a continuous input stream of sound, which provides the input to phonology. Phonology can be characterized as a body of knowledge which enables hearers to divide the input stream into phonological domains which provide lexical access. Lexical information provides the input to the building of the propositional form. The propositional form is established by using information from the lexicon and syntactically defined transition rules on the one hand and non-demonstrative inference on the other. Model-theoretic semantic interpretation is assigned to the propositional form, which is part of the interpretation of the utterance.

The syntactic aspect of utterance interpretation is modelled in DS as an incremental increase of information about the eventual propositional form. The syntactic vehicle for interpretation is tree structures for which a (operational) semantics is given in the form of a modal logic, the logic of finite

---

[5] As argued more extensively below, the motivation for a level of LF is more syntactic than pragmatic, so the real issue is to show that, from the point of view of syntax, it is not necessary or even possible to postulate such a level.

trees (LOFT). The growth of information in the process of utterance interpretation can be characterized as an increase in the information about the tree structure established at a given stage in the process. The formal tools of DS introduced in the next section thus make reference to trees and tree descriptions, and characterize the increase of information about a given tree, corresponding to the process of tree growth. Transitions from one partial tree structure to another, up to the establishment of the eventual tree representing the propositional form, are licensed by lexically encoded instructions and by syntactically defined, optional transition rules. Before introducing the formal details of this process, I summarize below the basic points made in this section.

The model of utterance interpretation discussed in this section reflects basic DS assumptions about linguistic structure and knowledge of language, in particular the view that linguistic knowledge reflects our ability to parse structures and process incoming information, and that linguistic knowledge of production is defined with recourse to perception.

DS shares with relevance theory the commitment to a representational theory of mind. The tree descriptions, with their corresponding tree structures built in DS, are structured representations of content, discrete from the natural language itself, and it is those representations over which the eventual semantic evaluation associated with the utterance is stated.

Furthermore, DS places emphasis on the dynamic process of how the representation of linguistic structure is established. The process of structure building is defined as a goal-driven incremental process, during which the information provided from lexical items is used to build increasingly more articulated structures. In this sense, the building of tree structure is dynamic, so that syntax can be characterized as a set of transitions, rather than (or in addition to) a set of constraints on well-formed structures.

In summary, DS is a formal model of utterance interpretation in which linguistic competence is analysed as the ability to dynamically build structured representations of content. In order to make these claims more specific, the next section introduces the tools necessary to make the model formally more explicit.

2.3 THE FORMAL TOOLS OF DYNAMIC SYNTAX

In order to model the process of incremental building of interpretations as a syntactic process, DS employs a number of formal tools, which are used in the analysis in Chapter 4 and are briefly introduced here.

2.3.1 Tree logic

The dynamic unfolding of structure is modelled in DS as tree growth, employing the logic of finite trees (LOFT) (Blackburn and Meyer-Viol 1994, Kempson et al. 2001). This is a modal logic which describes binary branching tree structures, reflecting the mode of semantic combination in function–application. Nodes in the tree may be identified by a numerical index ranging over 0 and 1:

(12)

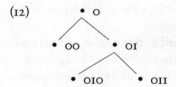

By convention, the left daughter node of a node n is assigned the index n0 and the right daughter is assigned the index n1. Information holding at a given node may be described by a node description, or declarative unit (DU). The location of a node, i.e. its index, may be expressed by the predicate Tn (tree node):

(13)

$$\{Tn(0), Q\}$$
$$\{Tn(00), P\} \quad \{Tn(01), P \to Q\}$$

The DUs in (13) specify the tree location and information holding at that node. A left daughter is defined as an argument node, a right daughter as a functor node.

An alternative way to express the location of a DU is by using a subscript:

(14) $\{_0 Q\}, \{_{00} P\}, \{_{01} P \to Q\}$

The DUs in (14) describe the tree in (13).

The relation between tree nodes can be described by modal statements. This provides a means to state that some information holds at a daughter or at a mother node:

(15) $\{_0 Q, \langle\downarrow_0\rangle P, \langle\downarrow_1\rangle P \to Q\}$

The DU in (15) states that at $Tn(o)$, Q holds, and that from the perspective of $Tn(o)$, at the left daughter P holds, and at the right daughter $P \rightarrow Q$ holds. The DU in (15) describes, again, the tree in (13). There are two basic modalities, one corresponding to the daughter relation ($\langle \downarrow \rangle$, 'down'), and one corresponding to the mother relation ($\langle \uparrow \rangle$, 'up'). These can be used with and without the numerical subscript, depending on whether it is important to distinguish between left and right branches. Furthermore, modality operators can be iterated, e.g. $\langle \downarrow \rangle\langle \downarrow \rangle$, $\langle \downarrow \rangle\langle \uparrow \rangle$, etc.

The system further allows for a weaker characterization of tree node relations, namely for saying that P holds somewhere down (or up), without specifying where exactly ('how deep down', or 'how high up') P holds. This is formally expressed by the 'Kleene star' operator, the reflexive transitive closure over the modalities $\langle \downarrow \rangle$ or $\langle \uparrow \rangle$:

(16) $\langle \downarrow^* \rangle P =_{\mathrm{def}} (P)$ or $\langle \downarrow \rangle\langle \downarrow^* \rangle(P)$

This recursive definition (and the analogous definition with the $\langle \uparrow \rangle$ operator) provides a means to express the underspecification of tree locations:

(17)   • $\{Tn(o), Q, \langle \downarrow^* \rangle R\}$

• $\{Tn(oo), P\}$ • $\{Tn(o1), P \rightarrow Q\}$
$\{Tn(o^*), R\}$

There are four DUs in (17), but only three of them are in fixed locations. The fourth DU is described as holding at $Tn(o^*)$, which is the numerical index indicating an unfixed daughter node of $Tn(o)$. Correspondingly, the modal statement at $Tn(o)$ indicates that at some unfixed daughter node R holds. This definition of underspecified tree location is the tool employed in DS for the analysis of preposed constituents such as *wh*-pronouns or left dislocated topics. The analysis of verbal underspecification developed in this study equally makes use of underspecified locations.

2.3.2 Declarative units

As pointed out in the last section, information holding at, or annotating, a tree node can be termed declarative units, or tree node descriptions. Next to the tree node predicate, DUs most commonly include a formula (Fo) and a type (Ty) value:

(18)   • {Tn(o), Fo(β(α)), Ty(t)}

        • {Tn(oo), Fo(α), Ty(e)}   • {Tn(o1), Fo(β), Ty(e → t)}

The tree in (18) shows how information from the functor node combined with
information from the argument node results in the complex formula value
at the mother node. Similarly to Categorial Grammar, application of modus
ponens over type values is paralleled by function–application over formula
values. Note, however, that DS types are conditional types without an implication for the order of natural language expressions.

A tree like the one in (18) could be, for example, a simplified representation
of a sentence with an intransitive predicate:

(19)   • {Tn(o), Fo(sing'(eve')), Ty(t)}

        • {Tn(oo), Fo(eve'), Ty(e)}   • {Tn(o1), Fo(sing'), Ty(e → t)}

Formula values are representations of the meaning of words. The notational
convention seen in (19) indicates an instruction to access a mental concept, for
example, in the case of Fo(eve'), the mental concept the hearer has of Eve. Not
all words encode instructions to access a named concept. Formula values of, for
example, pronominal expressions include a meta-variable Fo(U), indicating an
underspecified concept which encodes an instruction to the hearer to supply
the formula value from the (cognitive) context, guided by relevance considerations.[6] This search might be restricted, such as for the second person singular
pronoun *you*, which encodes Fo($u_{addressee}$), but the basic encoded meaning is
here, as in the unrestricted case, an instruction for a search for a suitable conceptual representation. An example of a non-conceptual formula value is the
encoded meaning of question pronouns, which encode a meta-variable
Fo(*WH*) possibly with a suitable restriction, e.g. +person, +thing, which is
required to remain open in the eventual representation.

Type values consist of the elements {cn, e, t}, standing for common noun,
entity, and truth-value (i.e. a proposition) respectively, and conditional types
formed from these elements. Conditional types are for example Ty(e → t), as in
the example above, or Ty(e → (e → t)) for transitive verbs.

---

[6] One of the arguments against LF in DS is that in VP ellipsis a suitable representation
for pronominal expressions has to be established before the tree structure is completed (see
Kempson et al. 2001).

Other predicates found in DUs include Category (Cat) which indicates clause type, for example in questions: Cat(+Q). This predicate is always associated at the mother node. Similarly, the representation of tense is expressed as values of predicates.[7]

2.3.3 Requirements and task states

The dynamics of the DS system result from characterizing how trees grow. This means that DS derivations, or parses, start from minimal trees and proceed through stages of partial trees until the tree is fully developed. The minimal initial tree of a derivation is a tree with only a root node, formally introduced into the derivation by a rule called Axiom:

(20) • {Tn(o), ?Ty(t)}

The information holding at the root node at the outset of a derivation is, apart from the location, a requirement to derive an expression of Ty(t). This means that not only information already established can be stated in a DU, but also information which needs to be established. In this case, the requirement to derive an expression of Ty(t) reflects the justified expectation of a hearer that the tree-building process will result in a (the) propositional form. At any stage in a derivation, some information might have been established, and some other information might still be required. Outstanding information is indicated by writing a question mark in front of it; in the example above, there is a requirement ?Ty(t) holding at Tn(o). The derivation is completed if, after all information from the lexicon has been incorporated into the tree, all requirements have been fulfilled.

For any stage in a derivation, a current node can be identified. The requirements holding at that node constitute the current task state:

(21)

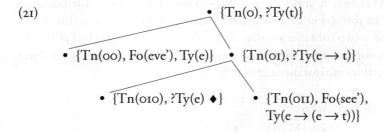

---

[7] A DS treatment of tense and temporal dependencies is developed in Perrett (2000).

The parse state in (21) holds after the tree structure for *Eve saw . . .* has been built. At this stage, there are three requirements, $?Ty(t)$ at $Tn(0)$, $?Ty(e \to t)$ at $Tn(01)$, and $?Ty(e)$ at $Tn(010)$. The pointer symbol ♦ indicates that the current node is $Tn(010)$, so that the current task state is $?Ty(e)$. If, in this situation, information from the lexicon provides an expression of $Ty(e)$, it can be introduced into the tree at $Tn(010)$, since it matches the current requirement. However, if the next word is *sing*, it cannot be introduced into the tree even though its type $Ty(e \to t)$ matches the requirement holding at $Tn(01)$. This is because the pointer is not at $Tn(01)$.

2.3.4 Transition rules

The development of tree structure involves the step from one parse state to another. This transition from one tree description to another can be licensed in two ways: either by one of a number of general transition rules, or by lexical instruction (cf. Kempson et al. 2001: 80–95).

2.3.4.1 *Introduction and Prediction*

A transition rule specifies the input tree, that is at which state in a derivation it may apply, and an output tree, that is, what the resulting state is. Transition rules are stated as tree descriptions, with the input tree on top and the output tree below:

(22) *Introduction*

$$\{\ldots ?Ty(Y) \ldots ♦\}$$

$$\{\ldots ?Ty(Y), ?\langle\downarrow_0\rangle Ty(X), ?\langle\downarrow_1\rangle Ty(X \to Y), \ldots ♦\}$$

Introduction licenses the introduction of modal requirements. If the current task is $?Ty(X)$ (where X and Y are any well-formed type values), Introduction licenses the introduction of two modal statements to the effect that at the daughter nodes two subtasks are required which together result in $Ty(Y)$. The rule licenses, for example, the introduction of the requirement for a subject when the variables are instantiated as follows:

(23) *Introduction (Subject)*

$$\{\ldots ?Ty(t) \ldots ♦\}$$

$$\{\ldots ?Ty(t), ?\langle\downarrow_0\rangle Ty(e), ?\langle\downarrow_1\rangle Ty(e \to t), \ldots ♦\}$$

The input tree in (23) corresponds to the minimal tree at the outset of a derivation:

(24)　　• $\{Tn(0), ?Ty(t) \blacklozenge\}$

In this situation, Introduction results in:

(25)　　• $\{Tn(0) ?Ty(t), ?\langle\downarrow_0\rangle Ty(e), ?\langle\downarrow_1\rangle Ty(e \rightarrow t) \blacklozenge\}$

The effect of this transition is that it introduces the statement that an expression of $Ty(t)$ can be derived if there is an expression of $Ty(e)$ at the argument daughter, and an expression of $Ty(e \rightarrow t)$ at the functor daughter.

Modal requirements, such as those being introduced by Introduction in (25), result in the building of tree structure by the application of Prediction:[8]

(26)　　*Prediction*

$$\frac{\{_n \ldots ?\langle\downarrow_\pi\rangle\phi, \blacklozenge\}}{\{_n \ldots ?\langle\downarrow_\pi\rangle\phi \ldots\}, \{_{n\pi} \ldots ?\phi, \blacklozenge\}}$$

where $\pi = 0$, or $\pi = 1$.

By Prediction, a new node is built. In a situation where at the current node a modal requirement holds, a new node can be built where this requirement minus the modal operator holds. This new node will then be the current node. By an application of Prediction, the tree in (25) can be developed into (27):

(27)　　　　　　• $\{Tn(0), ?Ty(t), ?\langle\downarrow_0\rangle Ty(e), ?\langle\downarrow_1\rangle Ty(e \rightarrow t)\}$

　　　• $\{Tn(00), ?Ty(e) \blacklozenge\}$

The new node $Tn(00)$ is licensed since $?\langle\downarrow_0\rangle Ty(e)$ holds at $Tn(0)$. Since transition rules are in general optional, an alternative development of (25) would be (28):

---

[8] This is a slightly simplified version of the rule given in Kempson et al. (2001: 80), since I do not define Prediction for LINK relations. The rule as given here is sufficient for the present discussion.

(28)   • $\{Tn(o), ?Ty(t), ?\langle\downarrow_0\rangle Ty(e), ?\langle\downarrow_1\rangle Ty(e \to t)\}$

           • $\{Tn(o1), ?Ty(e \to t) \blacklozenge\}$

Here $Tn(o1)$ is licensed since at $Tn(o)$ the requirement $?\langle\downarrow_1\rangle Ty(e \to t)$ holds. However, Prediction cannot apply to (25) twice, since after the first application, $Tn(o)$ is no longer the current node.

2.3.4.2 *Thinning, Elimination, and Completion*

While the rules discussed in the preceding section are concerned with unfolding of tree structure, the rules discussed in this section are concerned with the accumulation of established information.

The first rule provides a means for stating that requirements have been fulfilled:

(29)   *Thinning*

$$\{\ldots \phi \ldots ?\phi \ldots \blacklozenge\}$$
$$\overline{\{\ldots \phi \ldots \blacklozenge\}}$$

The rule simplifies DUs. If at a current node a DU holds which includes both a fact and the requirement to fulfil this fact, the requirement can be omitted. The node is still the current node.

The rule of Elimination can be regarded as the opposite of Introduction:

(30)   *Elimination*

$$\{\ldots \langle\downarrow_0\rangle(Fo(\alpha), Ty(X)), \langle\downarrow_1\rangle(Fo(\beta), Ty(X \to Y)) \ldots \blacklozenge\}$$
$$\overline{\{\ldots Fo(\beta(\alpha)), Ty(Y), \langle\downarrow_0\rangle(Fo(\alpha), Ty(X)),}$$
$$\langle\downarrow_1\rangle(Fo(\beta), Ty(X \to Y)) \ldots \blacklozenge\}$$

Elimination does not introduce a new node, but only changes annotations holding at one node. The rule states that if at a given node two modal statements hold which state that both the argument daughter and the functor daughter are annotated with a formula and a type value, and the two type values can combine by modus ponens, then the resulting type and the corresponding expression derived by function–application over the formula values hold at that node. For example, for a tree describing *Eve sings*, Elimination would license the following transition:

(31)   *Elimination* (Fo(sing'(eve')))

$$\frac{\{\ldots \langle\downarrow_o\rangle(\text{Fo(eve')}, \text{Ty}(e)), \langle\downarrow_1\rangle(\text{Fo(sing')}, \text{Ty}(e \rightarrow t)) \ldots \blacklozenge\}}{\{\ldots \text{Fo(sing'(eve'))}, \text{Ty}(t), \langle\downarrow_o\rangle(\text{Fo(eve')}, \text{Ty}(e)), \langle\downarrow_1\rangle(\text{Fo(sing')}, \text{Ty}(e \rightarrow t)) \ldots \blacklozenge\}}$$

Elimination licenses the combination of information present as modal requirements. Elimination is similar to Introduction in that both rules specify transitions involving modal statements holding at a given node, without any direct effect on tree structure (as opposed to tree descriptions).

The rule of Completion can be regarded as the inverse of Prediction:

(32)   *Completion*

$$\frac{\{_n \ldots\}, \{_{n\pi} \ldots \phi, \blacklozenge\}}{\{_n \ldots \langle\downarrow_\pi\rangle\phi, \blacklozenge\}, \{_{n\pi} \ldots \phi\}}$$

where $\pi = 0$ or $\pi = 1$.

Completion states that if at a daughter node some information holds, and the daughter is the current node, then that (i.e. mother) node may be annotated with the corresponding modal statement and become the current node. An example is given in (33):

(33) $\dfrac{\{_o \ldots ?\text{Ty}(t), \langle\downarrow_o\rangle(\text{Fo(eve')}, \text{Ty}(e))\}, \{_{o1} \ldots \text{Fo(sing')}, \text{Ty}(e \rightarrow t)) \blacklozenge\}}{\{_o \ldots ?\text{Ty}(t), \langle\downarrow_o\rangle(\text{Fo(eve')}, \text{Ty}(e), \langle\downarrow_1\rangle(\text{Fo(sing')}, \text{Ty}(e \rightarrow t) \blacklozenge\}, \{_{o1} \ldots \text{Fo(sing')}, \text{Ty}(e \rightarrow t))\}}$

The input state in the example in (33) is a tree description where at Tn(o) with the requirement ?Ty(t) a modal statement holds to the effect that at the argument node, Fo(eve') of Ty(e) holds (which in fact presupposes a previous application of Completion), and that at the (current) functor daughter Tn(o1), Fo(sing') of Ty(e $\rightarrow$ t) holds. The transition licensed by Completion is then that the presence of the information at Tn(o1) is recorded at Tn(o) as a modal statement, and that the pointer moves to Tn(o), making it the current node. This new description is then in turn suitable input to Elimination.

The rules Elimination and Completion provide the means to pass established information up the tree so that eventually an expression of Ty(t) can be derived. Although the rules are optional, in practice they apply as late as possible, (ideally) when all terminal nodes are filled.[9]

The rules introduced so far result, in conjunction with lexical instructions, in a complete parse. Modal requirements are introduced by Introduction, and the corresponding daughter nodes are built by Prediction. If lexical input fulfils a requirement, Thinning removes the requirement. After requirements have been fulfilled, Completion introduces modal statements at the mother nodes, and Elimination licenses the combination of formula values.

The next section introduces two more rules which are needed for more complex derivations.

2.3.4.3 **Adjunction and Merge*

The rules so far do not introduce unfixed nodes into the tree, or assign an unfixed node its place in the tree. The last two rules discussed in this section do this.

*Adjunction licenses the introduction of an unfixed node at the outset of the parse:

(34)   **Adjunction*

$$\{Tn(a), ?Ty(t), \blacklozenge\}$$

$$\{Tn(a), ?Ty(t)\}, \{\langle\uparrow^*\rangle Tn(a), ?Ty(e), \blacklozenge\}$$

At a given parse where the current node $Tn(a)$ has a requirement $?Ty(t)$, the introduction of an unfixed node lower than $Tn(a)$ is licensed, which becomes the new current node. This corresponds to a partial tree such as (35):

(35)   • $\{Tn(o), ?Ty(t)\}$

$\{Tn(o^*), ?Ty(e)\}$

The lower node is unfixed, and only encodes that its eventual position will be somewhere below the root node $Tn(o)$. The *Adjunction rule is more specific than the rules discussed so far. It can only apply at the beginning of the parse, and it specifies that the new node be of $Ty(e)$. This rule is needed to introduce fronted constituents such as question words into an unfixed node. *Adjunction and unfixed nodes in general will be discussed more fully in Chapter 4.

---

[9] More precisely, Elimination may apply after the tree is complete; the application of Completion is necessary at intermediate steps. This is shown in the sample derivation below, although in the remainder of this study I generally assume that both Completion and Elimination provide the final steps in a derivation.

The last rule introduced here licenses the resolution of the underspecified node and assigns it to a fixed position. Merge licenses the merging of two node descriptions, i.e. DUs:

(36)   *Merge*

$$\frac{\{\ldots \text{ND}, \text{ND'} \ldots\}}{\{\ldots \text{ND} \cup \text{ND'} \ldots\}}$$

The Merge rule is completely general. It simply states that two node descriptions can be combined into one. Although the rule overgenerates, it does ensure that an unfixed node can be merged with a fixed one, so that it is integrated into the tree.

2.3.5 Lexical entries

DS parses are essentially lexically driven. The model follows recent trends towards assigning lexical items a more important role in syntax, as found for example in Lexical Functional Grammar (LFG) or HPSG. Thus lexical information includes more than just decorations of terminal nodes: lexical information itself can build partial trees, up to full propositional structure (e.g. in a fully inflectional language such as Latin). The structure of lexical entries interacts with the general format of tree description introduced so far. Lexical information provides annotations on nodes, and specifies how a particular lexical item contributes to the process of structure building. The general format for lexical information is as follows:

(37)   *Format of Lexical Entries*

IF	Ty(X)
THEN	make(. . .),
	put(. . .),
	go(. . .)
ELSE	abort

Lexical entries consist minimally of three statements. The IF clause gives the condition under which the information provided by lexical entries can be introduced into the tree. For example, an expression of Ty(e) generally requires that there be a current requirement ?Ty(e) at the stage at which the lexical entry is scanned. The THEN statement lists the particular actions which are performed if the condition in the IF statement is met. THEN statements consist usually of three predicates. The predicate 'make' is an instruction to build a new node, which is further specified in the value of the predicate; for example 'make($\langle\downarrow_1\rangle$)' builds a new functor node. The predicate 'put' is an instruction to annotate an existing node, for example with a formula and a type value. Finally, 'go' is an instruction for pointer movement: it changes the current task state. Within lexical entries, the order of the predicates is important. For example 'put' before 'make' means 'put (. . .) at current node, then build a new node', while 'make' before 'put' means 'build a new node and put (. . .) there'. The ELSE clause specifies the actions to be performed if the IF condition is not met. Often this is 'abort', i.e. the premature end of the derivation, but the clause may be used otherwise. Finally, the clauses can be nested to result in more complex entries.[10]

This characterization of lexical entries is a minimal characterization in the sense that all lexical entries which contribute to tree building contain at least the three clauses discussed. However, the actual actions performed may be more complex than outlined here, since more idiosyncratic information may be associated with individual words in the lexicon. This point is further discussed in relation to the analysis presented in Chapter 4.

A sample lexical entry for *love* is given below:

(38)   *Lexical Entry for* love
    IF $?Ty(e \rightarrow t)$
    THEN $put(?\langle\downarrow_0\rangle Ty(e))$,
                $make(\langle\downarrow_1\rangle)$, $put(Fo(love'), Ty(e \rightarrow (e \rightarrow t)))$
    ELSE   abort

The condition for the introduction of the information from *love* is that the current task state is $?Ty(e \rightarrow t)$. If this condition is met, the current node is annotated with a modal requirement. Then a new functor node is built and annotated with the formula and type values specified. If *love* is scanned at a stage in the derivation when the current task does not include the requirement $?Ty(e \rightarrow t)$, the derivation ends. The entry for *love* is seen in use in the sample derivation in the next section.

2.3.6 Sample derivation

This section presents a sample derivation of a simple sentence to show how the step-by-step process of tree growth is expressed in the DS system. I display and

---

[10] The treatment of the lexicon here is compatible with arguments presented in Construction Grammar (see e.g. Fillmore 1988, Kay 1995) since lexical information includes (instructions to build) subtrees. In Construction Grammar, lexical entries may include larger syntactic structures (i.e. constructions) in which the lexical item is embedded.

comment on every step in the derivation, although I will give up this practice in the remainder of the study. The derivation here is merely meant to show how the rules discussed above work.

The example to be discussed is given in (39):

(39)   Sally loves chocolate.

The derivation begins with the introduction of the root node by Axiom:

(40a)   • $\{Tn(0), ?Ty(t) \blacklozenge\}$

At this stage, two rules may apply, Introduction and * Adjunction. This is a situation which often arises, since transition rules may apply optionally, and more than one rule might be applicable at any given stage of the parse.[11] In practice, I use the rules sensibly, so that in this case, Introduction applies:

(40b)   • $\{Tn(0), ?Ty(t), ?\langle\downarrow_0\rangle Ty(e), ?\langle\downarrow_1\rangle Ty(e \rightarrow t) \blacklozenge\}$

By Prediction, the argument daughter can be built:

(40c)   • $\{Tn(0), ?Ty(t), ?\langle\downarrow_0\rangle Ty(e), ?\langle\downarrow_1\rangle Ty(e \rightarrow t)\}$

         • $\{Tn(00), ?Ty(e) \blacklozenge\}$

At this stage the first word is scanned, namely *Sally*, for which I assume the following lexical entry:

(41)   *Lexical Entry for* Sally
        IF $?Ty(e)$
        THEN   put(Fo(sally'), Ty(e))
        ELSE   abort

The current task state matches the condition in the IF clause, so the formula value Fo(sally') and the type value Ty(e) can be introduced.

---

[11] However, application of 'wrong' rules leads to a situation where the derivation cannot be completed. Recall that DS does not model real time parsing, but characterizes the body of knowledge required for incrementally building interpretations.

(40d)　　　　● {Tn(0), ?Ty(t), ?⟨↓$_0$⟩Ty(e), ?⟨↓$_1$⟩Ty(e → t)}

　　　● {Tn(00), ?Ty(e), Fo(sally'), Ty(e) ◆}

At this stage, Thinning can apply to Tn(00) to remove the requirement:

(40e)　　　　● {Tn(0), ?Ty(t), ?⟨↓$_0$⟩Ty(e), ?⟨↓$_1$⟩Ty(e → t)}

　　　● {Tn(00), Fo(sally'), Ty(e) ◆}

The DU at Tn(00) now matches the tree description which licenses the application of Completion:

(40f)　　　● {Tn(0), ?Ty(t), ?⟨↓$_0$⟩Ty(e), ?⟨↓$_1$⟩Ty(e → t), ⟨↓$_0$⟩
　　　　　　(Fo(sally'), Ty(e)) ◆}

　　　● {Tn(00), Fo(sally'), Ty(e)}

At this stage, two rules could apply at Tn(0)—Thinning, since one requirement holding at Tn(0) has been fulfilled, and Prediction, since there is still the modal requirement of the functor node. However, while Prediction could apply after Thinning, which does not move the pointer, Thinning could not apply after Prediction, which does move the pointer. Thus for clarity of display, Thinning applies first:[12]

(40g)　　　● {Tn(0), ?Ty(t), ?⟨↓$_1$⟩Ty(e → t), ⟨↓$_0$⟩(Fo(sally'), Ty(e)) ◆}

　　　● {Tn(00), Fo(sally'), Ty(e)}

Now Prediction applies and builds the functor node:

(40h)　　　● {Tn(0), ?Ty(t), ?⟨↓$_1$⟩Ty(e → t), ⟨↓$_0$⟩(Fo(sally'), Ty(e))}

　　● {Tn(00), Fo(sally'), Ty(e)}　　● {Tn(01), ?Ty(e → t) ◆}

---

[12] Alternatively, Thinning would apply after Completion.

The next step is the scanning of the word *love*, which accesses the following information[13] (repeated here):

(42) *Lexical Entry for* love

IF   ?Ty$(e \rightarrow t)$

THEN   put(?$\langle\downarrow_o\rangle$Ty(e)),

make($\langle\downarrow_I\rangle$), put(Fo(love'), Ty$(e \rightarrow (e \rightarrow t))$))

ELSE   abort

The condition on the introduction of the lexical information from *love* is met, since the current node has a requirement ?Ty$(e \rightarrow t)$. The first 'put' statement annotates Tn(01) with a modal requirement, after which the 'make' statement results in the building of a new functor node which is annotated with the information specified in the second 'put' predicate:

(40i)   • {Tn(0), ?Ty(t), ?$\langle\downarrow_I\rangle$Ty$(e \rightarrow t)$, $\langle\downarrow_0\rangle$(Fo(sally'), Ty(e))}

• {Tn(00), Fo(sally'), Ty(e)}   • {Tn(01), ?Ty$(e \rightarrow t)$, ?$\langle\downarrow_0\rangle$Ty(e)}

• {Tn(011), Fo(love'),
Ty$(e \rightarrow (e \rightarrow t))$ ♦}

In this situation, Completion can apply to annotate Tn(01) with a modal statement registering the fulfilled requirement at Tn(011):

(40j)   • {Tn(0), ?Ty(t), ?$\langle\downarrow_I\rangle$Ty$(e \rightarrow t)$, $\langle\downarrow_0\rangle$(Fo(sally'), Ty(e))}

• {Tn(00), Fo(sally'),   • {Tn(01), ?Ty$(e \rightarrow t)$, ?$\langle\downarrow_0\rangle$Ty(e),
Ty(e)} $\langle\downarrow_I\rangle$(Fo(love'), Ty$(e \rightarrow (e \rightarrow t))$)) ♦}

• {Tn(011), Fo(love'), Ty$(e \rightarrow (e \rightarrow t))$)}

At this stage, Prediction applies at Tn(01) since there is a new modal statement, resulting from the lexical action from *love*. Thus Tn(010) can be built:

[13] I omit tense and agreement throughout.

(40k)   • $\{Tn(o), ?Ty(t), ?\langle\downarrow_1\rangle Ty(e \rightarrow t), \langle\downarrow_o\rangle(Fo(sally'), Ty(e))\}$

    • $\{Tn(oo), Fo(sally'),$ • $\{Tn(o1), ?Ty(e \rightarrow t), ?\langle\downarrow_o\rangle Ty(e),$
       $Ty(e)\}$ $\langle\downarrow_1\rangle(Fo(love'), Ty(e \rightarrow (e \rightarrow t)))\}$

          • $\{Tn(o1o), ?Ty(e) \blacklozenge\}$ • $\{Tn(o11), Fo(love'), Ty(e \rightarrow (e \rightarrow t))\}$

The next step is again scanning of lexical input, this time from *chocolate*. I assume here that mass nouns have at least one reading under which they are of $Ty(e)$, so that the lexical information can be introduced into the tree:[14]

(43)   *Lexical Entry for* chocolate
      IF $?Ty(e)$
      THEN $put(Fo(chocolate'), Ty(e))$
      ELSE   abort

Since the current node requires a $Ty(e)$ expression, the 'put' statement can be applied:

(40l)   • $\{Tn(o), ?Ty(t), ?\langle\downarrow_1\rangle Ty(e \rightarrow t), \langle\downarrow_o\rangle(Fo(sally'), Ty(e))\}$

    • $\{Tn(oo), Fo(sally'),$ • $\{Tn(o1), ?Ty(e \rightarrow t), ?\langle\downarrow_o\rangle Ty(e),$
       $Ty(e)\}$ $\langle\downarrow_1\rangle(Fo(love'), Ty(e \rightarrow (e \rightarrow t)))\}$

         • $\{Tn(o1o), ?Ty(e),$ • $\{Tn(o11), Fo(love'), Ty(e \rightarrow (e \rightarrow t))\}$
           $Fo(chocolate'), Ty(e) \blacklozenge\}$

At this stage, all lexical information has been scanned and the verb's lexical requirements are fulfilled. All nodes have been built, so that the remaining steps serve only to combine the accumulated information. The only rules applying are thus Thinning, Completion, and Elimination. The first step is the application of Thinning at $Tn(o1o)$, followed by the application of Completion to $Tn(o1o)$ and $Tn(o1)$. This results in an increase in modal statements at $Tn(o1)$:

---

[14] NP structure is not part of this study. I assume that NPs may have complex internal structure, but that they are uniformly of $Ty(e)$ (cf. Kempson et al. 2001: 223ff. for discussion).

(40m)

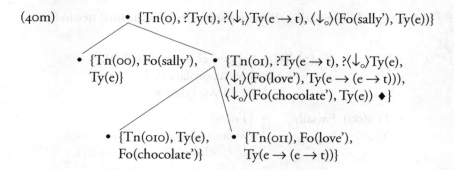

$\{Tn(0), ?Ty(t), ?\langle\downarrow_1\rangle Ty(e \to t), \langle\downarrow_0\rangle(Fo(sally'), Ty(e))\}$

$\{Tn(00), Fo(sally'), Ty(e)\}$

$\{Tn(01), ?Ty(e \to t), ?\langle\downarrow_0\rangle Ty(e), \langle\downarrow_1\rangle(Fo(love'), Ty(e \to (e \to t))), \langle\downarrow_0\rangle(Fo(chocolate'), Ty(e)) \blacklozenge\}$

$\{Tn(010), Ty(e), Fo(chocolate')\}$

$\{Tn(011), Fo(love'), Ty(e \to (e \to t))\}$

Next, Thinning applies at $Tn(01)$. I only reproduce $Tn(01)$, since the rest of the tree remains unchanged:

(40n) • $\{Tn(01), ?Ty(e \to t), ?\langle\downarrow_0\rangle Ty(e), \langle\downarrow_1\rangle(Fo(love'), Ty(e \to (e \to t))), \langle\downarrow_0\rangle(Fo(chocolate'), Ty(e)) \blacklozenge\}$

The $Ty(e)$ expression at the argument node fulfils the requirement $?\langle\downarrow_0\rangle Ty(e)$, which is removed. Elimination then applies to the values of the two daughter nodes:

(40o) • $\{Tn(01), ?Ty(e \to t), (Fo(love'(chocolate')), Ty(e \to t)), \langle\downarrow_1\rangle(Fo(love'), Ty(e \to (e \to t))), \langle\downarrow_0\rangle(Fo(chocolate'), Ty(e)) \blacklozenge\}$

The derived fact $Ty(e \to t)$ fulfils the requirement $?Ty(e \to t)$, which is removed:

(40p) • $\{Tn(0), ?Ty(t), ?\langle\downarrow_1\rangle Ty(e \to t), \langle\downarrow_0\rangle(Fo(sally'), Ty(e))\}$

$\{Tn(00), Fo(sally'), Ty(e)\}$

$\{Tn(01), (Fo(love'(chocolate')), Ty(e \to t)), \langle\downarrow_1\rangle(Fo(love'), Ty(e \to (e \to t))), \langle\downarrow_0\rangle(Fo(chocolate'), Ty(e)) \blacklozenge\}$

$\{Tn(010), Ty(e), Fo(chocolate')\}$

$\{Tn(011), Fo(love'), Ty(e \to (e \to t))\}$

Completion applied to $Tn(0)$ and $Tn(01)$ annotates $Tn(0)$ with a modal statement. I represent only $Tn(0)$:

(40q) • $\{Tn(0), ?Ty(t), ?\langle\downarrow_1\rangle Ty(e \to t), \langle\downarrow_0\rangle(Fo(sally'), Ty(e)), \langle\downarrow_1\rangle((Fo(love'(chocolate')), Ty(e \to t)) \blacklozenge\}$

By Thinning and Elimination the derivation ends with the final tree in (40r):

(40r)

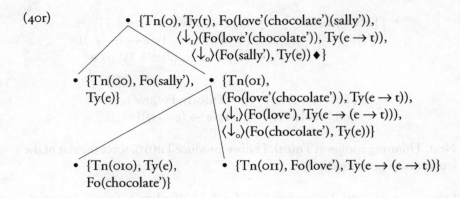

In the final tree, the last outstanding requirement, $?Ty(t)$ at the root node, has been fulfilled by the derivation of the corresponding formula value, $Fo(love'(chocolate')(sally'))$. The derivation shows that structure building is achieved by the rules Introduction and Prediction in conjunction with lexical information, while the combination of information in the tree is achieved by the rules Thinning, Completion, and Elimination.

In the remainder of this study I will display derivations in much less detail, and concentrate on the growth of tree structure, as opposed to the combination of information. I will also in general omit modal statements and pointer movement, unless necessary.

2.3.7 LINKed structures

A final extension of the DS system discussed so far is the LINK relation. A LINK relation can be established between two trees whose nodes then do not stand in a daughter or unfixed daughter relation. A LINK analysis is employed in DS for relative clause:

(44)   Sally, whom I admire, is leaving tomorrow.

The relative clause is in a LINK relation to the head noun, which means that it is an island for extraction (it is not a daughter relation—an unfixed node in the matrix clause cannot be fixed into a LINKed structure) but yet part of the tree in the sense that a copy of the formula value of the head noun has to be incorporated into the LINKed tree. The LINK relation is established as follows:

(45)   *LINK Induction*

$$\frac{\{_n \ldots \text{Fo}(\alpha), \text{Ty}(e) \ldots \blacklozenge\}}{\{_n \ldots \text{Fo}(\alpha), \text{Ty}(e) \ldots\}, \{_{nL} \ldots ?\text{Ty}(t) \ldots \blacklozenge\},}$$
$$\{_{nL^*} \ldots \text{Fo}(\alpha), \text{Ty}(e) \ldots\}$$

The rule states that from a Ty(e) expression with some formula value, a transition is licensed in which two new LINKed nodes are built: a new root node with ?Ty(t), and a new unfixed node below the new LINKed root node with the type and formula value being identical to those of the head noun. The corresponding tree structure is as follows:

(46)   • {Tn(o), ?Ty(t)}

    • {Tn(oo), Fo(sally'), Ty(e)}   • {Tn(o1), ?Ty(e → t)}

           LINK

                • {Tn(ooL), ?Ty(t) ♦}
        {Tn(ooL*), Fo(sally'), Ty(e)}

From this tree, the derivation proceeds standardly with the building of the relative clause. The unfixed node will be fixed in the gap position of the relative clause. After the due steps, subcategorization information from the verb *admire* leads to the building of a node with a requirement ?Ty(e), at which the unfixed node can be fixed. The derivation then continues with the development of the matrix clause.[15]

The LINK relation has been developed further by Swinburne (1999) in an analysis of secondary predication. While LINK relations are not of primary importance in this study, they are used to argue that adjuncts are daughters in Chapters 3 and 4.

2.4 CONCLUSION

The overall perspective within which the present study is located is now in place. It is a model of linguistic competence which is based on hearers' abilities

[15] The relevant pointer movement has to be added to the LINK rule above. Cf. the full treatment in Kempson et al. (2001: ch. 4), and Swinburne (1999).

to assign semantic representations to incoming sound strings. The primacy of perception is grounded—via relevance theory—in human cognition, which is viewed as essentially geared towards information processing. This essentially asymmetrical view of linguistic knowledge is further supported by the observation that production can be defined with recourse to processing, but not vice versa. The role of syntax in this set-up is to take lexical information and assemble increasingly large structured representations of content, which in conjunction with pragmatic processes of enrichment are developed to a propositional form, the vehicle over which further inferences can be made according to relevance considerations. The DS part of the model is formalized as a tree logic which can be used to state generalizations over natural language syntax.

The approach of DS, with its insistence on left-to-right structure building, provides, as I show in the following chapters, the right angle from which to see the problem posed by verb phrase adjunction, in particular since adjuncts threaten to undermine incrementality by requiring tree restructuring. On the other hand, it is the notions of dynamic structure building and syntactic underspecification which prove to be instrumental in developing a formal account of underspecified verbs which not only handles adjunction but also poses pertinent questions for the interpretation of verbs more generally. The specific proposal developed is the introduction of an underspecified semantic type for verbs which licenses the optional introduction of $Ty(e)$ expressions (i.e. NPs and PPs) as arguments of the verb. The type specification employs the Kleene star operation to give a type e^*. The embedding of DS in relevance theory will become the cornerstone of the treatment of the interpretation of underspecified verbs. Since verbal underspecification results in verbs with varying arities, depending on the occasion of use, it is difficult to develop a traditional semantics for them—these being based firmly on a static notion of arity, fixed a priori in the model against which the sentence is interpreted. The relevance-theoretic notion of concept, on the other hand, does provide the flexibility needed for the interpretation of underspecified verbs, and it is this notion which will be employed to develop an account of their interpretation.

Before starting on the formalization, however, the next chapter presents the evidence needed to establish that a new approach to adjunction, incorporating a notion of verbal underspecification, is needed to understand a range of cross-linguistic facts.

3

Arguments and Adjuncts

3.1 INTRODUCTION

This chapter presents the main empirical evidence for developing a notion of verbal underspecification as an analysis of adjunction. The thrust of the argument is that traditional notions of subcategorization entail a clear distinction between arguments and adjuncts, but that a number of morphological, semantic, and syntactic facts show that the distinction is not clear-cut, but rather that arguments and adjuncts behave alike in a number of respects. This observation is then taken as the starting point for an analysis which allows for the introduction of adjuncts into the verb phrase.

3.2 VERB PHRASE AND SUBCATEGORIZATION

To put the discussion about arguments and adjuncts into perspective, I provide an overview of the structure and role of the verb phrase and verbal subcategorization in particular in the DS model introduced in the last chapter.

3.2.1 Verb phrase

There is no primitive notion of verb phrase in the DS system, i.e. there is no rule, as for example found in phrase structure grammars, which specifies how a VP is built, nor is there a primitive notion of verb. Similar to Categorial

Grammar, verbs are analysed as predicates, which specify the number of nominal expressions with which they combine to yield a proposition. For example, a transitive verb may be associated lexically with a type specification such as (1):

(1)   *Type Specification for a Transitive Verb*
       $Ty(e \rightarrow (e \rightarrow t))$

The type in (1) indicates that two $Ty(e)$ expressions are required by the predicate to result in an expression of $Ty(t)$. However, there is one important difference between DS and Categorial Grammar with respect to typing, namely that DS has no general rules of type inference such as type shifting or function–composition (see e.g. Lambek 1958, McGee Wood 1993, Morrill 1994). This means that a DS derivation with a transitive verb always proceeds by first combining the verb with the object and then combining the verb plus object with the subject. If type shifting were allowed as one of a number of type inference rules, the subject could be assigned a higher type such as (2):

(2)   *Potential Type for Type-Shifted Subject*
       $Ty((e \rightarrow t) \rightarrow t)$

The type in (2) would by function composition license a derivation where the subject acts as a functor which takes a transitive verb as an argument, and where the subject plus verb then combines with the object to yield an expression of $Ty(t)$. But this means that there is no means to structurally define a VP, i.e. an expression which includes the verb and its object(s), but not the subject. It is because there are no type inference rules in DS that the notion of verb phrase can be defined structurally, namely as an expression of $Ty(e \rightarrow t)$. The corresponding notion of subject can thus be defined as that $Ty(e)$ expression which combines with a predicate to result (immediately) in an expression of $Ty(t)$. The corresponding tree relations are as follows:

(3)   • $\{Tn(o), Ty(t)\}$

       • $\{Tn(oo), Ty(e)\}$ • $\{Tn(o1), Ty(e \rightarrow t)\}$

              • $\{Tn(o1o), Ty(e)\}$ • $\{Tn(o11), Ty(e \rightarrow (e \rightarrow t))\}$

In the tree in (3), the expression at $Tn(oo)$ corresponds to the subject. A verb phrase is an expression holding at $Tn(o1)$. Constituents of the verb phrase can thus be characterized as Ty(e) expressions holding below Tn(o1). It is in the sense of this characterization that I employ the term 'verb phrase' here.

3.2.2 Subcategorization

Type information such as in (1), above, is used to specify the valency or transitivity of verbs. That is, DS assumes, following traditional grammar, that verbs specify in the lexicon how many nominal expressions can be associated with it in a clause, from which classifications of verbs into, for example, intransitive, transitive, and di-transitive verbs can be derived. Typing information is also used to distinguish between arguments and adjuncts: the former are the subcategorized NPs, while the latter are not, or at least not directly, licensed by the verb, so that their presence in a well-formed clause is regulated by some other principle of the grammar. For example, (4) shows that a putative lexical entry for *kiss* includes a statement to the effect that *kiss* both licenses and requires a subject NP and an object NP:

(4)   kiss, Ty(e → (e → t))

The subcategorization information associated with the verb accounts for the fact that only (5a) is grammatical, while in (5b) the object is missing, and in (5c), there is one NP too many, so that both these sentences are ungrammatical:

(5a)   Jill kissed Robert.

(5b)   *Jill kissed

(5c)   *Jill kissed Robert John

It also follows from (4) that the PP *in the garden shed* in (6) is an adjunct, and thus not directly licensed by the verb:

(6)   Jill kissed Robert in the garden shed.

In the following section, I briefly give a more general overview of how subcategorization information can be expressed, and then show in more detail how subcategorization information is expressed in DS.

3.2.2.1 *Means of expressing subcategorization*

In addition to the syntactic aspects of subcategorization information, there are semantic considerations. Thus, for example, in Categorial Grammar syntax and model-theoretic semantics are defined in tandem in analogy to the syntax and semantics of logical languages. From a Categorial Grammar perspective, the fact that *kiss* syntactically categorizes for two NPs follows from the fact that kiss' is a binary predicate in some model in which it receives its interpretation. That is, in addition to syntactic subcategorization, there is, in Categorial Grammar, semantic subcategorization. Thus, for example, a statement about syntactic subcategorization such as in (4) above corresponds to the statement (7) in the semantics:

(7) $\lambda x \lambda y kiss'(y,x)$

As stated in (7), the predicate kiss' combines with two expressions which are substituted for the variables to result in a proposition such as, for example, shown in (8):

(8)   kiss'(jill, robert)

Accordingly, ungrammatical sentences like (5b) and (5c) above are incomplete or ill-formed in the semantics, since they do not result in an expression of Ty(t).

Frameworks not, or less, based on logic often employ the term 'participants' for the semantic correlate of subcategorization. The idea here is that verbs have the valency they have because they refer to some semantic entity, for example a frame, event, or scenario which involves a number of participants some or all of which are identified as subcategorized NPs by the verb. Despite considerable differences between more formal and more functional approaches to natural language analysis, in this particular respect, both are fairly similar—the syntactic restriction on NPs encoded by the verb is, at least partly, explained with reference to the meaning the verb expresses, however this meaning is represented.

There is a third alternative to characterize the relation between syntactic transitivity and semantic arity or participants: to employ thematic roles (or, theta(θ)-roles, deep cases). Thematic roles can be viewed as expressions in an intermediate vocabulary expressing generalizations over both conceptual (and/or semantic) structure and syntax. The major motivation for thematic roles is that they make it possible to characterize discrepancies between syntax and semantics, as well as cross-linguistic variation as to which semantic argument is expressed by which syntactic expression. For example, in Government and Binding (GB) theory (Chomsky 1981), both theta theory and case theory regulate the occurrence of nominal expressions; correspondingly, verbal lexical entries include information about both thematic roles and case. DS, following the Categorial Grammar tradition, does not recognize this intermediate level and does not employ thematic roles. I therefore offer only a short discussion here, without attempting to review the considerable literature on thematic structure even in outline.[1]

The main reason for rejecting thematic roles as part of the analytical apparatus is the vagueness of that concept. Specifically, there is, first, no set of well-defined theta-roles, and, secondly, their status as syntactic or semantic primitives is unclear. The first point, that there is no well-defined set of thematic roles, has often been made. While most frameworks or analyses would include roles like agent and patient, other potential members, for example source, path, goal, location, or direction, are less firmly established. Furthermore, it is not clear what the exact distinction is between the (or some) members of a given set of thematic roles, nor is it always clear which role to assign to a given noun phrase in a given natural language expression. The more technical reason for excluding thematic roles on these grounds is that all expressions in the DS model have an operational semantics, which might, however, be difficult to formulate for thematic roles. At present, thematic roles are thus not part of the DS system.

The second point, the unclear status of thematic roles with respect to syntax or semantics, is apparent in the following two quotes: 'in GB the focus is on the semantic relations holding between heads and their syntactic complements. These relations, called *thematic roles*, are stored in the lexical entries of potential heads' (Ravin 1990: 3, emphasis original); 'the notion "θ-grid" is no more a semantic notion than θ-theory is a semantic theory' (Tomaselli 1997: 144). That is, on the one hand, thematic roles can be viewed as syntactic primitives, purely technical tools to determine syntactic well-formedness, while on the other hand names like 'agent' or 'experiencer' seem to imply that these roles refer to something more semantic or conceptual. Assuming that this indeterminate status is undesirable, one can divide the question of thematic roles into two parts; syntactically, they are not part of the DS system due to the difficulty in defining them, while semantically, they may be regarded as generalizations over mental representations, or concepts, but not as primitives (cf. Ladusaw and Dowty 1988). I thus assume that thematic roles play no role in the specification of verbal subcategorization in DS.

3.2.2.2 *Subcategorization in DS*

The analysis of subcategorization in DS is similar to the Categorial Grammar approach, in that there is no notion of participants, or thematic roles, and in

---

[1] See Campe (1994) for references. The following discussion is based on (among others) Ravin (1990), Ladusaw and Dowty (1988), and the papers in Butt and Geuder (1998).

that typing information is taken to reflect semantic arity. DS types can thus be defined in correspondence with lambda expressions as in Categorial Grammar, for example in (9):

(9)   kiss: $\{Fo(\lambda x\lambda y kiss'(x)(y)), Ty(e \rightarrow (e \rightarrow t))\}$

In (9) the conditional type corresponds to two steps of lambda reduction which are needed to derive a proposition.

There is however an important conceptual difference between Categorial Grammar and DS with respect to the relation between syntactic structure and semantic interpretation. In DS, there is considerable independence of the building of semantic trees and eventual model-theoretic evaluation, whereas in Categorial Grammar every operation in the syntax corresponds to an operation in the semantics. Since in DS the process of tree growth is defined syntactically, independent of the eventual semantic evaluation, there is no (model-theoretic) semantic correlate for tree underspecification, or any model-theoretic semantic interpretation for procedural aspects of lexical items such as *wh*-pronouns. For the same reason, subcategorization statements in DS are not so much concerned with how eventual semantic evaluation in a model is reflected as with the contribution of lexical items to the process of structure building. In addition to type information, lexical entries for verbs may thus include explicit instructions about the transitions licensed by the verb. As shown in Chapter 2, a transitive verb like *kiss* may lexically specify the following actions:

(10)   *Lexical Entry for* kiss

IF $?Ty(e \rightarrow t)$
THEN $put(?\langle\downarrow_o\rangle Ty(e))$,
          $make(\langle\downarrow_1\rangle)$, $put(Fo(kiss'), Ty(e \rightarrow (e \rightarrow t))$
ELSE   abort

The lexical entry does not only specify the type and formula value of the verb, but consists of a set of actions which are licensed by the lexical entry. In this case, the information from the verb results not only in the building of the verb's own node (the functor daughter) but also in the annotation of the VP node with a modal requirement, which effectively, given the availability of Prediction, licenses the building of the argument node as well. Lexical entries in DS do not only include the subcategorization requirements of a given verb, but in addition include instructions for the establishment of corresponding tree structure. Subcategorization thus plays an important part in the building of tree structure.

In view of this characterization, the relation between type information and eventual model-theoretic interpretation can be regarded as being mediated by the process of structure building, as well as possibly other processes relevant for the establishment of interpretation. The exact relation between the type information provided by verbs and their eventual semantic interpretation constitutes one of the main topics of this study, fully developed in the following chapters. In particular, I argue that verbal subcategorization determines only partly the arity of a given predicate, but that quite generally, information from words is subject to pragmatic enrichment, so that the eventual semantic representation of a verb is only determined in context. In order to express the possibility of structural and contextual contribution to the establishment of meaning in utterance interpretation, I follow the DS convention in representing formula values not as lambda expressions, but by writing, for example, Fo(kiss'), which indicates that the word *kiss* provides an instruction to the hearer to access the concept kiss'. It is this concept, rather than the instruction to access it, which can be characterized as being of a particular arity. Thus, in practice, the number of Ty(e) expressions with which a given verb can combine is stated in the type value, but not explicitly in the formula value, at least not unless necessary.

3.3 ARGUMENTS AND ADJUNCTS

One of the implications of a traditional view of subcategorization is that there is a clear distinction between arguments and adjuncts. The former are subcategorized, necessarily expressed nominal expressions, while the latter are optional, not always nominal expressions in a more loose relationship to the verb.[2] This distinction correlates to some extent with a difference in semantic function and morphological marking. Semantically, arguments often introduce the main participants of the event or action denoted by the verb, while adjuncts prototypically add further information which is not strictly speaking necessary—about place, time, purpose, instruments used, or other people involved. Morphologically, arguments tend to be marked with nominative (or ergative) and accusative case, or simply unmarked, while adjuncts are often marked with a non-core case, introduced by a preposition, or marked as

---

[2] The terminology is not always straightforward in this area, which reflects I think the main claim made in this chapter that the argument-adjunct distinction is blurred. I use the term 'argument' for an obligatory, subcategorized for Ty(e) expression in the VP, and 'adjunct' for an optional Ty(e) expression in the VP. I use the term 'complement' as a cover term for both.

adverbs. However, as has been discussed by among others McConnell-Ginet (1982) and Fillmore (1994), this correlation is not perfect, and the distinction between arguments and adjuncts might therefore not be as clear as implied by strict subcategorization.

3.3.1 Morphological marking

Leaving the semantics to one side for the moment, the argument/adjunct distinction is imperfect in the sense that a number of verbs require morphological adverbs as obligatory, rather than optional complements. Consider the following examples:

(11)   John behaved rudely to his mother-in-law.

(12)   The chancellor worded the bill carefully.

(13)   The secretary phrased the submission badly.

(14)   Given that he is a computer scientist, Sean dresses well.

The adverbs in (11)–(14) are clearly morphologically marked as such, but seem to be obligatory:

(11′)   *John behaved to his mother-in-law

(12′)   *The chancellor worded the bill

(13′)   *The secretary phrased the submission

(14′)   *Given that he is a computer scientist, Sean dresses

The sentences without the adverb are less well-formed than the corresponding sentences with adverbs, so that the adverbs appear to be subcategorized for by the verb.

Similarly, in (15)–(18) the prepositional phrases cannot be omitted:

(15)   Fran put the kettle on the stove.

(16)   Alex laid the book on the table.

(17)   Judy lives with her sister.

(18)   Donovan resides in Oyster Bay.

(15′)   *Fran put the kettle

(16′)   *Alex laid the book

(17′)   ?Judy lives

(18′)   ?*Donovan resides

As these examples show, the PPs in (15)–(18) behave as arguments rather than as adjuncts with respect to obligatoriness.

Finally, the examples in (19) and (20) show obligatory verb phrase constituents in German which are not accusative marked:

(19)   *Axel   half   dem   Jungen.*
        Axel   helped   the.DAT   boy.DAT
        'Axel helped the boy'

(20)   *Sie   gedachten   der   alten   Freunde.*
        they   remembered   the.GEN old.GEN   friends.GEN
        'They remembered the old friends'

The object in (19) is dative case marked, while the one in (20) is genitive marked. Although the canonical object case in German is accusative, the NPs in (19) and (20) cannot be omitted:

(19′)   *?Axel half*

(20′)   **Sie gedachten*

As in the preceding examples, the NPs here appear to be arguments, despite the fact that they are not marked with canonical argument case.

All the preceding examples show that the distinction between arguments and adjuncts is not co-extensive with any morphological distinction, so that neither the notion of argument, nor the notion of adjunct can simply be defined in terms of morphological coding.

3.3.2 Semantic function

From the point of view of subcategorization, adjuncts provide additional or circumstantial information, as opposed to core information provided by arguments of the predicate. For adverbial modification in general, a distinction can be made between sentence adverbs, verb phrase adverbs, and verb adverbs:

(21)   He will probably be late.

(22)   Jill put down the ring reluctantly.

(23)   He covered himself completely.

The sentence adverb in (21) adds information about the likelihood of the proposition expressed by the sentence. In (22), the adverb appears to modify the verb phrase, while the adverb in (23) seems to modify the verb. In addition, PPs functioning as adverbials can, in contrast to adverbs, modify a nominal expression:

(24)   I always liked to talk to the boys from South Dakota.

(25)   The man with the paper has just left.

In (24) the PP *from South Dakota* modifies the NP *the boys*, and in (25) the PP *with the paper* modifies the NP *the man*. The difference between PPs which modify NPs and those which function as complements to verbs will be discussed in more detail in Chapter 4.

On the other hand, PPs often resist a sentence adverbial reading available to an adverb, as shown in (26) and the parallel German example in (27):

(26a)   Carefully, David had cut all the bagels.

(26b)   With care, David had cut all the bagels.

(27a)   *Julia   stellte   die Blumen   sorgfältigerweise   auf den Tisch.*
          Julia   put   the flowers   carefully   on the table
          'Julia put the flowers carefully on the table'

(27b)   *Julia   stellte   die Blumen   mit großer Sorgfalt   auf den Tisch.*
          Julia   put   the flowers   with great care   on the table
          'Julia put the flowers with great care on the table'

While (26a) may have a reading 'it was careful of David . . .', (26b) can only mean that the act of cutting was done with care. Similarly, (27a) may mean that it was careful of Julia to put the flowers on the table, while (27b) can only mean that she did it carefully.

In this study I am mainly concerned with PPs which appear to be part of the verb phrase, as opposed to those functioning as sentence adverbial.

When modifying verbs or verb phrases, PPs express a variety of semantic functions, some of which are parallel to the semantic function of arguments as illustrated below:

Locative

(28a)   Jane was singing in the bathroom.

(28b)   Judy lives in Notting Hill.

Directional

(29a)   Olli is leaving for Tokyo tomorrow.

(29b)   Sara put the pizza into the oven.

Temporal

(30a)   I have to leave before midnight.

(30b)   The meeting lasted for six hours.

Commitative

(31a)   Sally went to the movies with James.

(31b)   I am staying with my parents.

The list could be expanded or refined, but it shows that the common characteristic of all these examples is that the optional PPs in the (a) sentences modify the action denoted by the verb, rather than the proposition expressed by the sentence, in a manner similar to the subcategorized PPs in the (b) sentences, so that there does not seem to be any obvious well-defined distinction between arguments and adjuncts on semantic lines.

Another semantic parallel between arguments and adjuncts has been noted by Tenny (1994), namely that both arguments and adjuncts may change the aspectual information of the verb:

(32a)   Sally painted for/*in an hour.

(32b)   Sally painted the picture *?for/in an hour.

(33a)   Rob pushed the table for/*in an hour.

(33b)   Rob pushed the table to the window *?for/in an hour.

Both the object *the picture* in (32) and the PP *to the window* in (33) change the aspectual status of the predicate from non-telic to telic, as is indicated by the temporal adverbial. I do not discuss aspect in detail here, but just note that arguments and adjuncts can have identical semantic functions with respect to aspectual information.

It is examples like those in (28)–(33) with which I am mainly concerned in this study, i.e. PPs which modify the action denoted by the verb. The relation between the analysis developed here and VP modification by adverbs and nominal adverbials (e.g. *yesterday*) is only discussed briefly at relevant junctures, as are PPs modifying NPs. I shall not, however, discuss sentence adverbials. The semantic aspect of VP modification by PPs is discussed in Chapter 5, whereas Chapter 4 is concerned with more syntactic aspects. The following section discusses relevant morphosyntactic evidence, which shows that in many languages which have constructions which encode extraction paths, there is no difference between arguments and adjuncts in this respect.

3.3.3   Morphosyntactic evidence

Hukari and Levine (1994, 1995) discuss constructions in a number of languages which exhibit particular morphosyntactic behaviour to mark extraction, or displacement structures ('Unbounded Dependency Constructions', UDC; see also Zaenen 1983). They then point out that in these constructions extraction is marked irrespective of whether the displaced element is an argument or an adjunct. I present here the evidence adduced by Hukari and Levine, as well as examples from other sources.[3]

3.3.3.1   *French stylistic inversion*

French permits optional subject–verb inversion in the context of extraction structures (discussed e.g. in Kayne and Pollock 1978), a process called 'stylistic inversion', and illustrated in (34) (Kayne and Pollock 1978, quoted from Hukari and Levine 1994: 285):

(34)   *Où   espéraient   dîner   tes   amis?*
        Where   hope.3PL   dine   your   friends
        'Where did your friends hope to dine?'

The subject *tes amis* follows the agreeing verbal complex, in contrast to the basic SVO order in French. Stylistic inversion is not triggered by the immediate presence of an interrogative pronoun (in this case *où*), but is sensitive to the displacement context, as can be seen from (35) (Kayne and Pollock 1978, quoted from Hukari and Levine 1994: 285):

---

[3] Similar data are also discussed in Bouma et al. (1997).

(35)   *Avec qui   croit-elle   qu'a   soupé   Marie?*
         With who   think-she   that-has dine   Marie
         'Who does she think that Marie has dined with?'

In (35) the subject *Marie* follows the verb *soupé* in the subordinate clause.
However, the interrogative PP (*avec qui*) is in the matrix clause. Thus, Hukari
and Levine conclude that stylistic inversion is licensed in the UDC, i.e. between the antecedent and its unification site (i.e. extraction site), and not
by the presence of a *wh*-word. The examples in (34) and (35) already show
that stylistic inversion is not restricted to arguments, but is also licensed
by extracted adjuncts. Further examples provided by Hukari and Levine
show the contrast in interpretation between non-inverted and inverted
structures (Kayne and Pollock 1978, quoted from Hukari and Levine
1994: 285):

(36a)   *Où/Quand   Marie   a-t-elle*
          Where/When   Marie   3.sg.aux-2.sg.cl-3.sg.fem.cl
          déclaré   que Paul était mort?
          declared that Paul was dead
          'Where/when did Marie declare that Paul had died?'

(36b)   *Où/Quand   Marie   a-t-elle*
          Where/When   Marie   3.sg.aux-2.sg.cl-3.sg.fem.cl
          déclaré   que était mort Paul?
          declared that was dead Paul
          'Where/when did Marie declare that Paul had died?'

The difference between these two sentences is that (36a) has the non-inverted
order subject–verb in the lower clause (. . . *Paul était mort*), while (36b) has
the inverted order verb–subject (. . . *était mort Paul*). The difference in interpretation follows from what has been said so far: (36a) is ambiguous between
a reading where the *wh*-phrase is interpreted in the main clause and a reading
where it is interpreted in the subordinate clause. (36b), on the other hand is
not ambiguous; the *wh*-phrase has to be interpreted in the lower clause, since
the lower clause is marked as lying within the UDC. Hukari and Levine
conclude (1994: 285–6):

These examples show quite clearly that French SI [Stylistic Inversion, LM]—a
construction which registers UDC paths—is quite sensitive to both argument and
adjunct unbounded dependencies constructions, thus providing unequivocal evidence
that the latter are bona fide instances of syntactic extraction.

3.3.3.2 Downstep suppression in Kikuyu

The Kenyan Bantu language Kikuyu provides further evidence for the identical behaviour of arguments and adjuncts in displacement contexts. The evidence concerns the tonal behaviour of sentence-final words in a tensed verb phrase. In sentences without extraction, words like *moanáké*, 'boy', and *káyokó*, 'chicken' retain their final high tone in sentence-final position. However, this rule does not apply within a displacement construction (data from Clements et al. 1983, quoted from Hukari and Levine 1995: 212):

(37) *né káyokó   karékó   móndo   ʹahéíʹ ré   moànàkè t*
      FP chicken   which   person   gave   boy
      'Which chicken did someone give to the boy?'

(38) *né ré   móndo   ʹahéíʹ ré   moanáké   káyòkò t*
      FP when   person   gave   boy   chicken
      'When did someone give the boy a chicken?'

In (37), the sentence-final *moànàkè* does not retain its high tone since it is within a displacement context—*káyokó* has been extracted. As (38) shows, *káyòkò* does not retain its high tone either, i.e. (38) behaves exactly as (37), although the fronted phrase in (37) is an argument, while the fronted phrase in (38) is an adjunct.

3.3.3.3 Agreement in Chamorro and Palauan

The next set of data presented by Hukari and Levine comes from the Austronesian languages Chamorro and Palauan. The relevant reflex of displacement constructions in these two languages is morphological: verbal agreement registers UCD paths. In Chamorro, verbs in displacement structures are marked by a nominalizer as in (39) (from Chung 1982, quoted from Hukari and Levine 1994: 286) and (40) (from Chung and Georgopoulos 1988, quoted from Hukari and Levine 1994: 287):

(39) *Hafa   puno'-mu   ni   lälu'?*
      what?   kill + Nmlz-your   Obl   fly
      'What did you kill the fly with?'

(40) *Taimänu   sagan-ña si   Juan __?*
      how?   say + Nmlz-his   Unm
      'How did Juan say it?'

Both (39) and (40) involve non-argument extraction, the first example an instrumental and the second a manner phrase.

In Palauan, displacement structures are marked by a difference in verbal mood. The verb is realis when the displaced phrase is nominative, irrealis for all other displaced phrases. The examples in (41) (from Georgopoulos 1985, quoted from Hukari and Levine 1994: 287) show nominative extraction, where the verb in irrealis (41b) is ungrammatical:

(41a) *ng-te'a$_i$* *[a kileld-ii a sub __ $_i$]*
       CL who   R-PF-heat-3s soup
       'Who heated up the soup?'

(41b) **ng-te'a$_i$* *[a le-kileld-ii a   sub __ $_i$]*
       CL who   IR-heat-3s   soup

Correspondingly, with an extracted object, irrealis mood is required and realis is ungrammatical (42a, b) (from Georgopoulos 1985, quoted from Hukari and Levine 1994: 287):

(42a) *ng-ngera$_i$* *[a le-silseb-ii __ $_i$ a se?el-il]*
       CL what   IR-3 PF-burn-3s friend 3s
       'What did his friend burn?'

(42b) **ng-ngera$_i$* *[a silseb-ii __ $_i$ a se?el-il]*
       CL what   R-3 PF-burn-3s friend 3s
       Int.: 'What did his friend burn?'

Finally, (43) (from Georgopoulos 1985, quoted from Hukari and Levine 1994: 287) shows that adjuncts behave like objects:

(43)   *ng- ker$_i$* *[a le- bilsk -au a buk er ngii$_i$ a Ruth]*
       CL where IR-3 gave 2s book P it
       'Where did Ruth give you the book?'

Thus, the data from both Chamorro and Palauan confirm Hukari and Levine's observation that both arguments and adjuncts are subject to syntactic extraction.

3.3.3.4 *Irish complementizers*

A further set of relevant data is the distribution of two different forms of the complementizer in Irish, discussed by McCloskey (1979), Hukari and Levine (1995), and Bouma et al. (1997). Irish has two different complementizers, *goN* and *aL*, where the former is found in non-displacement structures, while the latter registers extraction. The following examples illustrate this pattern (from McCloskey 1979, quoted from Hukari and Levine 1995: 205–6; in *goN*, N indicates nasal mutation and in *aL*, L indicates lenition):

(44) *Shíl   mé   goN   mbeadh   sé   ann*
      thought I   COMP   would-be   he   there
      'I thought that he would be there'

(45) *an fear   aL   shíl   mé   aL   bheadh   _   ann*
      [the man]ⱼ   COMP   thought I   COMP   would-be   eⱼ   there
      'the man that I thought would be there'

(46) *an fear   aL   shíl   _   goN   mbeadh   sé   ann*
      [the man]ⱼ   COMP   thought eⱼ   COMP   would-be   he   there
      'the man that thought he would be there'

The examples in (44)–(46) show the difference between the two Irish complementizers. In (44), *goN* is used, since the sentence does not involve a fronted phrase. In contrast, the example in (45) requires the complementizer *aL*, since *an fear*, 'the man' is extracted (relativized). Note that both complementizers register the extraction path. The sentence in (46) shows that *aL* and *goN* can cooccur, and that *aL* is used up to the extraction site of the fronted phrase, but that after the extraction site, *goN* is used. The following examples show that *aL* is used not only when an argument is extracted (as in (45) and (46)), but also when the fronted phrase is an adjunct (McCloskey 1979, quoted from Hukari and Levine 1995: 206):

(47) *I mBetlehem   aL   dúirt   na targaireachtaí   aL*
      [in Bethlehem]ⱼ   COMP   said   the prophecies   COMP
      béarfaí   an Slánaitheoir   _ .
      would-be-born   the Saviour   eⱼ
      'It was in Bethlehem that the prophecies said that the Saviour would be born'

(48) *Cén uair   aL   tháinig   siad   ńa bhaile   _ ?*
      [which time]ⱼ   COMP   came   they   home   eⱼ

The extracted element in (47) is a topicalized locative adjunct, while in (48) a temporal adjunct is questioned. In both cases the choice of the complementizer is *aL*, indicating that there is an extraction path between the adjunct and its eventual position lower in the tree. Thus the distribution of the two forms of the Irish complementizer shows that arguments and adjuncts behave alike in extraction contexts.

3.3.3.5 *The particle* no *in Duala*

In the Cameroonian Bantu language Duala, extraction is marked by a particle *no*, which is placed after the first verbal element (Biloa 1993: 68):

(49) *nja   o   bodi   no   moni?*
       who   you   give   *no*   money
       'Who did you give the money to?'

The particle does not occur in *wh*-in-situ structures, nor with subject extraction:

(50) *o   bodi   nja   moni?*
       you   give   who   money
       'Who did you give the money to?'

(51) *nja   a   poi?*
       who   s/he   come
       'Who came?'

The particle appears whenever a question word has been fronted from non-subject position, irrespective of the argument or adjunct status of the questioned constituent. It is thus found with all kinds of adverbial questions:

(52) *njika   wuma   w-en   no   mo?*
       wh-   place   you-see *no*   it
       'Where did you see it?'

(53) *njika   ponda   Kuo   a   wu   no   o   ngando?*
       wh-   time   Kuo   s/he return *no* from dance
       'When did Kuo return from the dance?'

(54) *onola   nje   nu   muna   a   kwedi   no   o   kekise?*
       for   what   that   child s/he   fail   *no*   in   examination
       'Why did that child fail his exam?'

Duala thus provides more evidence for the similarity of arguments and adjuncts since they are treated alike with respect to extraction and the particle *no* in that language.

3.3.3.6 *Finnish case assignment*

Case assignment in Finnish provides more evidence for the parallelism of arguments and adjuncts, since certain adjuncts are assigned syntactic case in the same way as arguments (data from Maling 1993, quoted from Przepiórkowski 1999: 239):

(55)   *Liisa   muisti   matkan   vuoden.*
        Liisa$_{NOM}$ remembered   trip$_{ACC}$ year$_{ACC}$
        'Liisa remembered the trip for a year'

The example in (55) shows that both the object *matkan*, 'trip' and the adjunct *vuoden*, 'year' are assigned accusative case in the presence of a nominative marked subject. In contrast, with a non-nominative subject, the object receives nominative case, and the adjunct alone receives accusative case:

(56)   *Lapsen   täytyy   lukea   yksi   kerta.*
        child$_{GEN}$ must   read   book$_{NOM}$ [third time]$_{ACC}$
        'The child must read the book for a third time'

Case assignment thus proceeds along a case hierarchy, where the default cases nominative and accusative are assigned to both arguments and adjuncts. That adjuncts play a part in the hierarchy like arguments is shown by the last example, where the adjunct receives nominative case with an illative marked subject:

(57)   *Kekkoseen   luotettiin   yksi kerta.*
        Kekkonen$_{ILL}$ trust$_{PASS}$ [one time]$_{NOM}$
        'Kekkonen was trusted once'

Case assignment in Finnish thus shows that arguments and adjuncts are treated alike. Similar evidence from case assignment can be found also in Korean, Chinese, and Polish (cf. Przepiórkowski 1999: 239). As a last set of data, the next section discusses examples from English.

3.3.3.7 *English*

English does not have extraction-sensitive morphological or syntactic alternations. Hence, to find evidence for the hypothesis that arguments behave like adjuncts proposed by Hukari and Levine (1994, 1995) is not as straightforward as in the cases considered so far. Hukari and Levine observe that despite the lack of obvious syntactic evidence, arguments and adjuncts behave alike in a way which would be unexpected if they resulted from different underlying structures. The parallel behaviour of arguments and adjuncts can be seen from the fact that both can be extracted out of identical environments, including 'finite and infinite interrogatives, finite and infinite relative clauses (with or without overt *wh*-phrases), topicalizations, clefts, exclamatory *wh*-constructions, free relatives, and so forth' (Hukari and Levine 1994: 289). Some of these parallel structures are illustrated below:

(58a)   What did Bill open GAP?

(58b)   What did Bill open the door with GAP?

(59a)   What does Sally believe Jim opened GAP?

(59b)   What bed does Mary believe Sue refuses to sleep in GAP?

(60a)   It was a sandwich Steve ordered GAP, not breakfast.

(60b)   It was a house we lived in GAP, not a flat.

(61a)   It is history I passed GAP, not maths.

(61b)   It is Dr Miller I have to finish this for GAP, not Dr Smith.

The examples above illustrate *wh*-questions and clefting, the (a) examples involving argument extraction, the (b) examples extraction out of adjunct position. Similarly, if extraction of arguments is not possible, neither is extraction of adjuncts:

(62a)   *What did Bill, who opened GAP, saw Mary?

(62b)   *What did Bill, who opened the door with GAP, saw Mary?

As Hukari and Levine (1994: 290) point out, adjunct extraction is subject to strong and weak crossover effects in the same way that argument extraction is:

(63a)   *?Who$_i$ did Mary claim he$_i$ asked Sarah to visit GAP$_i$?

(63b)   *?Who$_i$ did Mary claim he$_i$ asked Sarah to have lunch with GAP$_i$?

(64a)   ?Who$_i$ did Mary claim his$_i$ mother asked Sarah to see GAP$_i$?

(64b)   ?Who$_i$ did Mary claim his$_i$ mother asked Sarah to have lunch with GAP$_i$?

In the examples above, a co-indexed pronoun intervenes between a fronted phrase and the extraction site, creating a crossover configuration. Although judgements vary, differences in acceptability result from the position of the pronoun, i.e. whether it is embedded in a larger constituent or not, but are not affected by the status of the fronted phrase, i.e. whether an argument or an adjunct is extracted. That is to say, crossover data provide further evidence for the similarity between arguments and adjuncts.

To these distributional facts, the similarity of arguments and adjuncts in quantifier scoping can be added. An indefinite noun phrase in adjunct position can take wide scope over object and subject in the same way that an indefinite object may outscope its subject:

(65a)   Every student kissed a local boy.

$\exists x \forall y$ (local_boy(x) & (student(y) → kiss(y,x)))

(65b)   Every student kissed a local boy at a beach.

$\exists x \forall y \exists z$ (beach(x) & (student(y) → (local_boy(z) & kiss_at(y,z,x))))

Thus indefinite noun phrases can have wide scope both out of argument and out of adjunct position.

The examples in this section thus show that there are a number of contexts in English in which arguments and adjuncts behave alike.

3.3.4 Summary

The examples introduced in this section show that the distinction between arguments and adjuncts rests mainly on the obligatoriness of the former and the optionality of the latter. However, this distinction does not clearly correlate with any morphological, semantic, or syntactic distinctions. Morphologically, both adverbs and PPs can be obligatory, while semantically, optional PPs may have the same function as arguments. Finally, morphosyntactic evidence shows that arguments and adjuncts behave alike in languages which overtly indicate that a constituent has been extracted. This evidence taken together indicates that the distinction between arguments and adjuncts is weaker than implied by strict subcategorization.

3.4 PRELIMINARIES FOR AN ANALYSIS OF VERB PHRASE ADJUNCTION IN DS

The evidence considered so far shows that verb phrase adjuncts behave like arguments in several respects. An analysis of arguments and adjuncts should thus reflect their similarity, as well as the difference between the two with respect to optionality. The fact that both arguments and adjuncts extract alike means in DS terms that adjuncts have to be able to be projected into unfixed nodes, introduced by *Adjunction, and that they are in all likelihood of Ty(e).[4] This also means that adjuncts cannot be LINKed, since LINKed structures are extraction islands. In order to see this, consider how argument extraction is modelled by employing unfixed nodes.

3.4.1 Argument extraction

Displaced constituents such as question words and dislocated topics, are analysed by employing the Kleene star operation over tree modalities and the corresponding unfixed nodes. The relevant steps of an object extraction derivation are shown below:

(66)   What did Judy close?

In contrast to a declarative sentence, the first step is here not Introduction, but *Adjunction:

(67a)   • {Tn(o), ?Ty(t)}
          {Tn(o*), ?Ty(e)}

The relevant (abbreviated) lexical entry for *what* is given below:

(68)   *Lexical Entry for* what
         IF $\{_{n^*} ?Ty(e)\}$
         THEN   put(Fo(WH), Ty(e))
                  go($\langle \uparrow^* \rangle$), put(+Q)
         ELSE   abort

The IF clause requires a ?Ty(e) task to hold at an unfixed node. Since this condition is met, the node is annotated with the formula and type values given. The pointer then moves to the root node and puts a +Q feature to indicate that the proposition is a question:

(67b)   • {Tn(o), Cat(+Q), ?Ty(t)}
          {Tn(o*), Fo(WH), Ty(e)}

---

[4] *Adjunction can of course be defined for other types, but that would fail to bring out the parallelism with arguments, which are undoubtedly of Ty(e).

Ignoring the contribution of the auxiliary verb *did*, the next step is the scanning of the subject and the application of Introduction and Prediction to result in the building of the subject node for *Judy*:

(67c)   *Tree for* "What did Judy

$$\bullet \ \{Tn(o), +Q, ?Ty(t)\}$$

$$\bullet \ \{Tn(oo), Fo(judy'), Ty(e)\}$$
$$\{Tn(o^*), Fo(WH), Ty(e)\}$$

The next step in the derivation is the application of Introduction and Prediction, which results in the building of $Tn(o1)$ with a requirement $?Ty(e \rightarrow t)$:

(67d)   *Tree for* "What did Judy

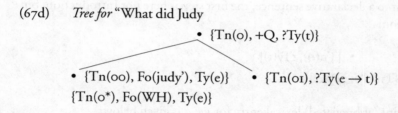

$$\bullet \ \{Tn(o), +Q, ?Ty(t)\}$$

$$\bullet \ \{Tn(oo), Fo(judy'), Ty(e)\} \quad \bullet \ \{Tn(o1), ?Ty(e \rightarrow t)\}$$
$$\{Tn(o^*), Fo(WH), Ty(e)\}$$

However, the type information from the verb *close*, i.e. $Ty(e \rightarrow (e \rightarrow t))$, does not match the requirement holding at $Tn(o1)$. The lexical information from *close* licenses in this situation the building of two new nodes, in accordance with the verb's subcategorization requirement:

(69)   *Lexical Entry for* close
    IF $?Ty(e \rightarrow t)$
    THEN · $put(?\langle\downarrow_o\rangle Ty(e))$
               $make(\langle\downarrow_1\rangle), put(Fo(close'), Ty(e \rightarrow (e \rightarrow t)))$
    ELSE   abort

The lexical information from *close* drives the process of tree building and ensures that its subcategorization requirements are projected into the tree by building a functor node for its formula and type value, and by building an argument node with the requirement $?Ty(e)$. Thus the following transition is licensed:

(67e)   *Tree for* "What did Judy close

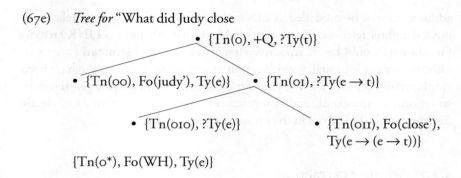

• {Tn(o), +Q, ?Ty(t)}

• {Tn(oo), Fo(judy'), Ty(e)}   • {Tn(o1), ?Ty(e → t)}

• {Tn(o1o), ?Ty(e)}   • {Tn(o11), Fo(close'), Ty(e → (e → t))}

{Tn(o*), Fo(WH), Ty(e)}

At this stage, the unfixed node has not yet been assigned its eventual location, but it is clear how this can be done. The *wh*-pronoun is of Ty(e), as indicated at Tn(o*). Furthermore, the DU has to be fixed at a position in the tree which is lower than Tn(o), that is, at a daughter node. These two specifications match exactly the information holding at Tn(o1o). It is a daughter node of the root node, and there is a requirement ?Ty(e). By merging Tn(o1o) with the under-specified node Tn(o*), the tree can be completed with no requirement out-standing, and all nodes being fixed:

(67f)   *Tree for* "What did Judy close?"

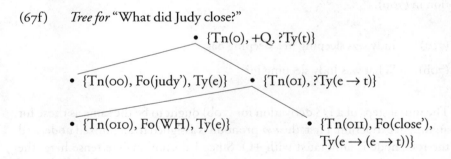

• {Tn(o), +Q, ?Ty(t)}

• {Tn(oo), Fo(judy'), Ty(e)}   • {Tn(o1), ?Ty(e → t)}

• {Tn(o1o), Fo(WH), Ty(e)}   • {Tn(o11), Fo(close'), Ty(e → (e → t))}

The information projected from the *wh*-pronoun is found in the eventual tree in object position. The analysis of displaced constituents thus exploits the possibility of underspecified tree node locations; this results in an unfixed node during the derivation, which only eventually is assigned a fixed place in the tree, before Completion and Elimination apply. The output trees of extraction structures and non-extraction structures are homomorphic modulo the pres-ence of the +Q feature and the presence of the WH variable at the Merge site. The real difference between these two sentence types is in the way the eventual tree structures are derived, with only the extraction structure involving an unfixed node.

Since argument extraction involves the intermediate use of unfixed nodes, and since unfixed nodes are defined as an infinite transitive daughter relation, adjuncts cannot be modelled as LINKed structures, since a LINK relation is not a daughter relation. This is remarkable in that otherwise a LINK analysis for adjuncts would be an attractive alternative. LINKed structures are in an informal sense additional, providing non-essential information, and have been employed not only for the analysis of relative clauses, but also for genitive constructions, conjunction, and parentheticals. Yet the extraction facts clearly disfavour a LINK analysis in the present context.

3.4.2 Adjunct extraction

Given the analysis of argument extraction discussed in the preceding section, and in view of the fact that arguments and adjuncts behave alike with respect to extraction, the first plausible analysis for adjunct extraction is to proceed along the steps described in the argument extraction derivation above. This leads to a discussion of how a DS analysis of verb phrase adjunction can be developed, a discussion which will form the background for the analysis proposed in Chapter 4.

As an example, consider the adjunct in (70a) and the corresponding question in (70b):

(70a)   Judy was sleeping in a sleeping bag.

(70b)   What was Judy sleeping in?

The initial steps of a DS derivation for (70b) ought to be the same as those for argument extraction. First, the *wh*-pronoun is assigned to an unfixed node, and the root node is annotated with +Q. Since I do not analyse tense here, the second step is—as above—the introduction of the subject and the building of the VP node by Introduction and Prediction:

(71a)   *Tree for* "What was Judy

$$\{Tn(0), +Q, ?Ty(t)\}$$

$\{Tn(00), Fo(judy'), Ty(e)\}$ $\{Tn(01), ?Ty(e \rightarrow t)\}$
$\{Tn(0^*), Fo(WH), Ty(e)\}$

This is the state of the derivation when *sleep* is scanned. I assume that *sleep* is intransitive, as stated in the following lexical entry:

(72)   *Lexical Entry for* sleep
    IF $?Ty(e \rightarrow t)$
    THEN   put(Fo(sleep'), $Ty(e \rightarrow t)$)
    ELSE   abort

The entry states that *sleep* can be introduced at a VP node, and that it annotates the node with its formula and type value, thereby fulfilling the requirement obtaining at that node:

(71b)   *Tree for* "What was Judy sleeping

$$\bullet \; \{Tn(o), +Q, ?Ty(t)\}$$

$\bullet \; \{Tn(oo), Fo(judy'), Ty(e)\}$ $\bullet \; \{Tn(o1), Fo(sleep'), Ty(e \rightarrow t) \; \blacklozenge\}$
$\{Tn(o^*), Fo(WH), Ty(e)\}$

Note that the pointer at this stage is still at $Tn(o1)$, so that Completion can apply to record the fulfilled requirement as a modal statement at the root node $Tn(o)$, where Elimination applies. With respect to subcategorized predicate–argument structure, the tree in (71b) is completed, since the combination of Fo(judy') and Fo(sleep') would result in a proposition of $Ty(t)$. Yet the derivation cannot be completed, since there is further input, namely the preposition *in*, and there is still an unfixed node, which needs to be fixed for the derivation to be successful. At this state, then, the parallelism between the derivation of argument extraction and the derivation of adjunct extraction ends. Whereas for the argument, the unfixed node could be located in the tree at an open daughter node resulting from the verb's subcategorization information, there is no obvious place in the tree in (71b) for the adjunct at the unfixed node. As it stands, the tree is unfinished and the derivation is aborted.

What can be done? There is still the preposition, which might lexically contribute to a resolution of the problem, for example, by building a new $Ty(e)$ node. Excluding the LINK operation, there are three general possibilities to expand a tree like the one in (71b), and I sketch them here so as to prepare for the discussion in the following chapter.[5]

The first possibility is inappropriate for the example discussed here, but should briefly be mentioned. This is to continue the tree after Completion has applied and the pointer has moved to the root node:

---

[5] Abstracting away from DS specific details, the alternatives illustrated here have been discussed in the literature. In Ch. 5, the analyses of Dowty (1979), McConnell-Ginet (1982), and Copestake et al. (1997) are discussed in more detail.

(73)

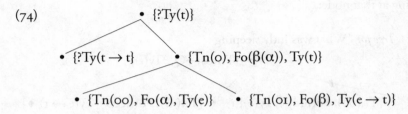

In a situation like this, the tree could be expanded upwards by building a new root node (a 'grandmother' node):

(74) • {?Ty(t)}

• {?Ty(t → t)}   • {Tn(o), Fo(β(α)), Ty(t)}

• {Tn(oo), Fo(α), Ty(e)}   • {Tn(oi), Fo(β), Ty(e → t)}

I have omitted several details in the tree in (74), such as the value of the tree node predicate, or how a Ty(e) expression could be integrated into the tree. However, for the example discussed here, this tree continuation is not possible, since the new nodes are not in a daughter relation to the original root node. Intuitively, the continuation shown in (74) could be employed for the analysis of sentence adverbials such as *possibly*, but it is not a viable option for adjuncts such as those discussed here.

Another possibility, and probably the most obvious analysis, is to integrate adjuncts somehow into the middle of a tree like in (71b), that is, to analyse the adjunct as operating on the VP node. Thus, a possible eventual tree for the example in (70b) might be the following:

(75) *Possible Tree for* "What was Judy sleeping in?"

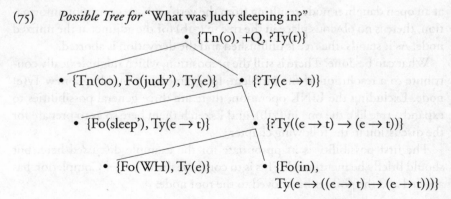

In the tree in (75) a new Ty(e) node is built which does stand in a daughter relation to the root node. The new functor node is built by the preposition, which acts as the main functor in the tree. Note that, as in the tree above, I have left out the tree addresses of the relevant nodes in (75). Although here it is clear what they should be, it is not clear how they are assigned; in particular the tree-node value for the DU introduced by the verb would have to be assigned a new address. In the next chapter, I argue that a continuation like the one in (75) is impossible in DS since it involves tree restructuring, so that it is not a viable analysis for verb phrase adjunction.

The third alternative to be considered here is the one which I argue in the next chapter to be the best solution, namely to analyse verb phrase adjuncts as optional arguments of verbs. A corresponding tree is shown below:

(76)   *Possible Tree for* "What was Judy sleeping in?"

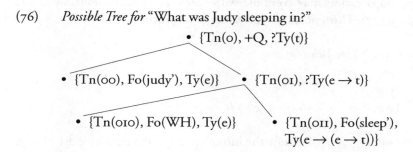

In (76), the verb appears as transitive, and a corresponding new argument node Tn(010) has been built at which the unfixed node has been located. The new node is a daughter of the root node and is below the original VP node, so that under this analysis adjuncts are transparently analysed as arguments of the verb. The syntactic contribution of the preposition can then be seen as licensing the necessary process of tree continuation. However, as pointed out in this chapter, adjuncts are not obligatory constituents of the verb phrase, and are not subcategorized for by the verb. A possible solution to this problem is simply to assume that there are two lexical entries for *sleep*, one intransitive one, and one which allows for the introduction of an argument. The derivation discussed above would then simply involve the right choice of predicate, for example in the case of *sleep* the 'transitive' one, which allows for the introduction of an additional Ty(e) expression. The difference between arguments and adjuncts would under this view result from different lexical entries for verbs. This would explain the optionality of adjuncts, since the choice of a particular lexical entry is in general optional.

However, while a lexical solution is an appropriate analysis for optional arguments of verbs with both an intransitive and a transitive use, for example *drink* or *read*, it is implausible for verb phrase adjunction in general, under the assumption that adjuncts are analysed as (non-lexical) optional arguments, as implied in the tree continuation in (76). Under this view, all verbs allow for the optional introduction of Ty(e) expressions, as seen in (77):

(77)   Mary was singing her favourite song at the top of her voice with her
        sister for their parents at Christmas in the drawing room.

In view of the generally free possibility of introducing Ty(e) expressions, which
I take here to include PPs, a point discussed in detail in the next chapter,
lexical subcategorization statements appear to be the wrong tool. Rather, a verb
such as *sing* may be lexically categorized as requiring at least one Ty(e) expression, or, in its transitive use, two Ty(e) expressions, but, given the view of
adjunction sketched here, there should in addition be the possibility of stating
that *sing* on occasion may combine with seven Ty(e) expressions, as in the
example in (77). Thus, possible type values of *sing* include:

(78)   *Possible Type Values of* sing
        $Ty(e \rightarrow t)$
        $Ty(e \rightarrow (e \rightarrow t))$
        $Ty(e \rightarrow (e \rightarrow (e \rightarrow (e \rightarrow (e \rightarrow (e \rightarrow (e \rightarrow t))))))$

The type values in (78) illustrate the intransitive and the transitive use of *sing*,
as well as the necessary type value for the analysis of the example in (77) under
the assumption that the Ty(e) expressions are introduced as arguments of the
verb. While the first two type specifications might be regarded as lexical information from *sing*, the last type is the result of the general process of adjunction.
In the next chapter I propose an analysis which models this general process of
adjunction as type underspecification, i.e. as an element of variability in verbal
subcategorization. The remainder of the study is then mainly concerned with
the formalization and implications of this view.

4

Verbal Underspecification

4.1 INTRODUCTION

The last chapter has presented evidence to support the view that the distinction between arguments and adjuncts mainly reflects the difference between obligatory and optional presence in the verb phrase, but that adjuncts behave syntactically like arguments once they are introduced. In this chapter I propose various ways in which these facts can be modelled in Dynamic Syntax, following on from the discussion which concluded the previous chapter, and in particular that basic DS assumptions about incrementality and underspecification lead naturally to the view that verbal subcategorization can be analysed as underspecified. The discussion in this chapter is concerned with the dynamics of tree building, while the interpretation of adjuncts in general, and of the specific analysis of verbal underspecification modelled in this chapter in particular, will be discussed in the following chapter.

4.2 TWO BASIC DS ASSUMPTIONS

As pointed out in Chapter 2, DS models the process of utterance interpretation which the hearer is required to perform in order to derive contextual effects. This process includes the combination of lexical building blocks (supplied by phonological accessing) into larger structural units. The process is strictly left-to-right in the sense that each lexical building block is taken in turn and, by application of relevant rules, integrated into the unfolding tree structure. More formally, the structure-building process is *incremental*. However, the mapping from 'surface structure', i.e. here the linear order of incoming lexical items, to conceptual structure, the output of the parse, is not one to one. Incrementality is achieved by allowing *underspecification* to be part of natural language expressions. These two assumptions are discussed in more detail here, since they are part of the motivation for the analysis of verbal underspecification proposed later in the chapter.

4.2.1 Incrementality

To say that the process of building interpretable structures is incremental reflects the observation, on the one hand, that hearers receive syntactic information in units, as accessed in phonological domains, one block after the other, and, on the other hand, that syntactic processing is fast and automatic. The model should thus reflect the fact that interpretations are built by knowing increasingly more about the eventual tree. I express this aspect of incrementality as 'informational incrementality' as in (1):

(1)   *Incrementality (informational)*
       Interpretation always involves an increase in information.

The aspect of incrementality expressed in (1) involves some idealization vis-à-vis human parsing as reported in the literature (e.g. Frazier and Fodor 1978, Berwick and Weinberg 1984, Fodor 1995, Gorrell 1995), where there is agreement that the human parser allows for local restructuring of already established structure, for example in certain types of garden-path utterances. This means that (1) is too strong as a statement of real time human parsing. It should be borne in mind, however, that the DS model is a model of competence in the sense discussed in Chapter 2, which by claim is amenable to psycholinguistic evidence, but that it is not a proper model of a parser. There are a number of avenues by which to incorporate the restructuring evidence into the model, for example by allowing for several parallel parses, or by relaxing the requirement of incrementality in certain respects. In the present context, however, it seems justified to maintain (1) as it stands, since it leads to the formulation of more precise syntactic and semantic characterizations of incrementality, as presented anon, and since it is warranted as a theoretical assumption by the overall cognitive argument presented in Chapter 2.

The strong version of informational incrementality in (1) is paralleled in the syntax of DS by the syntactic aspect of incrementality expressed here as (2):

(2)   *Incrementality (syntactic)*
        The process of building tree structure is defined as an incremental process. No process is defined which removes previously built structure.

This aspect of incrementality is the most important one in the following discussion of underspecified type values in the verb phrase. This syntactic restriction constrains the DS system considerably—both information from the lexicon and the transition rules have to be formulated such that they guarantee that all syntactic information is exploited at every step in a derivation, while at the same time ensuring that there is no 'back-tracking', that is, that every step in a derivation results either in leaving the tree as it is, or as developing it, but that no step in the derivation can ever remove nodes, or node descriptions from a given tree. The consequences of this restriction for the analysis of adjuncts will be discussed below.

Finally, the corresponding semantic notion of incrementality can be expressed as a requirement on tree structure:

(3)   *Incrementality (semantic)*
        Tree structure once built cannot be undone.

The notion of semantics invoked here is the structural notion of the semantics of tree structure—the 'operational' semantics of the DS system. The model-theoretic semantic interpretation of the natural language string is defined over the output of the structure-building process, in particular over the information from the formula values. For our purposes, it is the first, structural notion of semantics which is important.

Given the three aspects of incrementality discussed so far, the following 'principle of incrementality' in DS can be stated:

(4)   *Incrementality*
        The process of utterance interpretation as modelled in DS is informationally, syntactically, and semantically incremental.

Since the process of utterance interpretation in DS includes information provided in the lexicon as part of the tree building process, the following two corollaries result from (4):

(5)   *Corollary 1: The DS Projection Principle*
        Information which is established in the lexicon remains constant (unchanged) in a derivation.

(6)   *Corollary 2: Lexical Projection of Type Values*
       Type values established in the lexicon remain constant (unchanged) in a
       derivation.

That is, since lexical information is part of the derivation, it is subject to the
principle of incrementality. Lexical information cannot be changed during
a derivation (5). This includes in particular any type values established in the
lexicon (6). If some lexical information includes the predicate $Ty(e)$, it has to be
associated with a node with a requirement of $Ty(e)$, from which it follows that,
as discussed in the preceding chapter, type-shifting or function composition over
types are not recognized processes in DS, in contrast to Categorial Grammar.

The strong commitment to incrementality expressed in the principle of
incrementality in (4) has the immediate consequence that the question of
which information is available at a given step in a derivation is of central
importance to the DS enterprise. The answer to the question from a DS
perspective has predominantly to do with the underspecification of natural
language.

4.2.2 Underspecification

Certain instances of underspecification in natural language are widely regarded
as such—pronominal expressions, for example, do not fully encode their refer-
ential information; they are underspecified in regard to their (model-theoretic)
semantic contribution. In order to know what a pronominal expression refers
to, it has to be pragmatically enriched, exploiting contextual and background
knowledge. In DS, this is modelled as an underspecified formula value, such
that, for example, a personal pronoun encodes a meta-variable, possibly with
certain restrictions, as its formula value, which is taken to be an instruction to
the hearer to establish some suitable referent. While this treatment seems to be
rather uncontentious for the semantic interpretation of at least some pronouns,[1] it is not usually taken to be related to syntactic structure.

In DS, however, structural, syntactic underspecification is taken to be a key
feature of natural language, providing the basis for the analysis of a range of
syntactic phenomena, including topic structures and question formation,
where there is a mismatch between the surface position of a given constituent

---

[1] The analogy with the interpretation of pronouns depends on the particular analysis of
anaphoric expressions. While the analysis developed in Kempson et al. (2001) proposes a uniform analysis of all pronouns (or pronoun usages) as underspecified, alternative conceptions
may distinguish between different pronoun interpretations such as resumptive and bound-
variable interpretations. The DS view is discussed in more detail in Ch. 5, in connection with the
more general argument for mental representations.

in a natural language string and its eventual position in the semantic tree. As demonstrated in the preceding chapters, fronted constituents are modelled as having an initially underspecified tree location, which is only resolved at some later stage in the derivation. That is, question word 'movement' is in DS terms an instance of syntactic underspecification. It is to a large extent due to the possibility of having structural underspecification that the strong requirement of incrementality discussed in the preceding section can be maintained; a displaced constituent is not assigned an initial or intermediate place in the tree, but rather encodes the lack of any definite information as to its location. In that way, only weak tree structure specification is established, and resolving the final position of the displaced constituent can clearly be seen as an increase in information. The relevant steps of the derivation with unfixed constituents discussed in the last chapter demonstrate this:

(7a)   *Tree for* "What

         • {Tn(o), +Q, ?Ty(t)}

{Tn(o*), Fo(WH), Ty(e)}

The DU introduced by *what* is not integrated into the tree, since this is not warranted by the available information at this stage in the derivation. The syntactic information encoded by this DU is underspecified with respect to its eventual location in the tree. During the following transitions, the information that the DU is an as-yet-unfixed part of the tree is available at every step of the derivation. The DU is eventually assigned a fixed position in the tree when the underspecification is resolved:

(7b)   *Tree for* "What did Judy close?"

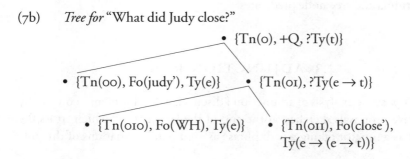

In the final stage of the derivation, the underspecification of Tn(o*) is resolved as Tn(o1o) by an application of Merge, and the DU is integrated into the tree. With regard to the present discussion, it is important that the resolution of Tn(o*) to Tn(o1o) is an increase in information, that no previously established tree structure has been changed, and that all semantic relations holding before the final step in the derivation still hold after that step. In other words, under-specification and the resolution of underspecification can be expressed within a derivation which is incremental in the sense defined in (4).

The discussion so far has highlighted the relation between incrementality and underspecification. We shall return to incrementality presently; a final observation is directed at the forms of underspecification introduced so far. As pointed out already, DS employs underspecified values of the formula predi-cate, for example Fo(WH) for an interrogative pronoun as English *who*, or Fo($U_{speaker}$) for a personal pronoun as English *I*. Additionally, there are under-specified values for the tree node predicate, as for example Tn(o^*) for a DU holding somewhere below the top node Tn(o), where $*$ is a short-hand nota-tion for the Kleene star operation over the daughter modality $\langle\downarrow\rangle$. This leads to the question of whether there are, analogously to the formula and tree node predicates, underspecified values for the type predicate. In other words, since underspecification is taken in DS to be a fundamental structural characteristic of natural language, expressed as underspecified values of structural predicates, it is a natural extension of the system to inquire into the underspecification of type values, which is indeed what I propose to do in the remaining sections of this chapter.

In summary, the discussion so far shows that a successful DS treatment of adjunction, to which I turn presently, has to provide an analysis which allows only incremental derivations, without tree restructuring or changing lexical information. In doing so, it might be helpful, but not necessary, to take advan-tage of the relation between incrementality and underspecification. There is, however, theory-internal independent motivation for exploring the possibility of underspecification of values for the type predicate, building on an analogy with formula and tree node predicates.

4.3 ADJUNCTION RULES

The first possible analysis of adjunction I discuss is a development of one of the alternative proposals sketched at the end of the last chapter, which treats the adjunct as a functor taking a verb phrase as argument.[2] Variations of this rule

---

[2] This analysis corresponds to the standard analysis of adjunction in the formal semantics tra-dition (e.g. Montague 1974, Morrill 1994). A particular formulation of it, the one proposed in Dowty (1979), is discussed in detail in the next chapter. Here the discussion focuses on the tree-theoretic aspects of adjunction. Kempson et al. (2001: 84–5) have an adjunction rule which builds adjuncts as functors without technically restructuring established tree structure. How-ever, they do not discuss the rule, or adjunction, in detail.

are discussed, including a version which assumes that the basic clausal relationship between a verb and subcategorized complements is fully specified, and that adjuncts can freely be added at several nodes of a tree. This is achieved by assigning an unspecified type value to prepositions, so that prepositional adjuncts can be added. However, this approach is problematic, since it implies that tree structure has to be undone.

4.3.1 Adjuncts as functors

To begin with, consider the example with a lexical adverb in (8):

(8)   Mary smiled nervously.

In (8), *nervously* might be analysed as acting as a modifier of the verb, which is of $Ty(e \to t)$. A possible derivation for the sentence might then proceed as follows:

(9a)   *Tree for* "Mary smiled

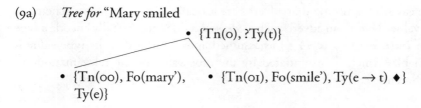

The stage of the derivation displayed in (9a) is reached after the information from *smile* is incorporated into the tree (again ignoring tense). The derivation cannot be completed here, since there is more lexical input, namely from *nervously*. On the assumption that *nervously* acts as a VP modifier, it is lexically of $Ty((e \to t) \to (e \to t))$. In order to incorporate the adverb into the tree, the DU holding at $Tn(01)$ has to be relocated so as to act as the argument to the modifier:

(9b)   *Tree for* "Mary smiled nervously

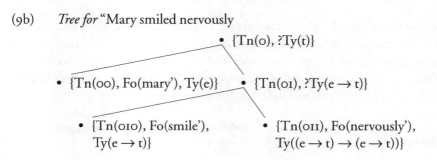

In (9b), the DU previously holding at Tn(01) is 'lowered' to Tn(010), a new node is created for the DU introduced by *nervously*, namely Tn(011), and a second new node is created, Tn(01), with a requirement of Ty(e → t), which can be satisfied by Completion. I will argue in the next section that this process of lowering is problematic, but assume for the moment that it is a possibility.

Under this analysis, then, the adverb is lexically of Ty((e → t) → (e → t)), that is a verb phrase modifier. However, the analysis could be extended to include examples such as those in (10):

(10a)   Mary looked out of the window nervously.

(10b)   Mary looked nervously out of the window.

(10c)   Nervously, Mary looked out of the window.

In (10), *nervously* seems to act as a modifier at different levels of clause structure, probably as a verb phrase adverb in (10a), as verb adverb in (10b), and as sentence adverb in (10c).[3] The analysis described here could be extended to these cases by assuming that adverbs are lexically associated with a schematic type value. That is, an adverb such as *nervously* does not lexically encode a type value Ty((e → t) → (e → t)) as assumed above, but rather, its type value is a variable, which is instantiated by the type value of the relevant node of attachment:

(11)   *Lexical Type for Adverbs*
         $Ty(X → X)$,   where X = any Type value.

         Possible Instantiations
         Sentence Adverb: $Ty(t → t)$
         VP Adverb: $Ty((e → t) → (e → t))$
         IntransV Adverb: $Ty((e → t) → (e → t))$
         TransV Adverb: $Ty((e → (e → t)) → (e → (e → t)))$
         Di-transV Adverb: $Ty(((e → (e → (e → t))) → (e → (e → (e → t)))))$

By assuming the schematic value in (11), the adverb can be introduced at any node in the tree, while adverbs can still be characterized as being lexically unambiguously of a single underspecified type. Note, however, that VP and intransitive verb adverbs are of the same type. The particular concept of type underspecification assumed in (11) is that adverbs have no type specification in

---

[3] I do not discuss these differences in detail, since I will not be concerned with (proper) adverbs any further.

the lexicon at all, and that their type value is specified according to the expression they modify. That is, type underspecification is here modelled as a variable over standard types.

On the analogy with adverbs, PPs in the verb phrase might be analysed as underspecified adverbials. This is the assumption underlying the possible tree for adjunct extraction discussed in the last chapter, repeated below:

(12)   *Possible Tree for* "What was Judy sleeping in?"

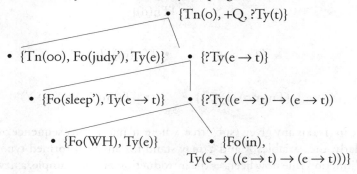

In (12), the preposition builds an argument node for the Ty(e) expression and combines with it to result in a verb phrase modifier. The preposition in (12) might thus be analysed as being lexically of the type below:

(13)   *Putative Type for Prepositions*
     $Ty(e \to (X \to X))$

Under this analysis, a preposition combines with a Ty(e) expression to result in an adverb. The underspecification can be resolved according to the node to be modified.

In summary, an analysis of adjuncts as functors can be formulated by assuming that an operation of tree stretching or lowering is possible, and by assuming that prepositions combine with a Ty(e) expression to result in an underspecified adverbial. In the following section I show that both these assumptions are problematic.

4.3.2 Adjunction with tree lowering

The analysis of adjuncts sketched in the preceding section can be formally stated by formulating an Adjunction rule which licenses an operation of 'subtree lowering' in order to introduce a new node in the middle of a tree.

(14)   *Adjunction*

$$\{Tn(a), Ty(X), Fo(\alpha) \blacklozenge\}$$

$$\{Tn(ao), Ty(X), Fo(\alpha)\}, \{Tn(a), ?Ty(X)\}, \{Tn(a1), ?Ty(X \to X) \blacklozenge\}$$

The rule is illustrated with abstract trees in (15):

(15a)   *Adjunction: Input Tree*

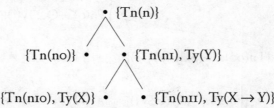

The tree in (15a) is any given (sub-)tree, where 'n' may be any sequence of 0 and 1. Similarly, the variables X and Y may stand for any well-formed type value. The Adjunction rule now licenses the introduction of, for example, a new node with a DU of type $Ty(Y \to Y)$, i.e. applying to the DU with $Ty(Y)$ at $Tn(n1)$ in (15a) at a stage in the derivation when this is the current node. The new node is thus a sister to $Tn(n1)$ and results, furthermore, in another new node of $Ty(Y)$ above the old $Tn(n1)$ and the new sister node:

(15b)   *Adjunction: Output Tree*

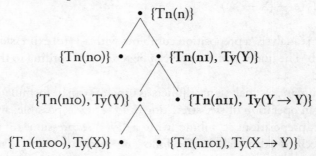

The new nodes introduced by the Adjunction rule are indicated in bold print; they are (the new) $Tn(n1)$ and (the new) $Tn(n11)$. As a result of this 'tree-stretching' operation, the old nodes $Tn(n1)$, $Tn(n10)$, and $Tn(n11)$ now become $Tn(n10)$, $Tn(n100)$, and $Tn(n101)$ respectively. The Adjunction rule thus licenses the introduction of new nodes 'into' an already established tree. However, the rule is problematic with respect to incrementality.

4.3.3 Adjunction as tree lowering and incrementality

On the surface, the Adjunction rule does not seem to respect incrementality, since it involves the restructuring of already established structure: already established tree node values are changed. However, it might be objected that the relative tree relations between the nodes already established remain unchanged. This means that, irrespective of the actual tree node values, the relation between nodes as expressed in the tree node modalities $\langle \downarrow \rangle$ and $\langle \uparrow \rangle$ remain unchanged. For example, from the position in the tree where the DU with $Ty(X)$ holds, it was and is true that the statement $\langle \uparrow \rangle Ty(Y)$ ('above me is a DU with $Ty(Y)$') is true, as is $\langle \uparrow \rangle \langle \downarrow \rangle Ty(X \rightarrow Y)$ ('at my sister $Ty(X \rightarrow Y)$ holds'). This is so, because all of these nodes have been lowered uniformly, namely 'one down'. Similarly, from the position of $Tn(n)$, it was and is true that $\langle \downarrow \rangle \ldots$ (meaning here 'below me holds whatever it is that holds below me'). This is true for two different reasons: for the left daughter, because both nodes have not been changed, and for the right daughter, because by definition the Adjunction rule introduces an identical node to the node the adjunct takes as an argument; i.e. since the adjunct is of type $Ty(Y \rightarrow Y)$, the type value holding at the sister node is identical to the type value holding at the mother node. For the nodes considered so far, it is thus indeed true that the relative tree positions hold. However, for the original node with $Ty(Y)$, it is not true; before adjunction, both $\langle \uparrow \rangle \ldots$ (here, 'above me holds whatever holds above me') and $\langle \uparrow \rangle \langle \downarrow \rangle \ldots$ (here, 'at my sister holds whatever holds at my sister') were true, whereas after adjunction $\langle \uparrow \rangle Ty(Y)$ ('above me is a DU with $Ty(Y)$') and $\langle \uparrow \rangle \langle \downarrow \rangle Ty(Y \rightarrow Y)$ ('at my sister $Ty(Y \rightarrow Y)$ holds') are true. One might argue that this particular difference is warranted, since it is after all the point of the rule to introduce these two DUs. But there is another problem. It is in general not true that relative tree relations are unchanged once the modality operators are iterated. For example, before Adjunction it was true for the node where $Ty(X)$ holds that $\langle \uparrow \rangle \langle \uparrow \rangle \ldots$ (here, 'above above me holds whatever holds above above me'), while after Adjunction the correct statement is $\langle \uparrow \rangle \langle \uparrow \rangle Ty(Y)$.[4] Similarly, from $Tn(n)$, before Adjunction $\langle \downarrow \rangle \langle \downarrow \rangle Ty(X)$ is true, whereas after Adjunction $\langle \downarrow \rangle \langle \downarrow \rangle Ty(Y)$ and $\langle \downarrow \rangle \langle \downarrow \rangle Ty(Y \rightarrow Y)$, as well as $\langle \downarrow \rangle \langle \downarrow \rangle \langle \downarrow \rangle Ty(X)$, but not $\langle \downarrow \rangle \langle \downarrow \rangle Ty(X)$ hold. Iteration of operators, however, cannot be excluded, since it is needed for the characterization of $\langle \downarrow^* \rangle$, i.e. for the characterization of underspecified tree locations, and since iterated modality statements are part of lexical instructions. It might be possible to introduce revisions into the DS system, so that no reference to iterated modality operators is necessary, other

---

[4] From now on I omit the English glosses.

than $\langle \downarrow^* \rangle$, by restricting lexical specifications.[5] This would mean that the tree restructuring involves only irrelevant information, and thus that the Adjunction rule does respect incrementality in the sense that relative, but not absolute, tree node locations count as established tree structure, and provided that relative tree locations are sufficiently described by modality statements with one modality operator only. The Adjunction rule discussed here, then, does provide a possible analysis of verb phrase adjunction, but it implies non-trivial revisions of the overall DS system and it does not, as it stands, respect incrementality in a clear sense. Thus, with respect to both conceptual assumptions and formal tools, the Adjunction rule does not present an optimal analysis of verb phrase adjunction in DS.

4.3.4 Adjunction as tree lowering and type values

In addition to the problems pointed out in the last section, there is the further problem that the Adjunction rule is not the right analysis for the adjuncts discussed in the last chapter. It results in problems with respect to the typing of prepositions, and with respect to the semantic structure assigned to PPs modifying the verb.

Under the Adjunction rule, PPs act as functors which take another functor as argument. For example, the relevant type information for the preposition *for* the tree in (12) is shown below:

(16) $\{Fo(in), Ty(e \rightarrow ((e \rightarrow t) \rightarrow (e \rightarrow t)))\}$

With the typing in (16) the preposition combines with a noun phrase (which is of $Ty(e)$) to give the necessary type $Ty((e \rightarrow t) \rightarrow (e \rightarrow t))$, which combines with an expression of $Ty(e \rightarrow t)$ to result in another expression of $Ty(e \rightarrow t)$, as required by the Adjunction rule. However, this analysis implies that PPs always act as modifiers, and is thus problematic for subcategorized PPs:[6]

(17a)   Jane put the book on the shelf.

(17b)   *Jane put the book

(17c)   *Jane put the book the shelf

---

[5] A possible way to do this is to use the 'go' predicate and specify pointer movement not in relation to tree nodes, e.g. $go(\langle \uparrow_i \rangle)$, but in relation to the intended endpoint of the movement, e.g. $go(\langle \uparrow^* \rangle ?Ty(X))$, i.e. 'go up to a node where $?Ty(X)$ holds'. It is not clear, however, if such an analysis could fully replace iterated modality operators.

[6] The same argument holds for subcategorized adverbs, illustrated in the last chapter.

The problem here is that, as discussed in the preceding chapter, the distinction between PPs and NPs is not co-extensive with the distinction between arguments and adjuncts, so that any attempt to derive the latter distinction from lexical typing of the former encounters problems with these cases. Similarly, distinguishing between arguments and adjuncts in terms of typing leads, as pointed out in the previous chapter, to problems for a uniform analysis of extraction.

A second point to note about the Adjunction rule is the formula value which it derives at the $Ty(t)$ node. Assuming that the typing problems mentioned above could be solved, a derivation with the Adjunction rule of an example like (18) looks as follows:

(18)   John baked a cake for Mary.

(19)   *Tree for* "John baked a cake for Mary"

$$\bullet\ \{Tn(o), Fo((for'(mary'))((bake'(cake'))(john'))), Ty(t)\}$$

$$\bullet\ \{Tn(oo), Fo(john'), Ty(e)\}\qquad \bullet\ \{Tn(or), Fo((for'(mary'))((bake'(cake')))), Ty(e \rightarrow t)\}$$

$$\bullet\ \{Tn(oro), Fo((bake'(cake'))), Ty(e \rightarrow t)\}\qquad \bullet\ \{Tn(orr), Fo(for'(mary')), Ty((e \rightarrow t) \rightarrow (e \rightarrow t))\}$$

$$\bullet\ \{Tn(oroo), Fo(cake'), Ty(e)\}\quad \bullet\ \{Tn(oror), Fo(bake'), Ty(e \rightarrow (e \rightarrow t))\}\quad \bullet\ \{Tn(orro), Fo(mary'), Ty(e)\}\quad \bullet\ \{Tn(orrr), Fo(for'), Ty(e \rightarrow (X \rightarrow X))\}$$

In the resulting structure in this derivation, the position of the adverb node $Tn(orr)$ is such that the adjunct acts as functor which takes the verb phrase at $Tn(oro)$ as argument. However, as noted in the previous chapter, some adjuncts behave as arguments to the verb, rather than as functors taking the verb, or the verb phrase, as arguments, so that for those adjuncts the Adjunction rule gives the wrong analysis. The semantic aspects of this distinction are discussed in the next chapter, but here it is worth noting that locating the underspecification of type values, as implied in the Adjunction rule, in the adjunct rather than in the predicate will always result in the adjunct acting as functor. In the next section I develop an analysis which locates the underspecification involved in adjunction in the verb, and which introduces adjuncts as optional arguments to the verb.

4.4 UNDERSPECIFIED VERBS WITH e*

In this section I come to the main proposal of this study. I propose a formalization of verbal subcategorization which treats verb-phrase adjuncts syntactically as arguments and, at least potentially, both arguments and adjuncts as being syntactically optional.[7] Following overall DS strategies, and similar to the Adjunction rule discussed above, the proposal involves the structural underspecification of lexical information. However, in contrast to the Adjunction rule, the underspecification is not located in the type information of the adjunct, but in the type information of the verb. The idea is that verbs structurally underspecify the number of $Ty(e)$ expressions, taken to include both NPs and PPs, with which they may combine to form a verb phrase. In addition to obligatorily required arguments, the type information of verbs which I propose thus explicitly encodes the possibility of adding $Ty(e)$ expressions optionally. If further $Ty(e)$ expressions are introduced, they are treated as arguments. The argument adding can be modelled as a step-by-step process, where the valency of the verb is increased in the context of suitable (in a sense left open at present) $Ty(e)$ expressions, so that verb phrase interpretation can then be seen to proceed incrementally. One consequence of this view is that the arity of a predicate introduced by a verb is in general determined anew at every occasion of its use.

4.4.1 Definition of $Ty(e^* \rightarrow X)$

The lexical type specification associated with verbs in DS is a conditional type specifying the number of $Ty(e)$ expressions required by the verb to give an expression of $Ty(t)$, as for example in $Ty(e \rightarrow t)$ for intransitive verbs. I retain this general format, but add to it the possibility of introducing additional expressions of $Ty(e)$. This is achieved by making use of the Kleene star operation, already employed in the system for the analysis of fronted constituents.

In particular, I define the type value $Ty(e^* \rightarrow X)$ as in (20):

(20)   *Definition of $(e^* \rightarrow X)$*
        $(e^* \rightarrow X) =_{def} \{(X) \text{ v } (e \rightarrow (e^* \rightarrow X))\}$
        where $X \in \{\text{TYPE}\}$

---

[7] This view of adjunction has been explored in the Categorial Grammar paradigm, notably by McConnell-Ginet (1982), whose analysis I discuss in the next chapter.

The definition in (20) states that 'if e-star, then (some type) X' is defined as 'X, or if e, then if e-star, then X'. The net effect of this definition is that e^* is under-specified as to how many e's it stands for. This is achieved by defining e^* disjunctively, where the left part of the disjunction corresponds to the case where e^* stands for zero e's, and the right part corresponds to the case where e^* stands for one e. Since the definition is recursive (the right part of the disjunction itself contains an e^* predicate), e^* can be interpreted as standing for an infinite number of e's.[8] Note that the definition in (20) does not enrich the set of types used in the system, since e^* is defined over types already employed.[9] In fact, starred types can be defined for all types by the generalized star definition in (21):

(21)   *Definition of* $(X^* \rightarrow Y)$
         $(X^* \rightarrow Y) =_{\text{def}} \{(Y) \text{ v } (X \rightarrow (X^* \rightarrow Y))\}$
         where $X, Y \in \{\text{TYPE}\}$

I do not explore the possibilities raised by the definition in (21). In this study I only employ e^* for verbs, so that the definition in (20) can be expressed more specifically as:

(22)   *Definition of* $(e^* \rightarrow t)$
         $(e^* \rightarrow t) =_{\text{def}} \{(t) \text{ v } (e \rightarrow (e^* \rightarrow t))\}$

From the definition in (22) it follows that the underspecification inherent in the starred type can be resolved to predicates of any arity:

(23)   *Resolution of* $Ty(e^* \rightarrow t)$
         $Ty(t)$
         $Ty(e \rightarrow t)$
         $Ty(e \rightarrow (e \rightarrow t))$
         $Ty(e \rightarrow (e \rightarrow (e \rightarrow t)))$
         $Ty(e \rightarrow (e \rightarrow (e \rightarrow (e \rightarrow t))))$
         . . .

Note that after the resolution of the underspecification, the starred type reduces to an ordinary type specification already employed in the DS system, which interacts with binary branching trees equally employed in the system.

---

[8] This is of course a very powerful characterization, a point which I discuss below.

[9] The disjunction symbol (vel) in the definition is not part of the type, but meta-vocabulary.

A possible alternative formulation would result in flat, *n*-ary branching trees. I introduce one such non-recursive formalization here for illustration purposes, although I do not develop it further in what follows:

(24)   *Definition of* $(e^n \rightarrow t)$

$(e^n \rightarrow t) =_{\text{def}} \{(t) \text{ v} ((e_1, e_2, \ldots e_n) \rightarrow t)\}$

where $n \in N$

The new aspect of (24) is that expressions of Ty(e) are added to an unordered set with little internal structure.[10] The disadvantage of this formalization is that it requires much more far-reaching revisions of the DS system than the alternative given in (22), since in (24) the vocabulary of the type predicate is enriched (by the comma), and corresponding tree relations are not defined. On the other hand, any advantages gained from either (22) or (24) can only be seen once the types are used, and the role of order of Ty(e) expressions for structure building and interpretation is explained. As it turns out, the formalization in (22) is completely adequate for the purposes I have in mind, so that I will in the remainder of this study only use the version given in (22).

4.4.2 e* introduction

In order to use the underspecified type e* in the DS system, it has to be stated how transitions from one parse state to another are licensed when predicates with e* are involved. The advantage of e* predicates is that they can be used with any number of arguments. However, in order for a derivation to be successful, we have to ensure that the underspecification is only fully resolved after all potential arguments are introduced into the tree. In other words, the predicate has to be fixed last in the derivation to ensure that it is associated at the lowest predicate node. Note the position of the resolved predicates in the two trees below:

(25)   *Tree for* "Judy was singing"

• {Tn(0), ?Ty(t)}

• {Tn(00), Fo(judy'), Ty(e)}   • {Tn(01), Fo(sing'), Ty(e → t)}

---

[10] The internal structure in (24) is expressed by a comma. I could equally well have used conjunctions, or required an ordered set.

(26)   *Tree for* "Judy was singing a song for her sister"

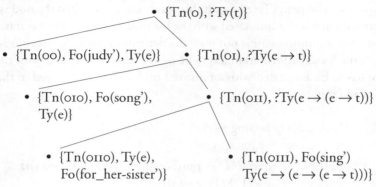

The intransitive use of *sing* in (25) shows that the predicate is associated at Tn(01). However, when the same predicate is combined with two optional Ty(e) expressions, and is consequently resolved as Ty(e → (e → (e → t))), it is associated at Tn(0111). In general, underspecified verbs will always be resolved at the lowest predicate node so as to ensure that they can combine standardly with their arguments. This means that until all arguments have been introduced, the verb has to be locally unfixed, awaiting resolution of the type, and therefore also of the location underspecification. In other words, transitions with e* can be characterized as subcases of transitions for underspecified tree nodes. There are two ways in which the association between the underspecified type e* and an underspecified tree location can be expressed with the resources given by the DS architecture. Either underspecified verbs are associated to an unfixed node via lexical instruction, or a general transition rule is defined which, similar to *Adjunction for Ty(e) expressions, introduces the unfixed node for the predicate. I discuss these alternatives in turn.

4.4.2.1 *e* introduction from the lexicon*

As outlined in Chapter 2, lexical entries in DS consist of a set of statements which define the particular context in which a lexical expression may be introduced into a derivation, and how it contributes to the development of tree structure. For example, the lexical entry for *sing* can be stated, without e*, as follows:

(27)   *Lexical Entry for* sing
IF	?Ty(e → t)
THEN	put(Fo(sing'), Ty(e → t))
ELSE	abort

According to (27), the condition for the introduction of the DU introduced by *sing* is a requirement ?Ty(e → t). If this condition is met, then the node with the requirement may be annotated with the formula and type values as stated in the entry. If the requirement is not met, the derivation ends. For the introduction of e*, the lexical information has to be modified, since the DU with the predicate has to be associated with an unfixed node. This is expressed in the lexical entry in (28):

(28)   *Lexical Entry for* sing *with e**

IF	?Ty(e → t)
THEN	make(⟨↓*⟩), put(Fo(sing'), Ty(e → (e* → t))), go(⟨↑*⟩ ?Ty(e → t))
ELSE	abort

The difference between these two specifications is that in (27), the DU from *sing* is associated directly at the node with the requirement, while in (28) a new unfixed node is built, where the DU is associated. The 'go' predicate indicates that the next lexical action proceeds from the requirement ?Ty(e → t), i.e. the pointer moves back to the point of origin.[11]

(29)   *Tree for* "Judy was singing . . ." *with e**

$$\{Tn(0), ?Ty(t)\}$$

$$\{Tn(00), Fo(judy'), Ty(e)\} \qquad \{Tn(01), ?Ty(e \to t) \blacklozenge\}$$
$$\{Tn(01^*), Fo(sing'), Ty(e \to (e^* \to t))\}$$

The type underspecification corresponds thus to an underspecification of location—it is as yet not known where in the eventual tree the DU from the verb is located. This situation means that there might be two locationally underspecified nodes in a given tree, since now both the verb and any unlocated nominal constituent (e.g. *Who*) are unfixed. However, the two nodes can always be distinguished by their type values, since constituents standardly analysed as being unfixed are Ty(e) expressions, while unfixed e* expressions always have a conditional type, so that no unwanted interaction between the two nodes results.

---

[11] Throughout this study I assume that statements such as go(⟨↑*⟩ ?Ty(e → t)) in the entry above are instructions for the pointer to move up in the tree to the *first* node with the relevant requirement. In Kempson et al. (2001) this is defined explicitly, but for the cases discussed here the formulation adopted is sufficient.

For a transitive verb like *close*, the relevant lexical entry and transitions are as follows:

(30)   *Lexical Entry for* close *with e**

IF $?Ty(e \rightarrow t)$

THEN $make(\langle\downarrow^*\rangle)$, $put(Fo(close'), Ty(e \rightarrow (e \rightarrow (e^* \rightarrow t))))$,
            $go(\langle\uparrow^*\rangle ?Ty(e \rightarrow t))$,
            $put(?\langle\downarrow_1\rangle Ty(e \rightarrow (e \rightarrow t)))$,
            $make(\langle\downarrow_0\rangle)$, $put(?Ty(e))$

ELSE   abort

In (30), it is part of the lexical specification of the verb to build the tree structure required to fulfil its subcategorization requirements. The entry licenses the building of three new nodes: an argument node ($\langle\downarrow_0\rangle$), a functor node ($\langle\downarrow_1\rangle$), both with the appropriate requirements, and an unfixed node for the verb. This means that both *sing* and *close*, and generally any verb, can be introduced at a requirement of $?Ty(e \rightarrow t)$. The corresponding tree structures are shown below:

(31a)   *Tree before the introduction of* close

$$\bullet \; \{Tn(0), \dots ?Ty(t)\}$$

$$\bullet \; \{Tn(00), \dots, Ty(e)\} \qquad \bullet \; \{Tn(01), ?Ty(e \rightarrow t) \; \blacklozenge\}$$

The tree in (31a) includes the requirement $?Ty(e \rightarrow t)$ at $Tn(01)$, which provides a suitable condition for the introduction of *close*. The lexical specifications of *close* in (30) then result in the following tree:

(31b)   *Tree after the introduction of* close

$$\bullet \; \{Tn(0), \dots ?Ty(t)\}$$

$$\bullet \; \{Tn(00), \dots, Ty(e)\} \; \bullet \; \{Tn(01) \, ?Ty(e \rightarrow t), \, ?\langle\downarrow_1\rangle Ty(e \rightarrow (e \rightarrow t))\}$$

$$\bullet \; \{Tn(010) \, ?Ty(e) \; \blacklozenge\}$$
$$\{Tn(01^*), Fo(close'), Ty(e \rightarrow (e \rightarrow (e^* \rightarrow t)))\}$$

As can be seen from (31b), the lexical specifications specify all required nodes; the unfixed node $Tn(01^*)$ and the argument node $Tn(010)$ are built directly, while the corresponding functor node is required by the modal statement holding at $Tn(01)$, which results by the application of Prediction in the building of this node.[12]

The introduction of underspecified predicates into a derivation at an unfixed node can thus be achieved by lexical instruction. A potential alternative to this solution is to devise a general rule which introduces unfixed nodes for predicates.

4.4.2.2 e^* *introduction by rule*

The alternative to the lexical introduction of e^* predicates is to define a transition rule for e^* which licenses the introduction of a DU with e^* type, and its association with an underspecified tree location. This can be done by defining a rule for e^* Adjunction, modelled on *Adjunction:

(32) e^* *Adjunction*

$$\frac{\{_n \ldots ?Ty(X \to Y)\}}{\{_n \ldots ?Ty(X \to Y)\} \ \{\langle \uparrow^* \rangle ?Ty(X \to (e^* \to Y))\}}$$

The rule states that at a parse state where at a given node $Tn(n)$ $?Ty(X \to Y)$ (where X, Y any type) holds, an unfixed node can be built lower than $Tn(n)$ with a DU with the underspecified type value $Ty(X \to (e^* \to Y))$ (where X, Y are the same type as at $Tn(n)$). The corresponding tree structure resulting from e^* Adjunction is given below:

(33) e^* *Adjunction: Tree*

$$\bullet \ \{Tn(n), \ldots ?Ty(X \to Y)\}$$
$$\{Tn(n^*), \ldots , ?Ty(X \to (e^* \to Y))\}$$

The e^* Adjunction rule ensures that verbs with an e^* type are introduced into the parse, by assigning them an underspecified tree node predicate $Tn(n^*)$. Due to the general format of the rule, it achieves the same result as the lexical alternative, namely to introduce e^* predicates from a VP node with a requirement $?Ty(e \to t)$.

There are two problems with defining a general rule for e^* introduction. The first is that the rule is specifically designed for underspecified types which are meant to be associated with verbs. However, despite involving type underspecification, verbs might still vary as to their strictly required arguments. For

---

[12] In the following discussions I occasionally assume that Prediction applies automatically, i.e. I omit the step from requirement to node building.

example, *sing* might be of Ty(e → (e* → t)), but *close* of Ty(e → (e → (e* → t))), but the rule is neutral with respect to this difference. Since idiosyncratic information of individual verbs has to be introduced from the lexicon, it seems more economical also to introduce their (underspecified) type value by lexical instruction, in which case a general introduction rule is unnecessary. In other words, the general aspect of verb phrase underspecification is that Ty(e) expressions may be introduced optionally. However, the contribution of the verb in this process is not in general optional, but rather to provide the (or one) necessary condition for the process, which might also include idiosyncratic information. The general rule does not adequately express the contribution of the individual verb, which can better be stated as lexical instructions.

Secondly, the rule e* Adjunction as it stands licenses the introduction of an underspecified location with an underspecified type at any parse stage. Although e* Adjunction is, like all transition rules, optional, this treatment still seems unnecessarily powerful. In a strict SVO language like English, for example, verbs are in general introduced at the VP node, i.e. at a node with the requirement ?Ty(e → t), which acts as a condition for the introduction of the verb from the lexicon, so that there are effectively no cases where the e* Adjunction rule would be needed. On the other hand, a general rule for verb adjunction might be needed to model word order variation, and in particular the position of the verb in languages with verb-second or verb-initial structures such as German (cf. Kempson et al. 2001: 172–3). I discuss this point in more detail in section 4.5, after the e* analysis has been more fully formulated, but I note here already that a general rule of e* introduction threatens to undermine an analysis of unfixed verbs for the phenomenon characterized in other frameworks as verb movement, and that, since the introduction of unfixed nodes from the lexicon provides a viable alternative to introduction by rule, it seems more cautious to reserve the general rule option for alternative applications.

4.4.3 Resolution with Merge

After e* predicates have been introduced into an unfixed node by lexical actions, they have to be assigned a fixed place in the tree after all arguments have been parsed, and the underspecification of their type has to be resolved. Since e* is defined as Kleene star operation, and since unfixed nodes are independently available in the system, the resolution of e* can be defined by exploiting independent DS operations. In particular, an unfixed node with e* provides suitable input for the transition rule Merge, which is used in the resolution of unfixed nodes, for example with question words. As pointed out in

Chapter 2, Merge is formulated completely generally, stating that two node descriptions (ND), corresponding to what is referred to as DU here, can be combined, so as to result in the union of whatever information is associated with the two DUs:

(34)   *Merge*

$$\frac{\{\dots ND, ND' \dots\}}{\{\dots ND \cup ND' \dots\}}$$

The rule licenses effectively the merging of the information from two distinct nodes into one node. In practice, the effect of the rule is restricted, since in most cases merging two nodes results in inconsistent information. However, in the case of underspecified nodes, it is exactly the combination of information which is required. Thus, in the case of e^*, Merge is instantiated as follows:

(35)   *Merge e^**

$$\frac{\{_n \dots ?Ty(X \to t)\}, \{_{n^*} \dots Ty(X \to (e^* \to t)\}}{\{_n \dots ?Ty(X \to t), Ty(X \to (e^* \to t))\}}$$

In this instantiation, the information from the unfixed node is merged with the requirement of a fixed node in the tree. If, by the definition of e^* in (22), above, $(e^* \to t)$ can be reduced to (t) in this situation, Thinning can apply, and the requirement is fulfilled. The effect of Merge e^* can be represented by two trees, corresponding to the input and to the output of Merge e^* respectively:

(36a)   *Merge e^* (before)*

$$\bullet \ \{Tn(n), \dots ?Ty(X \to t)\}$$
$$\{Tn(n^*), \dots, Ty(X \to (e^* \to t))\}$$

Before the application of Merge, the e^* predicate is at an unfixed node, and some requirement holds at a fixed node somewhere above the unfixed node. The application of Merge results in the merging of the information of the two nodes:

(36b)   *Merge e^* (after)*

$$\bullet \ \{Tn(n), \dots, Ty(X \to (e^* \to t)), ?Ty(X \to t)\}$$

The resolution of $Ty(e^*)$ predicates is thus achieved in the same way that underspecified nodes are resolved in general, namely by Merge. Thus, for example, a derivation for *John sang* with e* involves the introduction of an unfixed node, by the lexical information from *sing*, and the resolution of the underspecification by Merge:

(37a)　　*Tree for* "John sang

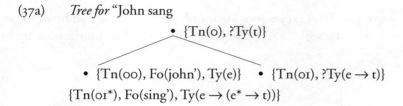

$\bullet$ {Tn(0), ?Ty(t)}

$\bullet$ {Tn(00), Fo(john'), Ty(e)}　$\bullet$ {Tn(01), ?Ty(e $\rightarrow$ t)}

{Tn(01*), Fo(sing'), Ty(e $\rightarrow$ (e* $\rightarrow$ t))}

The tree in (37a) is the result of building the tree structure specified in the lexical entry for *sing* in (28). In the absence of further input, Merge can apply to derive the tree in (37b):

(37b)　　*Tree for* "John sang"

$\bullet$ {Tn(0), ?Ty(t)}

$\bullet$ {Tn(00), Fo(john'), Ty(e)}　　　$\bullet$ {Tn(01), Fo(sing'),

Ty(e $\rightarrow$ (e* $\rightarrow$ t)), ?Ty(e $\rightarrow$ t)}

The information holding at Tn(01) is consistent, since Ty(e $\rightarrow$ (e* $\rightarrow$ t)) can be resolved as Ty(e $\rightarrow$ t), and thus Thinning can apply, which then leads to the completion of the derivation.

4.4.4　Introduction of optional Ty(e) expressions

The initial and the final steps in derivations with e* have so far been defined: the introduction of e* predicates from the lexicon, and the resolution of the underspecification by Merge. What needs to be defined is the introduction of additional Ty(e) expressions, and how they interact with the predicate. Again, I discuss two options, the first employing the general rule Introduction, and the second, better one employing lexical actions for prepositions.

4.4.4.1　*Ty(e) introduction by rule*

The optional intermediate steps in a derivation, in particular the optional introduction of Ty(e) expressions, can be stated by referring to the rules Introduction and Prediction, which are independently defined in the system. Consider a tree with an unfixed e* node:

(38a)   *Tree with unfixed e* node*

$$\bullet \ \{Tn(n), \dots ?Ty(e \rightarrow t)\}$$
$$\{Tn(n^*), \dots, Ty(e \rightarrow (e^* \rightarrow t))\}$$

When an incoming Ty(e) expression is scanned, the tree is updated by Introduction of the requirement $?\langle\downarrow\rangle Ty(e)$ and the building of the requisite node by Prediction:

(38b)

$$\bullet \ \{Tn(n), \dots ?Ty(e \rightarrow t)\}$$

$$\bullet \ \{Tn(no), \dots, Ty(e)\}$$
$$\{Tn(n^*), \dots, Ty(e \rightarrow (e^* \rightarrow t))\}$$

Similarly, Introduction and Prediction result in the building of a new functor node with the requirement $?Ty(e \rightarrow (e \rightarrow t))$:

(38c)

$$\bullet \ \{Tn(n), \dots ?Ty(e \rightarrow t)\}$$

$$\bullet \ \{Tn(no), \dots, Ty(e)\} \qquad \bullet \ \{Tn(nI), ?Ty(e \rightarrow (e \rightarrow t))\}$$
$$\{Tn(n^*), \dots, Ty(e \rightarrow (e^* \rightarrow t))\}$$

Two further applications of these two rules would result in two new nodes, one of which carries a requirement of $?Ty(e \rightarrow (e \rightarrow (e \rightarrow t)))$. This process could go on until no further Ty(e) expressions are scanned. At every step, Merge could apply to resolve the underspecification. This solution would drive derivations with e* with no changes to the overall system—the introduction of the DU with e* at an unfixed node would be followed by possibly several applications of Introduction and Prediction, and the resolution of the underspecification by Merge.

However, this solution threatens to be too powerful. Lexical information merely requires the presence of a given number of Ty(e) expressions. If further Ty(e) expressions could be freely introduced without any restrictions, as is indeed the case in this solution with Introduction, there would be no means of excluding strings like the following:

(39)   *John met Mary Bill the house

(40)   *Sally closed the window the kitchen

(41)   *Allan put the flowers the table

The strings in (39)–(41) would go through since the noun phrases are introduced by Introduction, and e* allows for the introduction of Ty(e) expressions into the predicate. However, what is missing is a preposition:

(39′) John met Mary with Bill in the house.

(40′) Sally closed the window in the kitchen.

(41′) Allan put the flowers under the table.

From the contrast between (39)–(41) and (39′)–(41′), it appears that prepositions function to license the introduction of further Ty(e) expressions. In the next section, I discuss how this function can be best expressed in the present context, and how the analysis of prepositions can be used to provide an alternative to the analysis employing the Introduction rule.

4.4.4.2 *Ty(e) introduction from the lexicon*

I have so far at least tacitly assumed that PPs are of Ty(e). It is only under this assumption that an e* analysis could be employed for PPs which behave as an argument of the verb:

(42) Fran opens bottles with her teeth.

(43) The Bakers travelled to Paris in their van.

(44) They discovered the corpse in the fridge.

The idea is that the verb is underspecified, and that all post-verbal constituents in (42)–(44) can be introduced as arguments to the predicate.[13] Given the definition of e*, both NPs and PPs have to be of Ty(e) for this analysis to work. But this state of affairs, in conjunction with the unrestricted availability of Introduction, leads to the undesirable results illustrated at the end of the last section—that not only PPs but both PPs and NPs can freely be added into the VP—which by and large is not true.

One possible solution to this problem would be to say that PPs are not of Ty(e) after all, but of a discrete type, say, for the sake of argument, of Ty(pp), so that it is not Ty(e) expressions but Ty(pp) expressions which can be freely added and incorporated into the predicate by a corresponding type, say,

---

[13] In the relevant reading, that is. PPs may modify NPs, a case discussed below.

$Ty(e \rightarrow (pp^* \rightarrow t))$. But that would take almost all of the original motivation for e^* out of the picture, since it is exactly PPs which appear most clearly to modify verbs in an argument-like fashion and which thus should be treated in a similar way. In addition, it would increase the available types in DS without proper motivation.

A better way to go seems to be to make prepositions the licensors of Introduction, for example by saying that $Ty(e)$ expressions can only be introduced if they are marked by a preposition. But that runs into problems for the main context where Introduction is needed—the building of the subject node in English. Introduction licenses the transition from a requirement $?Ty(t)$ to the building of a $Ty(e)$ node:

(45a)   • $\{Tn(o), ?Ty(t)\}$

The application of Introduction and Prediction at a parse stage like (45a) results in a tree such as (45b):

(45b)   • $\{Tn(o), ?Ty(t)\}$

          • $\{Tn(oo), ?Ty(e)\}$

The rule Introduction is needed to ensure that an initial $Ty(e)$ expression in a string of words can be assigned a position in the tree. Clearly, in this environment the $Ty(e)$ expression, i.e. the subject, need not, in fact cannot, be licensed by a preposition. Since I want Introduction to take care of the structure-building in cases like (45), I cannot restrict it to be licensed by prepositions. This means that I cannot use Introduction for the introduction of optional $Ty(e)$ expressions, and that optional $Ty(e)$ expressions have to be introduced into the tree by some other means. I thus pursue the idea that optional $Ty(e)$ expressions are introduced by the lexical instructions of prepositions, and not by a general rule.

Consider a case like (46):

(46)   Sandy opened the window with the broom.

Given the lexical definitions for verbs above, the NP *the window* is licensed in the tree since the $Ty(e)$ node has been built from lexical instructions. Furthermore, the predicate has been assigned to an unfixed node, resulting in a parse state like (47a):

(47a)   *Tree for* "Sandy opened the window

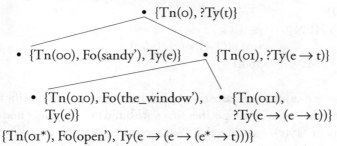

- {Tn(o), ?Ty(t)}
- {Tn(oo), Fo(sandy'), Ty(e)}   • {Tn(o1), ?Ty(e → t)}
- {Tn(o1o), Fo(the_window'),   • {Tn(o11),
  Ty(e)}   ?Ty(e → (e → t))}
{Tn(o1*), Fo(open'), Ty(e → (e → (e* → t)))}

The next step in the derivation should result in the introduction of the PP at a new argument node Tn(o11o). I assume for the moment that Introduction is blocked from applying in this situation (in a sense to be made more precise soon). The sensible assumption, then, is that it is the preposition *with* which builds the necessary node, to result in a tree like (47b):

(47b)   *Tree for* "Sandy opened the window with

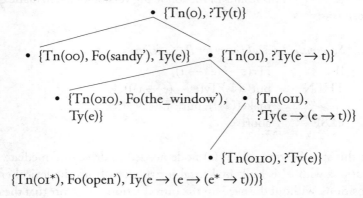

- {Tn(o), ?Ty(t)}
- {Tn(oo), Fo(sandy'), Ty(e)}   • {Tn(o1), ?Ty(e → t)}
- {Tn(o1o), Fo(the_window'),   • {Tn(o11),
  Ty(e)}   ?Ty(e → (e → t))}
- {Tn(o11o), ?Ty(e)}
{Tn(o1*), Fo(open'), Ty(e → (e → (e* → t)))}

The tree in (47b) is identical to a potential tree where Tn(o11o) would have been introduced by Introduction. Thus, it can be developed further without problems. Prediction results in the building of a functor node Tn(o111) with ?Ty(e → (e → (e → t))), and the DU from *the broom*, an expression of Ty(e), fulfils the requirement at Tn(o11o). Finally, Merge applies, and the derivation is finished.

The claim is thus that Tn(o11o) is built not by Introduction but from the lexical information from the preposition *with*. This can be achieved with the following lexical entry:

(48)   *Lexical Entry for* with

  IF $?Ty(e \rightarrow (e \rightarrow t))$

  THEN $put(?\langle\downarrow_1\rangle Ty(e \rightarrow (e \rightarrow (e \rightarrow t))))$,

       $make(\langle\downarrow_0\rangle), put(?Ty(e))$

  ELSE   abort

While some modifications are still needed, it is clear that this specification does what is needed—the entry specifies that *with* builds an argument node with the requirement $?Ty(e)$. I assume that lexical entries for prepositions consist minimally of such an instruction to build a $?Ty(e)$ node. There are two further points. The first concerns the condition (i.e. IF) for the introduction of the preposition. In (48), the preposition can be introduced if there is a requirement $?Ty(e \rightarrow (e \rightarrow t))$ at the relevant parse state, as was the case in the example discussed, (47). In general, however, PPs can be introduced at any stage with the requirement for a predicate, e.g. $?Ty(e \rightarrow t)$, $?Ty(e \rightarrow (e \rightarrow t))$, $?Ty(e \rightarrow (e \rightarrow (e \rightarrow t)))$, etc. But this is exactly the range of cases covered by $Ty(e^* \rightarrow t)$. Thus e^* can be used here as a requirement. Given that the relevant PPs here are introduced into the VP, the universal condition for the introduction of PPs is $Ty(e \rightarrow (e^* \rightarrow t))$. This results in the following version of a schematic entry for prepositions:

(49)   *Schematic Lexical Entry for Prepositions*

  IF $?Ty(e \rightarrow (e^* \rightarrow t))$

  THEN $put(?\langle\downarrow_1\rangle Ty(e \rightarrow (e \rightarrow t)))$,

       $make(\langle\downarrow_0\rangle), put(?Ty(e))$

  ELSE   abort

With this specification, the $Ty(e)$ node needed to drive intermediate steps in derivations with e^* is built by lexical instructions from the lexical entries of prepositions, without the need for the Introduction rule. Note that the requirement obtaining at the argument daughter here implies the resolution of the underspecified requirement; in particular, it has to be read not as an absolute statement, but as the resolved type specification relative to the parse state. Thus for a requirement such as $Ty(e \rightarrow (e \rightarrow (e^* \rightarrow t)))$, the first action is $put(?\langle\downarrow_1\rangle Ty(e \rightarrow (e \rightarrow (e \rightarrow t))))$. In this way, the preposition requires the building of a corresponding functor node by Prediction.[14]

---

[14] This could equally be expressed more formally by having an underspecified node built from the lexical action in (49), i.e. $put(?\langle\downarrow_1\rangle Ty(e \rightarrow (e \rightarrow (e^* \rightarrow t))))$ instead of $put(?\langle\downarrow_1\rangle Ty(e \rightarrow (e \rightarrow t)))$, to indicate that the node being built has one more e than the trigger.

A second point relevant for the lexical entry of prepositions is their 'semantic' contribution, since the entry thus far only specifies that prepositions build nodes. I will here not provide a detailed discussion of the meaning of prepositions in English (or in general). Rather, I simply show how the semantic contribution of prepositions can be encoded into lexical entries of the kind discussed here in general. The easiest way to do this is to employ features which specify that the $Ty(e)$ expressions be of a particular semantic/thematic kind. In the example considered above, *with the broom* may be regarded as an 'instrument', so that the preposition in this case requires the $Ty(e)$ node to be annotated with a feature '+instr'. This may simply be written into the lexical specification:

(50)   *Lexical Entry for* with *(with 'instr' feature)*

IF $?Ty(e \rightarrow (e^* \rightarrow t))$

THEN $put(?\langle \downarrow_I \rangle Ty(e \rightarrow (e \rightarrow t)))$,

            $make(\langle \downarrow_o \rangle), put(_{+instr}, ?Ty(e))$

ELSE   abort

A feature like '+instr' in (50) can be thought of as a language-specific set of words, e.g. the feature '+loc' in English would be something like {*in, on top of, behind, under,* . . . }, or it can be given a specific semantic interpretation, e.g. in terms of force dynamics, or lexical-conceptual structures. However, I am not developing such an account here, nor do I review the available literature. Although formal semantic accounts have been developed for temporal and spatial prepositions,[15] the analysis of instruments or comitatives as in (51) and (52) appears to be much more intricate:

(51)   Fran wrote her dissertation with an ink pen.

(52)   John went to the party with Mary.

Rather than defining the particular semantic contribution of the preposition in cases like these, I simply use features, and, since I do not go into further details here, I prefer to use one feature per preposition, that is, for example, *with* annotates the $Ty(e)$ node with a 'feature' '+with'. On occasion, I use a general feature '+prep', meaning a $Ty(e)$ expression with a preposition, i.e. a PP. For our purposes, the main contribution of prepositions in cases where PPs function as arguments to the verb is to license the introduction of their object (i.e. the

---

[15] For example, Dowty (1979), Gawron (1985), Pratt and Francez (1997), Zwarts (1997), as well as several non-formal approaches, e.g. Bennett (1975) and Jackendoff (1983).

noun phrase) into the predicational range of the verb—i.e. prepositions may function, in conjunction with the verb, as instructions for argument adding. In this sense, the use of prepositions corresponds to the function of case in languages like Finnish or German, which mainly signals the relation of the noun phrase with the verb without any clear semantic contribution, at least with respect to tree building, which is the focus of this chapter.[16] In the cases in (51) and (52), for example, the contribution of the prepositions is intuitively to allow the construction of a three-place semantic writing relation between Fran, her dissertation, and an ink pen for (51) and the construction of a three-place semantic going relation between John, the party, and Mary for (52). This process of constructing semantic relations will be discussed more extensively in the next chapter. For the present, I assume that the information from the preposition is projected into the formula value of the Ty(e) expression, so that *with the broom* results in a Ty(e) expression with a formula value Fo(with_the_broom). The interpretation of formula values in general will be discussed in more detail in the following chapter, so that I assume here that prepositions minimally build a Ty(e) node and provide some annotation on it.

The lexical treatment of the introduction of a Ty(e) node provides an alternative to the introduction of Ty(e) expressions by Introduction discussed in the last section. However, the analysis is not yet a solution to the problem of the unwanted optional NPs. This is because general rules can apply at any stage in the derivation. Thus, although Ty(e) nodes can now be built from the lexicon, they still can be built by Introduction. What is missing is a statement to the effect that Ty(e) expressions can *only* be built from the lexicon; in other words, the assumption I have made in this section that Introduction is blocked has to hold. It is, however, difficult to block a rule from applying, since rules, including Introduction, are not context sensitive in the relevant sense. Rather, what this analysis of e* entails is that there is no general rule Introduction. As pointed out above, Introduction is needed for the introduction of subjects in English. But this is, as far as I can see, the only context where the rule is required. If this turns out to be true, Introduction can be replaced by (53):

(53)   *Subject Introduction*

$$\frac{\{_n \ldots ?Ty(t) \; \blacklozenge\}}{\{_n \ldots ?Ty(t), ?\langle\downarrow_o\rangle Ty(e), ?\langle\downarrow_1\rangle Ty(e \rightarrow t) \; \blacklozenge\}}$$

[16] This position seems also plausible with respect to language change, since it has been noted especially in the grammaticalization literature that case markers diachronically develop out of prepositions (cf. e.g. Heine et al. 1991, Hopper and Traugott 1993). Prepositions, in turn, develop often from nouns—supporting an analysis with a nominal type for PPs.

The rule Subject Introduction licenses the introduction of a Ty(e) node, which then can be built by Prediction, only in the context of a Ty(t) task, i.e. at the root node. This still licenses the introduction of subjects (in languages where this is necessary), but does not interfere with the introduction of Ty(e) expressions at any other position in the tree. This is in fact the only major revision of the overall DS architecture required by the analysis of adjunction by e* developed here, and for the purposes of this study I assume that Introduction is replaced by Subject Introduction.

Before progressing, I shall briefly mention two implications of this analysis of prepositions. The first concerns the lexical entry for verbs like *put*, obligatorily requiring a PP. Lexical entries for ditransitive verbs such as *put* or *give* pose a problem for DS, since they induce the building of complex tree structure. This leads not only to rather complex lexical entries, but also to a situation where computational rules, lexical instructions from the predicate, and lexical input from associate Ty(e) expressions interleave in complex ways. The e* approach offers a good way to model ditransitive verbs with prepositional arguments, since the verb can be projected into an unfixed node as with any other verb, while argument tree structure is built by the preposition. The only lexical constraint is that there be a PP. This can be expressed by a constraint such as $?\downarrow^*_{+prep}$, which queries the existence of a prepositional feature in the tree.[17]

(54)   *Lexical Entry for* put *with e**

IF	$?Ty(e \rightarrow t)$
THEN	$put(?\downarrow^*_{+prep})$,
	$make(\langle\downarrow^*\rangle), put(Fo(put'), Ty(e \rightarrow (e \rightarrow (e \rightarrow (e^* \rightarrow t)))))$,
	$go(\langle\uparrow^*\rangle?Ty(e \rightarrow t))$,
	$put(?\langle\downarrow_1\rangle Ty(e \rightarrow (e \rightarrow t)))$,
	$make(\langle\downarrow_0\rangle), put(?Ty(e))$
ELSE	abort

Except for the requirement for a preposition in the tree, the entry is identical to a corresponding entry for a transitive verb. Since with e*, PPs can be built by lexical actions from the preposition, no lexical actions for the structure building need to be included in the entry for *put*. Similarly, no special statement has to be made for the building of the functor node, which is built by prediction. The type value of *put* does of course encode the verb's requirement for at least two objects. The entry leads to the following partial tree:

---

[17] Cf. Kempson et al. (2001: 48–9) for discussion of this 'external' variant of tree modality. It is here employed to indicate that the requirement for a +prep feature can be satisfied along fixed tree relations, i.e. by the PP argument.

(55)

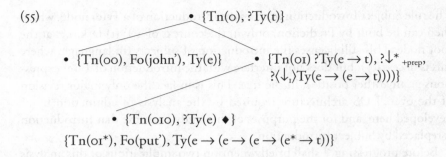

$$\bullet \; \{Tn(o), \; ?Ty(t)\}$$

$\bullet \; \{Tn(oo), \; Fo(john'), \; Ty(e)\}$ \qquad $\bullet \; \{Tn(oI) \; ?Ty(e \rightarrow t), \; ?\downarrow^*_{+prep},$
$?\langle\downarrow_I\rangle Ty(e \rightarrow (e \rightarrow t))))\}$

$\bullet \; \{Tn(oIo), \; ?Ty(e) \; \blacklozenge\}$

$\{Tn(oI^*), \; Fo(put'), \; Ty(e \rightarrow (e \rightarrow (e \rightarrow (e^* \rightarrow t))))\}$

That is, no node is built, but its presence is indirectly required. Again, there is some uncertainty about the feature value. The way the entry reads now results in a successful derivation of, for example, (56):

(56)   ?Sally put the books at noon.

The question is whether (56) is ungrammatical or just semantically odd. According to (54), (56) is grammatical, because I have opted for a more liberal characterization of the lexical syntactic requirements. Alternatively, one might use a feature +loc again, which would block (56). Since I am here concerned with general characterizations of tree growth, I leave the question open. The important point here is that in a derivation involving *put* and a PP, some tree building comes from the lexical entry from *put*, and some from the preposition, where the latter is restricted by the lexical requirements imposed by *put*. Subcategorization can thus be characterized either as building nodes or merely as requiring nodes to be present.

   A second implication of this analysis is that some NPs may lexically be characterized as building nodes. I am thinking here of adverbials like *yesterday*, *tomorrow*, or possibly *home*. For these, their lexical entries may specify that they effectively are like PPs without preposition, so that they may be freely introduced:

(57)   I saw him yesterday.

(58)   They will leave from Manchester tomorrow.

(59)   I walked her home.

A lexical characterization in the Ty(e) expressions in these examples guarantees that they, at least on some readings, can be introduced as optional arguments to a given predicate. However, I leave this as a possibility here.

   Overall, then, an analysis where optional Ty(e) expressions are introduced into the tree structure by instructions from the lexicon seems to have advantages over a rule analysis. The lexical treatment captures formally the intuition that prepositions function as licensors of Ty(e) expressions, and does not overgenerate widely. It additionally allows for a simplification of the lexical entries for ditransitives.

A complete DS derivation with e* thus involves the building of an unfixed node for the predicate, which is achieved by lexical instructions, the optional building of Ty(e) nodes by prepositions which are filled by their NP objects, and finally, the application of Merge which results in the resolution of the underspecification of the type, and the assignment of a fixed position in the tree of the unfixed node. Note that under this characterization, the underspecified type is resolved 'in one go'—i.e. only with the application of Merge is the underspecified type resolved to whatever the current requirement is. Although I think this is ultimately correct, the next section discusses a rule which allows for the incremental partial resolution of e* predicates, where every introduction of an expression of Ty(e) is 'registered' at the unfixed node. This incremental notion of e* resolution is needed for the semantic analysis developed in the next chapter, although it is not needed for the ultimately favoured pragmatic analysis.

4.4.5 Incremental transition rule for e*

As just noted, the definitions discussed in the preceding sections imply that the underspecification of e* is resolved at once, with the application of Merge. If, for example, there is a node with the requirement ?Ty(e $\rightarrow$ (e $\rightarrow$ (e $\rightarrow$ t))), the underspecified type Ty(e* $\rightarrow$ t) can be resolved as meeting this requirement. For some applications, however, it might be useful to have a more context-sensitive rule for e* which states that the underspecification is partially resolved with every instance of the introduction of a Ty(e) expression. The choice depends really on the interpretation of underspecified verbs, which is discussed in the next chapter. In this chapter, I formulate a rule which allows for partial resolution of e* predicates as a more specific characterization of its syntax.

The rule for partial resolution applies after the introduction of e* and before the application of Merge and can be stated as follows:[18]

---

[18] The pointer movement defined in the rule is needed to prevent recursion of the rule. However, as it stands, it conflicts with Completion, which equally needs to apply whilst the pointer is still at the argument daughter. A possible solution is to define a complex variant of Completion which includes e* Partial Resolution. Doing this here, however, would lead us too far afield.

(60) e^* *Partial Resolution*

$$\{_{n^*} \ldots Ty(X \to (e^* \to t))\}, \{_n \ldots ?Ty(Y)\}, \{_{no} \ldots Ty(e) \; \blacklozenge\}$$

$$\{_{n1^*} \ldots Ty(X \to (e \to (e^* \to t)))\}, \{_n \ldots ?Ty(Y) \ldots \blacklozenge\}, \{_{no} \ldots Ty(e)\}$$

The rule licenses the following transition. Given a parse state with a DU with underspecified type $Ty(e^* \to t)$ at an underspecified location $Tn(n^*)$ and the current task state at an argument node where a DU of $Ty(e)$ holds, the underspecified node can be updated to (1) holding at or below the corresponding functor node $Tn(n1)$ and (2) being minimally reducible to an expression with $Ty(e \to t)$, but not simply to $Ty(t)$. The pointer then moves from the argument daughter to its mother node at $Tn(n)$. According to this rule, the introduction of the $Ty(e)$ expression is 'registered' at the unfixed node by partially resolving the underspecification, and the unfixed node is 'passed down' the tree to its lowest possible resolution site. The following tree illustrates the transition licensed by e^* Partial Resolution:

(61a) e^* *Partial Resolution: Tree (before)*

$$\bullet \; \{Tn(n), \ldots ?Ty(Y)\}$$
$$\bullet \; \{Tn(no), \ldots, Ty(e) \; \blacklozenge\}$$
$$\{Tn(n^*), \ldots, Ty(X \to (e^* \to t))\}$$

(61b) e^* *Partial Resolution: Tree (after)*

$$\bullet \; \{Tn(n), \ldots ?Ty(Y) \; \blacklozenge\}$$
$$\bullet \; \{Tn(no), \ldots, Ty(e)\}$$
$$\{Tn(n1^*), \ldots, Ty(X \to (e \to (e^* \to t)))\}$$

The effect of the rule is to update the information at the unfixed node. The rule may apply after every introduction of a $Ty(e)$ expression into the tree. The final resolution of the underspecification of e^* is achieved by Merge, as before.

4.4.6 Sample derivation

The combination of the definition of e^*, the lexical specifications, and the rules discussed in the preceding sections together define complete derivations with e* predicates, so that their role in the DS system can now be illustrated with a sample derivation. I assume that at least one Ty(e) expression is lexically required by every verb, a point discussed in more detail in the next section. On the other hand, I assume that all verbs allow for the introduction of optional Ty(e) expressions. Thus, the lexical entry for the (transitive)[19] verb *bake* can be represented as in (62):

(62)   *Lexical Entry for* bake *with e**

    IF   ?Ty(e → t)
    THEN   make(⟨↓*⟩), put(Fo(bake'), Ty(e → (e → (e* → t)))),
                go(⟨↑*⟩ ?Ty(e → t)),
                put(?⟨↓₁⟩Ty(e → (e → t))),
                make(⟨↓₀⟩), put(?Ty(e))
    ELSE   abort

The important part of the entry in this context is the underspecified type value Ty(e → (e → (e* → t))), which states that the DU introduced by *bake* minimally requires two expressions of Ty(e), i.e. a subject and an object, and that it allows for a potentially unlimited number of optional Ty(e) arguments. With this entry in mind, consider the following example in (63), involving *bake*, and how the definitions for e* are used in the unfolding tree structure:

(63)   John was baking a cake for Mary in the kitchen.

The example in (63) involves two prepositional VP adjuncts, the benefactive *for Mary* and the locative *in the kitchen*. The relevant derivational steps are as follows:

(64a)   *Tree for* "John

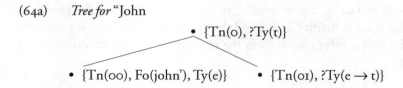

The first steps in the derivation up to the scanning of the verb are familiar. The requirement ?Ty(e → t) holding at Tn(01) is the condition for introducing the

---

[19] See the section on optional arguments below.

information from *bake*. Thus, two fixed daughter nodes are built, as well as an unfixed node for Fo(bake'):

(64b)   *Tree for* "John was baking

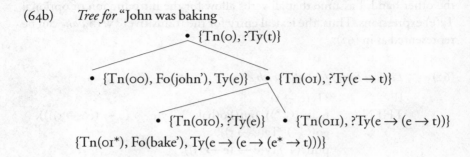

$$\bullet \; \{Tn(o), ?Ty(t)\}$$

$$\bullet \; \{Tn(oo), Fo(john'), Ty(e)\} \quad \bullet \; \{Tn(o1), ?Ty(e \rightarrow t)\}$$

$$\bullet \; \{Tn(o1o), ?Ty(e)\} \quad \bullet \; \{Tn(o11), ?Ty(e \rightarrow (e \rightarrow t))\}$$

$$\{Tn(o1^{*}), Fo(bake'), Ty(e \rightarrow (e \rightarrow (e^{*} \rightarrow t)))\}$$

The next expression in the string, *a cake* (I ignore the internal structure of the NP throughout), is of Ty(e) and thus fulfils the requirement holding at Tn(o1o):

(64c)   *Tree for* "John was baking a cake

$$\bullet \; \{Tn(o), ?Ty(t)\}$$

$$\bullet \; \{Tn(oo), Fo(john'), Ty(e)\} \quad \bullet \; \{Tn(o1), ?Ty(e \rightarrow t)\}$$

$$\bullet \; \{Tn(o1o), Fo(a\_cake'), Ty(e)\} \; \bullet \; \{Tn(o11), ?Ty(e \rightarrow (e \rightarrow t))\}$$

$$\{Tn(o1^{*}), Fo(bake'), Ty(e \rightarrow (e \rightarrow (e^{*} \rightarrow t)))\}$$

At this stage in the derivation Merge could apply, so that the underspecification would be resolved and the unfixed node is merged with Tn(o11). This would in fact be the derivation of *John was baking a cake*. However, in this case there is further input, and the application of Merge is prevented due to the lexical information from the next word, *for*, the lexical entry for which is:

(65)   *Lexical Entry for* for
   IF $?Ty(e \rightarrow (e^{*} \rightarrow t))$
   THEN $put(?\langle \downarrow_{1} \rangle Ty(e \rightarrow (e \rightarrow (e \rightarrow t)))),$
              $make(\langle \downarrow_{o} \rangle), put(_{+for}, ?Ty(e))$
   ELSE   abort

If Merge applied before the introduction of *for*, the condition for introducing *for* would not be met, since there would be no requirement ?Ty(e → (e* → t)), so that, by the ELSE clause, the derivation would be aborted. Since the application of Merge is optional, it is enough to say that here it does not apply, without any need to specify this further.[20] The information from *for*, then, results in the building of a new argument node:

(64d) *Tree for* "John was baking a cake for

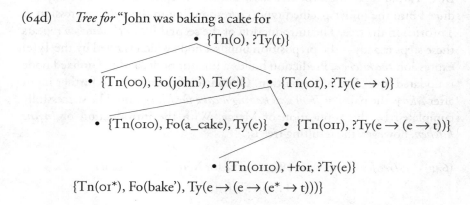

The new node Tn(0110) is built and annotated according to the lexical instructions from the preposition. The corresponding functor node Tn(0111) can be built by Prediction, and the next word in the string, *Mary*, of Ty(e), can be associated at Tn(0110), resulting in the following state:

(64e) *Tree for* "John was baking a cake for Mary

$$\bullet \ \{Tn(o), ?Ty(t)\}$$

$$\bullet \ \{Tn(oo), Fo(john'), Ty(e)\} \qquad \bullet \ \{Tn(o1), ?Ty(e \to t)\}$$

$$\bullet \ \{Tn(o1o), Fo(a\_cake'), Ty(e)\} \qquad \bullet \ \{Tn(o11), ?Ty(e \to (e \to t))\}$$

$$\bullet \ \{Tn(o11o), Ty(e), \qquad \bullet \ \{Tn(o111),$$
$$Fo(for\_Mary')\} \qquad ?Ty(e \to (e \to (e \to t)))\}$$

$$\{Tn(o1^*), Fo(bake'), Ty(e \to (e \to (e^* \to t)))\}$$

---

[20] Note that this works here, since the application of Merge would result in the application of the ELSE clause in the entry of *with*. The problem with the rule Introduction discussed above is different, since its unrestricted use would not automatically result in abort.

At this stage, e* Partial Resolution can apply to partially update the unfixed node,[21] which then becomes (I reproduce only the unfixed node here, since the rest of the tree does not change):

(64f) $\{\text{Tn}(\text{0111*}), \text{Fo}(\text{bake'}), \text{Ty}(e \rightarrow (e \rightarrow (e \rightarrow (e^* \rightarrow t))))\}$

By e* Partial Resolution the tree node location is updated, and one e is introduced into the underspecified type, corresponding to the Ty(e) expression at Tn(0110) in the tree. The introduction of the second PP *in the kitchen* repeats these steps exactly—the preposition builds a node which is filled by the Ty(e) expression *the kitchen*, Prediction builds a functor node, and the unfixed node is updated by e* Partial Resolution. Of course, if there were no further input after *Mary*, the parse of *John was baking a cake for Mary* would be successfully completed by the application of Merge. With the introduction of *in the kitchen*, however, the resulting tree is:

(64g)   *Tree for* "John was baking a cake for Mary in the kitchen

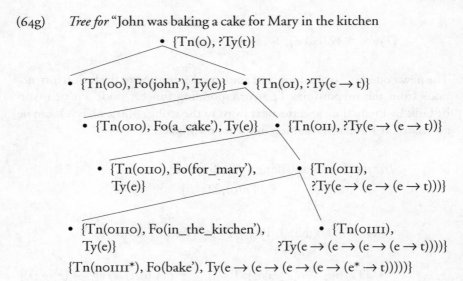

The tree in (64g) represents the parse state after introducing *in the kitchen*, the building of Tn(01111), and the updating of the underspecified type value. Since there is no further input, Merge applies and the underspecification is resolved in the manner defined in the definition of e*. The DU provided by *bake* is then associated at Tn(01111), fulfilling the requirement holding at that node, and Completion can apply:

---

[21] This step only occurs if the rule e* Partial Resolution is operative. Without it, nothing would happen at the unfixed node at this juncture.

(64h)   *Tree for* "John was baking a cake for Mary in the kitchen"

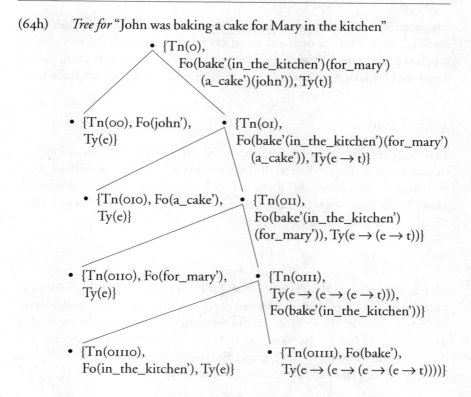

$\bullet$ {Tn(0),
        Fo(bake'(in_the_kitchen')(for_mary')
        (a_cake')(john')), Ty(t)}

$\bullet$ {Tn(00), Fo(john'), $\bullet$ {Tn(01),
Ty(e)}   Fo(bake'(in_the_kitchen')(for_mary')
                                        (a_cake')), Ty(e → t)}

$\bullet$ {Tn(010), Fo(a_cake'), $\bullet$ {Tn(011),
Ty(e)}   Fo(bake'(in_the_kitchen')
                                        (for_mary')), Ty(e → (e → t))}

$\bullet$ {Tn(0110), Fo(for_mary'), $\bullet$ {Tn(0111),
Ty(e)}   Ty(e → (e → (e → t))),
                                        Fo(bake'(in_the_kitchen'))}

$\bullet$ {Tn(01110), $\bullet$ {Tn(01111), Fo(bake'),
Fo(in_the_kitchen'), Ty(e)}   Ty(e → (e → (e → (e → t))))}

This derivation of *John was baking a cake for Mary in the kitchen* with the underspecified type value e^* shows how the lexical type information of *bake* is underspecified and that it is resolved in the context of the utterance within which it is used. The definition of e^*, together with lexical information and transition rules, results in a parse where Ty(e) expressions can be introduced into the tree as arguments to the underspecified verb, and where the underspecification is incrementally resolved, depending on the input to the parse.

4.5 DISCUSSION

The e^* formalization for verbal subcategorization provides an elegant and efficient way to encode the idea that verbs may be combined with a number of Ty(e) expressions within DS, as has been shown in the main outlines in the chapter so far. Before turning to the question of how underspecified verbs are interpreted, a number of loose ends related to the tree-theoretic side of e^* are addressed in the following discussion. These include the notion of subjects and optional arguments, as opposed to adjuncts, as well as some issues already touched upon, namely how to model extraction with e* and how the approach proposed here relates to the analysis of verb-second languages such as German.

4.5.1 Subjects

Thus far, e* predicates have been introduced which require at least one expression of $Ty(e)$, corresponding to the logical subject. This does not follow, however, from the definition of e* given in (22). In fact, it is tempting to think of an example like *sing* that it lexically encodes the weaker type $Ty(e^* \rightarrow t)$, so that the following parse could be derived:

(66)   • $\{Tn(o), Fo(sing'), Ty(t)\}$

The 'tree' in (66) could be thought of, for example, as the representation of imperatives like *Sing!*, since no element of type $Ty(e)$ is in the utterance, and the underspecification of *sing* could, under this assumption, simply be resolved to $Ty(t)$. The problem in the structure in (66) is that there is no expression in the tree corresponding to the logical subject—in the case of imperatives, the addressee. The preferred parse tree for *Sing!* is rather:

(67)   • $\{Tn(o), Fo(sing'(U_{addressee})), Ty(t)\}$

      • $\{Tn(oo),$ • $\{Tn(oi), Fo(sing'),$
        $Fo(U_{addressee}),$ $Ty(e \rightarrow t)\}$
        $Ty(e)\}$

In (67), the subject position is annotated with a formula value with a meta-variable, indicating an instruction to the hearer to search for a suitable representation, and a restriction on that variable to the effect that the interpretation of the meta-variable be the representation of the addressee. For this example, imperatives in English, the licensing and annotating of the subject node involves several sources of information; the formula value results presumably from the information from the paradigm,[22] while the licensing of the node as such might be regarded as resulting from an Introduction rule such as Subject

---

[22] For example, 'mood', or 'clausal typing'; in fact this might be even more clearly expressed by a category feature similar to the Cat(+Q) feature in questions, e.g. as Cat(+Imp).

Introduction. Yet intuitively, the presence of the subject node results partly from verbal information. Furthermore, on the technical side, it is not clear if the introduction of one e into the underspecified type (i.e. the application of the right disjunct of the definition) is licensed by the node built due to Introduction, or by the grammatical information from the paradigm, or both. To avoid this problem, and to capture the intuition about the relation between information from the verb and the subject, the underspecification in verbal subcategorization information will be restricted to the verb phrase, i.e. including objects and VP adjuncts but excluding subjects. This is partly in order to restrict the scope of inquiry in this study, but also because it seems correct that verbal information includes the requirement of the presence of a subject. I thus assume that all lexical specifications for verbs include a statement that at least one Ty(e) expression, directly dominated by the node with Ty(t), which is the position of the logical subject, be present.[23]

4.5.2 Optional arguments

Under the analysis developed here, Ty(e) expressions can be introduced into the verb phrase either by lexical instructions from the verb or by lexical instructions from prepositions, and possibly, in some restricted cases, by lexical specification of bare Ty(e) adverbs. However, this means that optional arguments such as in (68)–(70) are not covered by the analysis:

(68a)   Kelly was singing.

(68b)   Kelly was singing a song.

(69a)   Mr Yu spent the whole afternoon baking.

(69b)   Mr Yu spent the whole afternoon baking cakes.

(70)   Everybody was eating, but only Billy was eating pasta.

The optional objects in these examples are not introduced by a preposition, and they are not of the kind such that one would want to say that they build

---

[23] Two further related problems are not discussed in this study: the analysis of 'weather' verbs which possibly do not have a logical subject; and the much bigger problem of grammatical functions, including grammatical function-changing, i.e. the relation between grammatical and logical subjects and grammatical expressions which appear to encode/change this relation. Both problems have not been addressed in detail, to my knowledge, in the DS literature in general.

their own node by lexical specification. This leaves, under the proposal developed here, only the possibility that optional arguments are in fact introduced by lexical specification from the verb. This is partly warranted by the fact that in general there are semantic restrictions on which optional arguments go with which predicate, whereas these restrictions are much weaker for true optional $Ty(e)$ expressions. Optional arguments are thus encoded in the lexical specifications of verbs, so that a verb like *sing*, for example, has a disjunctive lexical entry, specifying the intransitive and the transitive use:

(71)　　*Disjunctive Lexical Entry for* sing *with e^**

IF	$?Ty(e \rightarrow t)$
THEN	$make(\langle \downarrow^* \rangle)$, $put(Fo(sing'), Ty(e \rightarrow (e^* \rightarrow t)))$,
	$go(\langle \uparrow^* \rangle \, ?Ty(e \rightarrow t))$
OR	$make(\langle \downarrow^* \rangle)$, $put(Fo(sing'), Ty(e \rightarrow (e \rightarrow (e^* \rightarrow t))))$,
	$go(\langle \uparrow^* \rangle \, ?Ty(e \rightarrow t))$,
	$put(?\langle \downarrow_1 \rangle \, ?Ty(e \rightarrow (e \rightarrow t)))$,
	$make(\langle \downarrow_0 \rangle)$, $put(?Ty(e))$
ELSE	abort

As was the case with prepositions, the argument node may be annotated with further restrictions specifying that the expression of $Ty(e)$ denote something singable, e.g. a song or an aria. This analysis of optional arguments as disjunctive lexical entries is in fact not quite as desired, since optional arguments can be regarded as a clear case of verbal underspecification, and should thus be more amenable to the general analysis proposed here. However, I leave this question for future research, and keep the lexical analysis.

4.5.3 Extraction

Evidence from extraction presented in the previous chapter provided the strongest empirical support for the claim that arguments and adjuncts behave in parallel, and that, consequently, verbal subcategorization needs to be modelled as underspecified. With the e^* analysis sufficiently developed, this evidence can be revisited and extraction with e^* demonstrated.

4.5.3.1 *Extraction out of PPs*

In DS, extraction is permitted along a path of functor–argument relations. Since by e^*, NPs introduced by a preposition are associated at an argument node in the tree, they can be extracted.

(72a)   I went to the movies with Jane.

(72b)   Who did you go to the movies with?

In DS terms, this means that the unfixed constituent introduced by the *wh*-pronoun can be merged with a requirement ?Ty(e) if this requirement is introduced by the preposition under e*. The following parse stage shows the relevant tree configuration:

(73)   *Tree for* "Who did you go to the movies with?"

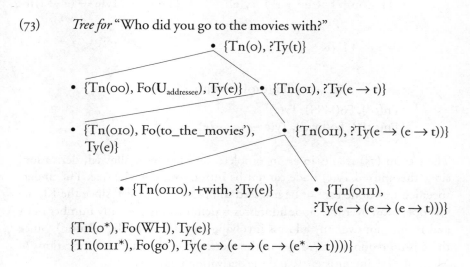

- $\{Tn(o), ?Ty(t)\}$

- $\{Tn(oo), Fo(U_{addressee}), Ty(e)\}$ • $\{Tn(o_1), ?Ty(e \rightarrow t)\}$

- $\{Tn(o_{10}), Fo(to\_the\_movies'), Ty(e)\}$ • $\{Tn(o_{11}), ?Ty(e \rightarrow (e \rightarrow t))\}$

- $\{Tn(o_{110}), +with, ?Ty(e)\}$ • $\{Tn(o_{111}), ?Ty(e \rightarrow (e \rightarrow (e \rightarrow t)))\}$

$\{Tn(o^*), Fo(WH), Ty(e)\}$
$\{Tn(o_{111}^*), Fo(go'), Ty(e \rightarrow (e \rightarrow (e \rightarrow (e^* \rightarrow t))))\}$

The tree in (73) illustrates the derivation just before the unfixed nodes are merged. The Ty(e) node Tn(o_{110}) has been built by lexical instructions from the entry for *with*. Note that now two unfixed nodes are in the tree, the unfixed Ty(e) node from *Who* and the unfixed e* node from the verb. By two applications of Merge, the nodes are associated at Tn(o_{110}) and Tn(o_{111}) respectively. The tree shows clearly why adjunct extraction works like argument extraction—the relevant tree configurations are identical.

Note, in contrast, how an NP-modifying PP cannot be extracted if it is assumed that PPs are LINKed to NPs:

(74a)   I love the girl with red hair.

(74b)   *What do you love the girl with?

The unfixed Ty(e) node cannot be assigned an eventual location in a tree with LINKed NP adjunct:[24]

(75)   *Attempted tree for* "*What do you love the girl with?*"

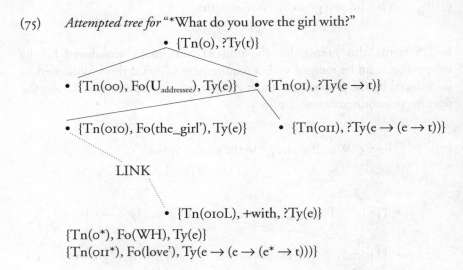

- {Tn(o), ?Ty(t)}

- {Tn(oo), Fo(U$_{addressee}$), Ty(e)}   • {Tn(o1), ?Ty(e → t)}

- {Tn(o1o), Fo(the_girl'), Ty(e)}   • {Tn(o11), ?Ty(e → (e → t))}

LINK

- {Tn(o1oL), +with, ?Ty(e)}
{Tn(o*), Fo(WH), Ty(e)}
{Tn(o11*), Fo(love'), Ty(e → (e → (e* → t)))}

The tree in (75) results in an incomplete, and hence disallowed, derivation, since the unfixed Ty(e) node cannot be introduced into the tree. The underspecified tree node cannot be resolved to hold at Tn(o1oL), since the Kleene star operation over tree node addresses is defined only over any number of os and 1s, but not over any address involving an L (i.e. a LINK relation). Since there is no requirement ?Ty(e) in the matrix tree, all putative applications of Merge lead to inconsistency, and the derivation is aborted.

4.5.3.2 *PP extraction*

Next to preposition-stranding structures, adjuncts can be extracted together with their (pied-piped) preposition.

(76)   With whom did you go to the movies?

Examples like (76) should be subject to the same analysis as standard object extraction and NP extraction as discussed in the last section, namely as involving an unfixed Ty(e) node which is integrated into the tree by e* and Merge, so that before Merge the following parse state obtains:

---

[24] The exact details of NP modification are of course not addressed here, and the tree is merely intended to show how that different extraction facts can be accommodated by invoking the notion of LINK; cf. Kempson et al. (2001: ch. 4), Swinburne (1999).

(77)　　*Tree for* "With whom did you go to the movies?

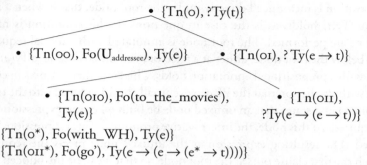

The problem PP extraction poses is that the PP is introduced into the parse much earlier than needed for building the $Ty(e)$ node for its argument. While intuitively, it is clear that the argument node, and the corresponding functor node, have to be built if the derivation is to be successful, it is not clear how this can be achieved given the lexical characterization of node building I have given for prepositions. I assume here, in (78), that Prediction can build nodes from (internal) modality statements at the root node, and that Introduction introduces a functor node in the presence of an (independently built) argument node. A further challenge posed by PP extraction is that the lexical instructions of prepositions as currently formulated state that the condition for their introduction into the tree is that there be a requirement $?Ty(e \rightarrow (e^* \rightarrow t))$. In question formation, however, the preposition is found at the outset of the parse, where the requirement $?Ty(t)$ holds. In the light of the tree in (77), the lexical entry for prepositions has to be modified such that they can be introduced at the beginning of the parse, and that if they are, they are integrated into the verb phrase. This can be achieved by a disjunctive lexical entry for prepositions, which is, however, activated by a uniform condition:

(78)　　*Schematic Disjunctive Lexical Entry for Prepositions*

IF　　　　　$?Ty(e^* \rightarrow t)$
THEN IF　　　$?Ty(t)$
　　　　　　　$put(?\downarrow^* (_{+prep}, Ty(e)))$
　　　　　　　$make(\langle \downarrow^* \rangle), put(_{+prep}, ?Ty(e))$
　　ELSE　　　$put(?\langle \downarrow_{\mathrm{I}} \rangle Ty(e \rightarrow t)),$
　　　　　　　$make(\langle \downarrow_{0} \rangle), put(_{+prep}, ?Ty(e))$
ELSE　　　　abort

The lexical entry in (78) states firstly the condition for the introduction of prepositions, where the definition of e^* is finally fully exploited, since now possible instantiations include a simple $Ty(t)$. However, two cases are distinguished by the two clauses under THEN. The first case is where the preposition is introduced directly under the root node, that is when a requirement $?Ty(t)$ holds, as is the case in questions. If this condition is met, two actions are performed. The root node is annotated with a modal requirement that below the root node, either at a fixed or at an unfixed node, a $Ty(e)$ expression with a prepositional annotation holds. This statement ensures in conjunction with Prediction that the PP can eventually be introduced into the tree. The second clause states that an unfixed node be built where an expression of $Ty(e)$ is required. At this node, the interrogative pronoun, a $Ty(e)$ expression, is introduced. The resulting expression at the unfixed node meets the requirement which the first clause puts at the root node, so that it can be introduced into the tree later. The ELSE clause is the ordinary case where the preposition builds a node for an optional $Ty(e)$ expression. This clause remains unchanged. The relevant parse states are given below:

(79a)   • $\{Tn(o), ?Ty(t)\}$

The initial state of a parse provides the condition for the introduction of a preposition. This results in (79b):

(79b)   • $\{Tn(o), ?Ty(t), ?\downarrow^*(_{+prep}, Ty(e))\}$

          $\{Tn(o^*), {}_{+prep} ?Ty(e))\}$

The following *wh*-pronoun fulfils the requirement at $Tn(o^*)$ and annotates the root node with the question feature $+Q$ (as standardly assumed):

(79c)   • $\{Tn(o), +Q, ?Ty(t), ?\downarrow^*(_{+prep}, Ty(e))\}$

          $\{Tn(o^*), {}_{+prep}, Fo(prep\_WH), Ty(e))\}$

The following steps proceed in a standard fashion to result in a tree like (79d), which is identical, in the relevant respects, to the tree in (77) above:

(79d)   • $\{Tn(o), +Q, ?Ty(t), ?\downarrow^*(_{+prep}, Ty(e))\}$

     • $\{Tn(oo), Ty(e),$ • $\{Tn(o1), ?Ty(e \rightarrow t)\}$
     $Fo(U_{addressee})\}$

               • $\{Tn(o10), Ty(e),$ • $\{Tn(o11), ?Ty(e \rightarrow (e \rightarrow t))\}$
               $Fo(to\_the\_movies')\}$
     $\{Tn(o^*), {}_{+prep}, Fo(with\_WH), Ty(e))\}$
     $\{Tn(o11^*), Fo(go'), Ty(e \rightarrow (e \rightarrow (e^* \rightarrow t))))\}$

The next step in the derivation is the application of Prediction, which results in the building of a node with the requirement specified in the root node:

(79e)
$\quad\bullet\ \{Tn(o), +Q, ?Ty(t), ?\!\downarrow^*(_{+prep}, Ty(e))\}$

$\bullet\ \{Tn(oo), Ty(e),\ \ \bullet\ \{Tn(o1), ?Ty(e \rightarrow t)\}$
$Fo(U_{addressee})\}$

$\bullet\ \{Tn(o1o), Ty(e),\ \ \bullet\ \{Tn(o11), ?Ty(e \rightarrow (e \rightarrow t))\}$
$Fo(to\_the\_movies')\}$

$\bullet\ \{Tn(o11o), ?\ _{+prep}, Ty(e))\}$
$\{Tn(o^*),\ _{+prep}, Fo(prep\_WH), Ty(e))\}$
$\{Tn(o11^*), Fo(go'), Ty(e \rightarrow (e \rightarrow (e^* \rightarrow t))))\}$

At this stage, Merge applies to Tn(no*) and Tn(o11o) so that the underspecified Ty(e) node is introduced into the tree:

(79f)
$\quad\bullet\ \{Tn(o), +Q, ?Ty(t), ?\!\downarrow^*(_{+prep}, Ty(e))\}$

$\bullet\ \{Tn(oo), Ty(e),\ \ \bullet\ \{Tn(o1), ?Ty(e \rightarrow t)\}$
$Fo(U_{addressee})\}$

$\bullet\ \{Tn(o1o), Ty(e),\ \ \bullet\ \{Tn(o11), ?Ty(e \rightarrow (e \rightarrow t))\}$
$Fo(to\_the\_movies')\}$

$\bullet\ \{Tn(o11o),\ _{+prep},$
$Fo(prep\_WH), Ty(e))\}$
$\{Tn(o11^*), Fo(go'), Ty(e \rightarrow (e \rightarrow (e^* \rightarrow t))))\}$

With this step, the requirement introduced by the preposition at Tn(o) is fulfilled, since a Ty(e) expression with a +prep feature holds below Tn(o). The derivation can now be completed by Introduction and Prediction, which license the building of the functor node, and Merge, and eventually by Completion.

With the disjunctive lexical definition of prepositions as given in (78), both question patterns of PP adjuncts can now be derived. For PP extraction, however, two further assumption are necessary: that Prediction builds nodes from modal statement at the root node, and that Introduction may introduce functor nodes if the corresponding argument node is independently available. Both these assumptions, while acceptable from the point of view of the overall system, are only necessary for the derivation here and are not needed elsewhere, and there is thus scope for the development of a better analysis of PP extraction, which does not need any extra assumptions.

4.5.3.3 *Registration of extraction paths*

A final point to be addressed with respect to extraction is the explicit syntactic or morphological marking of argument and adjunct extraction as discussed in the preceding chapter. Given the important role of lexical instructions for the analysis presented here, cross-linguistic differences are expected to reside to some extent in the characterization of prepositions, case, and NPs, as well as general rules of tree building. Thus, no full analysis can be produced here of the languages discussed in Chapter 3 showing marking of adjunct extraction. Rather, I just show how the symmetrical behaviour can be stated, irrespective of the actual analysis of the morphological or syntactic reflex.

Consider again the case of the Irish complementizers (McCloskey 1979, quoted from Hukari and Levine 1995: 206):

(80) *I mBetlehem   aL   dúirt   na targaireachtaí   aL*
      [in Bethlehem]$_j$ COMP   said   the prophecies   COMP
      béarfaí   an Slánaitheoir
      would-be-born   the Saviour   e$_j$
      'It was in Bethlehem that the prophecies said that the Saviour would be born'

(81) *Cén uair   aL   tháinig siad   ná bhaile*
      [which time]$_j$ COMP   came   they   home   e$_j$

As seen in the examples, the complementizer is *aL* if an argument or an adjunct is extracted. In DS terms, in (80) and (81) an unfixed Ty(e) node (and an appropriate +Q feature) has been introduced into the tree, as opposed to the non-extraction environment, where all Ty(e) nodes are fixed. A possible lexical analysis of the complementizer *aL* in Irish could express this as follows:

(82) *Lexical Entry for Irish Complementizer* aL

IF	$?Ty(t \to (e \to (e^* \to t)))$	
THEN	IF	$exist(\{Tn(n^*), Ty(e)\})$
	THEN	$make(\langle\downarrow_o\rangle), put(?Ty(t), ?\langle\downarrow^*\rangle Ty(e)))$
ELSE	abort	

The entry in (82) assumes that *aL* is a context-sensitive allomorph of an 'abstract' lexical complementizer. The entry states the condition for the existence of an unfixed node, which does not need to be fulfilled in sentences without extraction using *goN* as complementizer. In the main condition, I have included a tentative type for verbs taking sentential complements which allow for the introduction of $Ty(e)$ expressions before the introduction of the sentential complement. What is more relevant in (82) is that the condition stated for the introduction of *aL* in the lexical entry is sensitive to unfixed $Ty(e)$ expressions, so that *aL* is used for both extracted arguments and extracted adjuncts.

The evidence from Duala, an SVO language, shows clearly how under-specified verbs are lexically introduced and how the marking of extraction paths—in Duala by the particle *no*—is sensitive to unfixed nodes and not, for example, to the presence of a question feature. Recall the basic facts about Duala. Both *wh*-extraction and *wh*-in-situ are possible; however, only when non-subject constituents, either argument or adjunct, are extracted is the par-ticle *no* found immediately following the verb. In order to understand this pat-tern, assume that subjects are introduced in Duala by a subject introduction rule,[25] and that questioned subjects are projected onto an unfixed node while annotating the root node with a question feature.

(83) nja   a   poi?
      who   s/he   come
      'Who came?'

(84) *Tree for* "nja . . .

$$\bullet \ \{Tn(o), +Q, ?Ty(t)\}$$

$$\bullet \ \{Tn(oo), ?Ty(e)\}$$
$$\{Tn(o^*), Fo(WH), Ty(e))\}$$

---

[25] Alternatively, the subject is lexically introduced from the agreement marker, similar to the case in Swahili, discussed in Ch. 6. Another alternative is to assume that subjects in Duala are always LINKed and that the agreement functions as pronominal subject. In either case, by the time the main verb is parsed, the unfixed node has been fixed.

At this stage in the parse, the underspecification can already be resolved, and the unfixed node can be located at the subject position. This means that by the time the verb is scanned, there is no unfixed node present in the tree. Similarly, in *wh*-in-situ structures the question pronoun is never projected onto an unfixed node, but rather fills the requirement at the current parse stage like any other $Ty(e)$ expression. Thus, the environments where *no* does not appear are exactly those where there is no unfixed node in the derivation at the time when the verb is introduced. In contrast, *no* is triggered whenever there is an unfixed node at the time when the verb is introduced.

(85)　　*njika　wuma　w-en　　no　mo?*
　　　　wh-　　place　you-see　　*no*　it
　　　　'Where did you see it?'

(86)　　*Tree for* "njika wuma w-. . .

$$\bullet \ \{Tn(o), +Q, ?Ty(t)\}$$

$\bullet \ \{Tn(oo), Ty(e),$　　$\bullet \ \{Tn(o1), ?Ty(e \rightarrow t)\}$
$\quad Fo(\mathbf{U}_{addressee})\}$
$\{Tn(o^*), Fo(WH\_place), Ty(e))\}$

The unfixed node in (86) has to be kept unfixed, since the subject node has been filled from the inflection. This means that it has to be fixed within the VP. Since the VP is being built from the verb, it is at the introduction of the verb that this information is relevant. The particle *no* is thus a morphological sign that an unfixed node is present when the verb is introduced.

　　The evidence from extraction thus confirms the e^* analysis of verbal underspecification, which provides a means to introduce optional $Ty(e)$ expressions into the verb phrase as arguments, so that optional and obligatory $Ty(e)$ expressions can be seen to behave alike with respect to extraction.

4.5.4 e^* and unfixed verbs in German

In the discussion so far, a number of points have been discussed mainly with English in mind. A different problem is posed by languages with flexible verb positions like German, since unfixed verbs may be employed for an account of word order. It was this consideration which led to the analysis of the introduction of e^* predicates from the lexicon in English. The point taken up here is, then, how e^* predicates interact with the generally unfixed nature of verbs in

German. For the purposes of this discussion I assume that German is rigidly verb-second/verb-final, i.e. that the tensed verb, including tensed lexical verbs, is found either after the first constituent of the clause or in final position.[26] Furthermore, I ignore issues involving auxiliary and modal verbs, including cross-modal dependencies (see e.g. Hinrichs and Nakusawa 1994).

As in English, PPs can freely be added into the VP in German, both in main and in subordinate clauses:

(87) *Frank sang.*
      Frank sang
      'Frank was singing'

(88) *Frank sang Arien.*
      Frank sang arias
      'Frank was singing arias'

(89) *Frank sang in der Wanne.*
      Frank sang in the.DAT tub.DAT
      'Frank was singing in the bath-tub'

(90) *Frank sang aus vollem Halse Arien in der Wanne.*
      Frank sang out full.DAT throat.DAT arias in the.DAT tub.DAT
      'Frank was singing arias at the top of his voice in the bath-tub'

(91) ... *daß Frank   aus vollem Halse   Arien   in der Wanne*
           that Frank   out full.DAT throat.DAT arias   in the.DAT tub.DAT

      sang.
      sang

      'that Frank sang arias at the top of his voice in the bath-tub'

The examples show *singen*, 'sing', with different arguments and adjuncts; the intransitive use (87), transitive use with optional argument (88), with a locative adjunct (89), with optional argument, locative, and manner adverb in main

---

[26] These assumptions are too strict, as can be seen from the examples below:

(i) *Den Peter, den habe ich schon ewig nicht mehr gesehen.*
     the-ACC Peter the-ACC have I already forever not anymore seen
     'Peter I haven't seen in ages'

(ii) *Petra glaubt, daß Sonja gesagt hat, daß Holland morgen gewinnt.*
     Petra believes that Sonja said has that Holland tomorrow win
     'Petra believes that Sonja said that Holland will win tomorrow'

In (i), two NPs precede the tensed verb in a main clause, while in (ii) the sentential complement of *sagen*, 'say', follows the verb. However, I will not discuss examples like these here.

(90) and subordinate clause (91). The order of the VP constituents is, at least syntactically, unfixed:

(92)   *Frank sang Arien aus vollem Halse   in der   Wanne.*
       Frank sang arias out full.DAT throat.DAT in the.DAT tub.DAT
       'Frank was singing arias at the top of his voice in the bath-tub'

(93)   *Frank sang in der   Wanne Arien aus vollem   Halse.*
       Frank sang in the.DAT tub.DAT arias out full.DAT throat.DAT
       'Frank was singing arias at the top of his voice in the bath-tub'

(94)   *. . . daß Frank in der   Wanne   aus   vollem*
       that   Frank in the.DAT tub.DAT out full.DAT

       Halse   Arien sang.
       throat.DAT arias sung
       'that Frank sang arias at the top of his voice in the bath-tub'

Furthermore, the position of the tensed verb varies between second and final position in main and subordinate clause. A more idiomatic, attested example with the same verb is given in (95):[27]

(95)   *Ein pausbäckiges   Mädchen mit   karierter Bluse   und*
       a   chubby-faced   girl   with   checked   blouse and

       Zahnspange singt, unsicher und kokett   zugleich,
       braces   sings insecure and flirtatious at-the-same-time

       in einer Art Privatkaraoke   einen Popsong in   die Kamera.
       in a   kind private karaoke a.ACC pop song into the camera
       'A chubby-faced girl in a checked blouse and with braces is singing, insecure and flirtatious at the same time, in a kind of private karaoke, a pop song into the camera.'

The PP *mit karierter Bluse und Zahnspange*, 'with checked blouse and braces' is a nominal modifier of the subject, and falls outside of the analysis presented here, as does the adverbial phrase *unsicher und kokett zugleich*, 'insecure and flirtatious at the same time', although there is at least one reading where it modifies the verb. Yet the analysis of adverbs in German is beyond the scope of this study. This leaves *singen*, 'sing' here still as a quaternary predicate, with both the adverbial PPs *in einer Art Privatkaraoke*, 'in a kind of private karaoke' and *in die Kamera*, 'into the camera', and the optional object *einen Popsong*, 'a pop song', as part of the verb phrase.

[27] From a review of Rineke Dijkstra's video installation 'Annemiek', *Die Welt*, 24 Feb. 2001.

Given the data in (87) to (95), I assume that the e* analysis of verbal under-specification holds for German, including the analysis of optional arguments as involving disjunctive lexical entries, and the general requirement that Ty(e) expressions need to be licensed to be introduced into the tree. However, in con-trast to English, the structure-building process cannot be characterized as pro-ceeding to a large extent from lexical information from the verb, but has to be achieved in a way similar to how I have characterized the introduction of adjuncts in English, namely by structure-building operations from prepo-sitions and case. From this perspective, the final position of the verb can be taken to be basic, so that subcategorization requirements can be checked against already established tree structure.

Consider for example a parse for a simplified version of (94):

(96)   . . . *daß   Frank   in der   Wanne   Arien   sang.*
          that   Frank   in the.DAT   tub.DAT   arias   sung
       'that Frank sang arias in the bath-tub'

The corresponding tree just before the introduction of the verb is given in (97a):

(97a)   *Tree for* ". . . Frank in der Wanne Arien

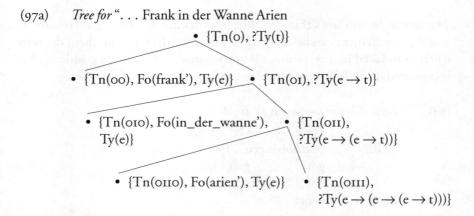

In order to ensure a particular order relation on the introduction of Ty(e) expressions, an explicit characterization of the function of prepositions and case in German has to be given, as well as an additional notion of locally unfixed Ty(e) nodes. Although these are interesting questions, I assume that Ty(e) expressions are introduced into the tree in the order in which they appear, since I am here interested in the introduction of the verb. The next step in the derivation in (97) is the scanning of the verb. On the assumption that *singen* is transitive in the relevant reading here, it specifies the obligatory presence of the subject and the object, and is thus of Ty(e $\rightarrow$ (e $\rightarrow$ (e* $\rightarrow$ t))). The important point with respect to this final position is that the verb does not have to be assigned to an unfixed position: when the verb is introduced in final position, no more Ty(e) expressions can be introduced—all expressions which determine the predicate's eventual arity are already in the tree. The derivation thus proceeds immediately with the association of the DU introduced by the verb at Tn(0111):

(97b)   *Tree for* "... Frank in der Wanne Arien sang

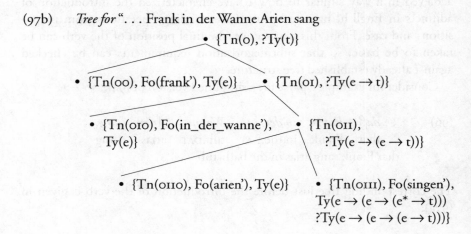

The tree in (97b) shows this step. The information at Tn(0111) is consistent, and the requirement can be checked by Thinning. In German, then, the verb when introduced in final position is not assigned to an unfixed position. This is expressed in the following lexical entry:

(98)   *Lexical Entry for* singen *(V-final)*

    IF $?Ty(e \rightarrow (e \rightarrow (e^* \rightarrow t)))$
    THEN $put(Fo(singen'), Ty(e \rightarrow (e \rightarrow (e^* \rightarrow t))))$,
                $go(\langle \uparrow^* \rangle_{+ACC}), go(\langle \uparrow^* \rangle_{+NOM})$,
                $go(\langle \uparrow^* \rangle ?Ty(t))$.
    ELSE   abort

The requirement in (98) indicates that transitive *singen* cannot be introduced into the tree unless at least two Ty(e) expressions have been introduced into the tree. This is important, since, as already pointed out, no further Ty(e) expressions can be introduced at this stage, so all required Ty(e) expressions have to be present. If this condition is fulfilled, the formula and type values of the verb are introduced at the node where the requirement holds. The 'go' predicates have two functions. The first two ensure that the Ty(e) expressions are indeed the ones required by the verb, and not optionally introduced ones. The instructions cause the pointer to go up the tree to check for the case feature +ACC and +NOM, where the object is lower than the subject. The third 'go' predicate causes the pointer to go to the mother node $Tn(0)$ where $?Ty(t)$ holds. This is to ensure that no further expressions can be introduced into the tree. The combined effect of this definition is that the verb is introduced directly at a fixed position in the tree, and that subcategorization requirements are checked, since they have to be met at this stage.

The lexical definition given so far has now to be extended to cover V2 cases. It is for the analysis of V2 that a general e* Adjunction rule is needed. The first additional observation in this respect is that the initial position in German is not reserved for subjects. Rather, in principle any constituent may be introduced into the parse initially:

(99a) *Frank sang aus vollem Halse   Arien   in der   Wanne.*
       Frank sang out full.DAT throat.DAT   arias   in the.DAT   tub.DAT
       'Frank was singing arias at the top of his voice in the bath-tub'

(99b) *In der Wanne sang Frank Arien aus vollem Halse.*

(99c) *Arien sang Frank in der Wanne aus vollem Halse.*

(99d) *Aus vollem Halse sang Frank Arien in der Wanne.*

The data in (99) show that all constituents can be found before the verb. In DS terms this can be analysed by saying that the initial position is a locally unfixed position which will be fixed only at some later stage during the parse, i.e. that the initial constituent is projected onto an unfixed node built by *Adjunction. This in turn means that the verb in V2 is introduced at a stage where $?Ty(t)$ holds. The condition for the introduction of the verb in V2 position can be stated as a requirement $?Ty(t)$:

(100) *Lexical Entry for* singen

    IF $?Ty(e^* \rightarrow t)$

    THEN IF $?Ty(t)$

          THEN $make(\langle \downarrow^* \rangle)$,

                     $put(Fo(singen'), Ty(e \rightarrow (e \rightarrow (e^* \rightarrow t)),$

                         $\langle \uparrow^* \rangle_{+ACC}, \langle \uparrow^* \rangle_{+NOM})$

                     $go(\langle \uparrow^* \rangle \, ?Ty(t))$

          OR $?Ty(e \rightarrow (e \rightarrow (e^* \rightarrow t)))$

          THEN $put(Fo(singen'), Ty(e \rightarrow (e \rightarrow (e^* \rightarrow t)))),$

                     $go(\langle \uparrow^* \rangle_{+ACC}), go(\langle \uparrow^* \rangle_{+NOM}),$

                     $go(\langle \uparrow^* \rangle \, ?Ty(t)).$

    ELSE   abort

The new part of the entry, the first disjunct of the main THEN statement, licenses the building of an unfixed node for the verb. The 'go' statements of the verb-final entry are now modal requirements, ensuring that both subject and object are found above the verb's eventual position in the tree. The second part of the entry remains unchanged. The new entry licenses the following step in the derivation of a V2 verb:

(101)   *Tree for* "In der Wanne sang

$$• \{Tn(o), ?Ty(t)\}$$
$$\{Tn(o^*), Fo(in\_der\_wanne'), Ty(e)\}$$
$$\{Tn(o^*), Fo(singen'), Ty(e \rightarrow (e \rightarrow (e^* \rightarrow t)))\}$$

The remaining steps in the derivation proceed standardly, i.e. the tree is developed similarly to derivations with final verb, where the only difference is that the verb has already been assigned to an unfixed position. From the perspective of the verb, the derivation proceeds exactly as in English in that Merge applies after all Ty(e) expressions have been scanned. I thus do not give the remaining steps of the derivation.

What this brief consideration has shown is that e^* can be used for languages with verb movement, under an analysis which specifies different conditions of introduction in a disjunctive lexical entry. There are two important points to note for the e^* analysis. The first is that it is not always the case that underspecified types and unfixed location go together. Although they do go together in English and in V2 in German, the final verb is introduced into the tree directly. This is the reason for introducing e^* predicates from the lexicon, rather than by general rule, since this treatment ensures that the two kinds of underspecification can be separated. The second point to note is that incremental interpretation of e^* predicates does not work for final verbs in German, since in these cases the predicate is introduced directly, so that no application of Merge is necessary. Rather, the underspecification of underspecified predicates is resolved simply by Thinning. This fact lends some support to the view that the interpretation of e^* predicates is achieved in one step of resolution, and not, as implied in the Partial Resolution rule, step-by-step for every new Ty(e) expression introduced.

4.6 CONCLUSION

The main finding of the discussion so far is that verbal subcategorization information is lexically underspecified. This result, and its formalization as e^*, follows from the empirical evidence presented in the last chapter, and from the overall perspective adopted, in particular the idea that hearers build semantic representations incrementally, on-line. The definition and description of the syntax of e* in this chapter provides a theory of adjunction for DS and at the same time an exploration of the notion of structural underspecification and its application to predicate–argument structure. Consonant with proposals in the literature, the e* approach models VP adjuncts as optionally introduced arguments, standing in the same structural relation to the predicate as obligatory, subcategorized for arguments, leading to the derivation of propositional forms where the predicate is combined with different numbers of arguments, varying from utterance to utterance. The important question to be considered now is how these predicates are interpreted.

5

The Interpretation of Underspecified Verbs

5.1 INTRODUCTION

The central idea developed so far is that verbs are lexically underspecified. While they require a minimum number of Ty(e) expressions to occur with them in the verb phrase they are heading, they allow for any number of optional Ty(e) expressions to be introduced into the VP as well. The formal reflex of this observation is the type characterization of verbs with the underspecified value e*. Underspecified verbs can be introduced into a derivation at an unfixed node, so that all complements are fixed at their respective argument nodes before the verb is fixed and the type underspecification is resolved. The projection of verbs into unfixed nodes will usually occur in verb-initial and SVO structures, but not, for example, in verb-final structures in German, where the verb is projected into its fixed, eventual position directly.

One advantage of this approach is that it can be implemented into the DS model without much modification. It only requires a particular analysis of prepositions, which are, at least in English, analysed as building the argument node for their complement, and some restriction on the scope of the Introduction and Prediction rules to environments where nodes can be built freely, for example in subject position. Because of this conservative view of VP structures—fully resolved underspecified verbs result in ordinary binary trees—no special operational, tree-theoretic semantics for e* needs to be given in addition to the definitions already introduced, and parses with e* will always result in well-formed predicate–argument structures. The next step in the investigation is to think about the real-world semantics of these output structures, about how predicates with varying complement arrays are interpreted. Resultant structures with e* include propositional structures such as the following, where the predicate is combined with both arguments and adjuncts:

(1)   *John was baking a cake for Mary in the kitchen.*
       Fo(bake'(in_the_kitchen')(for_mary')(a_cake')(john'))

(2)   *I went to the movies with Jane.*
       Fo(go(with_jane')(to_the_movies')($U_{speaker}$))

(3)   *Fran wrote her dissertation on a Mac.*
       Fo(write'(her_dissertation')(on_a_mac')(fran'))

(4)   *Frank sang aus vollem   Halse   Arien   in der   Wanne.*
       Frank sang out full.DAT   throat.DAT   arias   in the.DAT   tub.DAT

       'Frank was singing arias at the top of his voice in the bath-tub'
       Fo(sing'(in_der_wanne')(arien')(aus_vollem_halse')(frank'))

The predicates in these examples can of course be combined with any other array of Ty(e) expressions. Furthermore, if adjuncts are differently ordered in two utterances, these different orders are projected into the propositional structure.

(5a)   *Joan was singing Danish Christmas songs for the whole street with the twins.*
       Fo(sing'(with_the_twins')(for_the_street')
       (Danish_Christmas_songs')(joan'))

(5b)   *Joan was singing Danish Christmas songs with the twins for the whole street.*
       Fo(sing'(for_the_street')(with_the_twins')
       (Danish_Christmas_songs')(joan'))

(6a)   *Robert was waiting for his cousin in the departure lounge.*
       Fo(wait'(in_the_departure_lounge')(for_U's_cousin')(robert'))

(6b)   *Robert was waiting in the departure lounge for his cousin.*
       Fo(wait'(for_U's_cousin')(in_the_departure_lounge')(robert'))

The different orders of adjuncts result in different propositional structures for the (a) and (b) sentences. It is not clear how an interpretation of these structures can be achieved in a traditional model-theoretic way, where a model is specified a priori, including the arity of its predicates and the order of the arguments. After considering—and rejecting—two possible approaches to specify a standard model-theoretic interpretation for underspecified verbs, this chapter will be concerned with developing an alternative pragmatic approach which it is argued is better suited to modelling the context sensitivity of verbal subcategorization.

5.2 MODIFIER SEMANTICS

The starting point for a discussion of the semantics of adjuncts, and the best-known analysis of the semantics of adjuncts and adverbial expressions more generally, is to treat the adjunct as a functor, taking a verb or a verb phrase as argument, as is the case in Montague (1974). In this way the verb keeps its original arity, and the complex expression is interpreted as a function from verb (or verb phrase) denotation to another verb (or verb phrase) denotation. A specific variety of this approach has been proposed by Dowty (1979), who also provides a detailed discussion of PP adjuncts. This makes his proposal especially pertinent to the present discussion, and it is therefore, and because of its historical importance, presented here in some detail, despite the fact that it presupposes also that syntactically adjuncts are analysed as functors and not, as proposed here, as arguments. Dowty combines Montague Grammar with the lexical decomposition approach advocated within Generative Semantics (see e.g. Lakoff 1971). Following Montague, Dowty develops a possible-world semantics for a type-logical system, and combines this with the 'abstract' underlying predicates CAUSE and BECOME introduced within Generative Semantics. These predicates are, together with the temporal predicates such as PRES, FUT, and PAST, defined in a temporal possible-world semantics.

5.2.1 Dowty's IV/IV and TV/TV analysis

In the light of examples like (7) and (8), Dowty (1979: 207–8) proposes to distinguish between intransitive verb and transitive verb modifiers:

(7a)   John walked.

(7b)   John walked to Chicago.

(8a)   John moved the rock.

(8b)   John moved the rock to the fence.

The PPs in (7b) and (8b) are similar in that they turn an activity verb into an accomplishment verb, i.e. in Dowty's system, they add a BECOME predicate to the verb. However, (7b) entails that the referent of the subject ends up in Chicago, while (8b) entails that the referent of the object is at the fence, which can be expressed with a CAUSE predicate. Thus, there are two prepositions *to*: the first denotes a function from intransitive verbs to intransitive verbs (IV/IV), the second denotes a function from transitive verbs to transitive verbs (TV/TV). The first of these is illustrated in the analysis tree below (Dowty 1979: 211):[1]

(9) *Analysis Tree for* "John walks to Chicago"

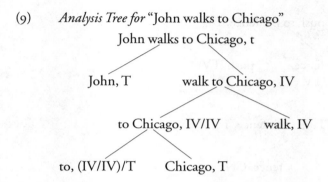

The most interesting step to note here is the combination of the verb and the PP, where the PP acts as functor which takes the verb as argument. The preposition is correspondingly typed. The semantics for the preposition, a complex lambda expression, results after appropriate conversion in the translation in (10):

(10) *Translation for* "John walks to Chicago"
       walk'(j) & BECOME [be-at'(j, c)]

The preposition introduces the BECOME predicate (which is interpreted as meaning intuitively a temporal 'before–after' sequence) and the locational predicate be-at', which is not further analysed, although Dowty indicates ways to provide a more detailed analysis by employing a LOC function assigning positions to individuals in a (every) model. The sentence is interpreted as a conjunction of two predicates, where walk' remains unary, and the relation

---

[1] I have omitted references to the syntactic rules licensing steps of combination which are given in the original. Though obviously related, the Montagovian type system is different from the types employed in DS, as briefly pointed out above; here, approximate correspondences are t = Ty(t), T = Ty(e), IV = Ty(e → t), and (IV/IV)/T = Ty(e → ((e → t) → (e → t))).

between the referents of subject and object is expressed by be-at' (hence the preposition is 'transitive').

The second *to* is illustrated in (11):

(11)   *Analysis Tree for* "John pushes a rock to the fence"

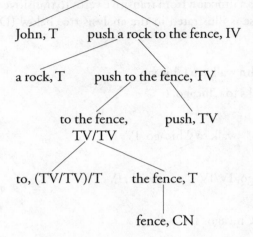

In (11), in contrast to (9), the preposition combines with its object to form the transitive verb modifier *to the fence*. There is the technical problem that when the 'transitive verb' *push to the fence* combines with the object of *push*, i.e. *a rock*, the object has to be 'inserted' between the verb and the PP, which have already combined—the solution being a 'wrap' operation without semantic content (cf. McGee Wood 1993, Morrill 1994). The translation corresponding to (11) is then:

(12)   *Translation for* "John pushes a rock to the fence"

$\exists x \, [rock'(x) \, \& \, \exists y [\forall z \, [fence'(z) \leftrightarrow y = z] \, \&$
$push'_*(j, x) \text{ CAUSE BECOME } [be\text{-}at'(x, y)]]]$

As (12) shows, the transitive modifier preposition introduces, in addition to BECOME, a CAUSE predicate into the translation, indicating that it is the object which moves, and not the subject. In that way, the verb remains transitive.[2]

---

[2] The clause $\forall z \, [fence'(z) \leftrightarrow y = z]$ indicates that *the fence* is definite, the notation push'. means that *push* translates into an extensional predicate, in contrast to e.g. *seek*. Both points are irrelevant here.

The two translations for prepositions (*to* is just an example) as IV/IV and TV/TV lead to a systematic ambiguity in the lexicon in that there are (at least) two entries for each preposition. Dowty proposes a translation rule, which translates intransitive modifiers into transitive modifiers, so that prepositions only need to be listed as IV/IV. This means that the semantic operation associated with TV/TV can be defined on the operation IV/IV.[3] Verbs subcategorizing for a PP such as *put*, *set*, *lay*, Dowty translates as requiring a modifier as argument, so as to give a consistent interpretation of PPs as modifiers. For example, *put* is of category TV/(TV/TV), requiring a transitive verb modifier to yield a transitive verb, corresponding to a DS type $Ty(((e \rightarrow (e \rightarrow t)) \rightarrow (e \rightarrow (e \rightarrow t))) \rightarrow (e \rightarrow (e \rightarrow t)))$.

There are some problems with this approach, as noted by Dowty himself. Since TV/TV results from a translation rule applying to IV/IV, all PPs can function as IV/IV, since the translation rule is optional. For example, the PP in (13) can apply as IV/IV to the verb:

(13)   John threw the letter into the wastebasket.

The preferred interpretation here is that the PP is a TV/TV so that the letter ends up in the wastebasket. However, the PP might equally well function as IV/IV, which, given the semantics for intransitive verb modifiers given in (10) above, results in a reading where it is John who comes to be in the wastebasket. These two readings will be generated by the semantic algebra, but one reading is highly unlikely for pragmatic reasons. A slightly different situation arises with (14):

(14)   John drove his car to Chicago.

In (14), both interpretations seem to be possible (or, maybe, required) since both John and his car end up in Chicago. Dowty proposes that sentences like (14) 'may well be syntactically (and semantically) ambiguous, though the two readings are indiscernible for pragmatic reasons' (1979: 209). The role of pragmatics in this situation is thus to select among several readings generated by the grammar, as in other cases of disambiguation, despite the fact that an example such as (14) does not intuitively seem to be ambiguous. In addition, it is not

---

[3] I do not reproduce the translation rule here, nor for that matter the actual translation rules for prepositions. For the present discussion, the difference between IV/IV and TV/TV as the absence or presence of the CAUSE predicate is all that is needed. The actual rules involve the intensional interpretation of all expressions. However, the issue of intensionality is not relevant here.

clear how the role of the predicate, i.e. the verb, in these entailment relations can be expressed, since the analysis assigns semantic operations of PP modification to the preposition. For example, the contrast between (14) and (15) seems to result from the choice of the predicate, and not from the PP:

(15)   John wrote a letter to the editor.

That is, the particular pragmatic knowledge about who and what ends up where involved in these cases includes knowledge about driving and writing, i.e. about concepts addressed by the verbs, yet by treating PPs as functors, this observation is not expressed directly.[4]

5.2.2 Minimal Recursion Semantics and the dissociation of syntax and semantics

Dowty's analysis, like all analyses treating adjuncts as functors, is not very compatible with the syntax of e*, which treats adjuncts as arguments. Intuitively, the appropriate syntax for the semantics proposed by Dowty is the Adjunction rule discussed in Chapter 4. Yet even with a more harmonious syntax, some problems arise for Dowty's analysis from a DS perspective. For example, the definition of verbs as requiring a modifier presupposes a type system which supports inferences over types, which, as discussed above, DS does not have. Similarly, it is not possible to change lexical types by translation rules, since once established, lexical information cannot be changed. For e*, the problem is of course much bigger, since the syntactic structure runs against the semantic structure. This problem would be almost enough to force abandonment of the idea of using modifier semantics for adjunction and verbal underspecification if it were not for the development of recent approaches of dissociation between syntactic argument structure and semantic representation within HPSG (Bouma and van Noord 1994, Bouma et al. 1997, Copestake et al. 1997).[5]

Several works in the HPSG literature include a discussion of the status of adjuncts as syntactic arguments, based on data similar to those discussed in Chapter 3.[6] A formal reflex of this observation is, for example, the lexical rule

---

[4] A more detailed analysis of PP modifiers similar to Dowty's approach is found in Keenan and Faltz (1985), who also discuss valency changing operations such as passives.

[5] For work on HPSG (Head-Driven Phrase Structure Grammar) more generally, see Pollard and Sag (1994), Sag and Wasow (1999), Levine and Green (1999), and also Horrocks (1987) and Lappin and Johnson (1999) for discussions of HPSG and its relation to other theoretical approaches.

[6] The majority of data in Ch. 3 are in fact from this literature.

provided by Sag (1998: 10), following Bouma et al. (1997), by which a verb can take any modifier occurring with it as a syntactic argument:[7]

(16)
$$
\begin{bmatrix} vb\text{-}lxm \\ \text{ARG-ST } \boxed{1} \end{bmatrix} \Rightarrow LR \begin{bmatrix} word \\ \text{HEAD } \boxed{3} \\ \text{ARG-ST } \boxed{1} \otimes \text{list} \begin{bmatrix} \text{MOD} \begin{bmatrix} \text{HEAD } \boxed{3} \\ \text{CONT } \boxed{2} \end{bmatrix} \end{bmatrix} \\ \\ \text{CONT } \boxed{2} \end{bmatrix}
$$

The lexical rule in (16) states that for any given verb with a given argument structure, a new word can be derived which is like the input verb, but where the argument structure is supplemented with a list of modifiers. The amend symbol ($\otimes$) indicates an addition to a list, since argument structure in general is modelled as a list. The head feature of the modifier unifies with the head feature of the derived word, i.e. whatever the (syntactic) head of the modifier (for example, a preposition) is, it is dominated by the verb, and, similarly, the content of the modifier is represented in the content list of the derived form. The syntactic effect of (16) is similar to the e* formalization. Under both formalizations a sentence like (17) will have three arguments:

(17)   The Sheriff of Nottingham sentenced Robin Hood for three years.

In both approaches, the modifier *for three years* can be analysed as an argument of the verb *sentence* under the same structural configuration as *Robin Hood*, at some level of syntactic description. The difference between the two approaches is that (16) is formulated as a lexical rule, while e* is defined syntactically and does not change lexical information. The lexical rule in (16) results furthermore in unordered lists of arguments without internal structure. The reason for this liberal treatment of syntactic structure is that it is coupled with a corresponding semantic analysis, Minimal Recursion Semantics (MRS, Copestake et al. 1997), which establishes semantic relations, especially scope relations among quantified NPs, but also head–modifier relations, independently of syntax. Minimal Recursion Semantics allows for a flat representation of sentences, represented as simple lists under conjunction (symbolized here by $\wedge$), where all constituents are introduced with a numerical index, a 'handle':[8]

---

[7] A number of alternative formulations are discussed in Sag (1998) and elsewhere, some of them restricting the introduction of modifiers as arguments to slash values (i.e. extracted modifiers), some of them including a separate DEP(endent) feature, in addition to argument structure.

[8] The examples are from Copestake et al. (1997). The quantified NPs in the second example

(18)   The Sheriff of Nottingham sentenced Robin Hood for three years.

$\wedge$ {2:sentence', 1:sheriff_of_nottingham', 3:Robin_Hood',
4:for_three_years'}

(19a)   Every dog chased some cat.

(19b)   top 5

$\wedge$ {1:every(x, 3, 4), 3:dog(x), 7:cat(y), 5:some(y, 7, 1), 4:chase(e, x, y)}

(19c)   top 1

$\wedge$ {1:every(x, 3, 5), 3:dog(x), 7:cat(y), 5:some(y, 7, 4), 4:chase(e, x, y)}

In particular, quantified expressions can be represented with underspecified scope relations, which are resolved by designating one handle value as the top value, which will identify the expression with the widest scope. For example, (19b) represents the wide-scope subject, (19c) the wide-scope object reading of (19a). The choice of the handle value thus implies the scope of the quantifiers. More generally, the choice of handles and their mutual relations (e.g. 'outscope') determine semantic relations between constituents independent of their syntactic relations.

For the analysis of adjuncts, Minimal Recursion Semantics can be employed under the assumption that predicate–argument relations can equally be represented as a relation between handles, i.e. if, for example, scope relations are translated into attribute–value relations. By making the handle value of adjuncts bound by the top node ('implicit top-level binding'), the adjunct will be interpreted as modifying the lower constituents, i.e. the VP. The HPSG analysis of adjuncts as arguments, on the one hand, but as semantically acting as modifiers on the other, combines the syntactic generalization that adjuncts act as arguments with traditional semantic analyses such as Dowty's.

Given the underspecified nature of the syntactic representation of MRS structures, the system can easily be extended to underspecified verbs, and although I will ultimately propose a different analysis, I provide a sketch here of how this can be done. Since in DS, all tree positions are uniquely identified by their tree address, these could be used as handles. However, the more explicit solution is to introduce a new predicate named Handle (Hd(x)), with its value as part of the formula value.

(20)   {Hd(1), Fo(1: sing), Hd(2), Fo(2: john)}

are represented as generalized quantifiers (see e.g. Barwise and Cooper 1984, Keenan 1996, Cann 1993: 187ff.). The analysis of quantification has no bearing on the present discussion.

Handle values can be projected directly at the top node, Tn(0), by introducing a predicate σ({x, y, z, . . .}), where handle values are recorded. The rule in (21) defines that lexical action add_handle:

(21) *Handle Rule*

    (1)   IF   T

          THEN   . . . add_handle . . .

    where T an arbitrary trigger

    (2)   add_handle: 1) put(Hd(x)), where x = 1, 2, . . . and x is fresh

                        2) σ := σ ∪ (x),

    where σ is the set of handles at Tn(0).

The first clause of the Handle rule states that add_handle is a possible lexical action. The second clause of the rule states that the action to be carried out consists of introducing a handle predicate and a new value for it, i.e. a value which has not yet been assigned in the tree, and, secondly, to introduce the value into the set σ where all handle values which have been assigned are recorded.[9] The rule results in representations where the presence of adjuncts is recorded at the top node Tn(0). This does not interfere with the syntax of e*, since the handle rule simply adds a new action predicate to the set of actions stated in the lexicon.

A derivation for (22) thus results in a tree like (23) before completion:

(22) John was singing with Mary in the kitchen.

(23) *Tree for* "John was singing with Mary in the kitchen" *(with e* and MRS)*

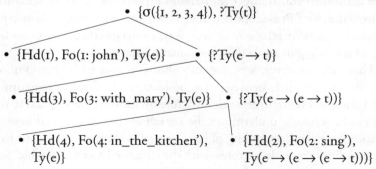

---

[9] I have not included an explicit statement for pointer movement, which could be added by employing the 'go' predicate and an appropriate modal operator. I also assume that new (fresh) values can be identified.

According to the e* rule, all PPs have been introduced as arguments. The underspecification in the verb has been resolved, and a place in the tree has been assigned. The new feature in the tree is that all expressions are represented at $Tn(0)$ by their handle value. In a tree like (23) explicit reference can be made to the members of σ, so that semantic scope can be stated independently of the syntactic underspecification. Of course, as it stands, it is not clear what sort of semantic interpretation is assigned to e* with MRS—all that has been done is to introduce a new predicate and a lexical rule. But with this modification it is possible to model an analysis of adjuncts both as functors and as arguments if these relations are regarded as scope relations. For example, in (23), *in the kitchen* might be taken as a functor to the predicate, while *with Mary* may be an argument, which can be expressed as handle scoping at $Tn(0)$:

(24)   *Tree for* "John was singing with Mary in the kitchen"
        (with e*/MRS, scoped)

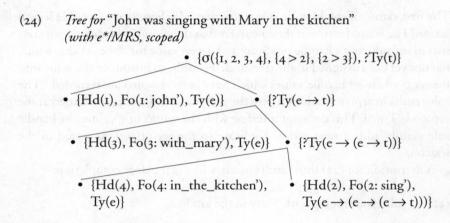

The additional constraints over handles express the different semantic functions of the two PPs as scope constraints, where the relation '>' is interpreted as functor–argument relation. In that way, underspecified verbs can be interpreted according to any traditional semantic approach.

There are, however, some serious shortcomings with this solution. Any postulated mismatch between tree building and syntactic structure on the one hand and eventual semantic structure on the other, as implied in the MRS approach, seriously undermines the overall enterprise pursued here, namely to come to an understanding of how natural language can be used to express the meanings that it does express with the structural means available. Secondly, as it stands, the proposal equates predicate–argument structure with scope statements, despite the fact that the scope relation of, for example, quantified expressions, though dependent on the structure of the VP, is a different relation from that between a verb and its argument, and it can be argued that it is better analysed by a distinct formalism. Thirdly, the analysis presupposes that adjuncts really are semantically modifiers. For the cases discussed in this study, however, there is a strong intuition that e* predicates denote *n*-ary relations.

(25)   She was driving to Spain with Sarah in her old Toyota.

In (25), for example, there is an intuitive 'driving' relation between the protagonist, Spain, Sarah, and the old Toyota. This indicates that also, semantically, adjuncts which have been introduced by e* should be analysed as arguments, and it is an approach which reflects this intuition to which I now turn.

5.3 ARGUMENT SEMANTICS

An alternative approach to the semantics of adjuncts has been proposed by McConnell-Ginet (1982), where adjuncts are treated both syntactically and semantically as arguments of the predicate. In fact, some of the syntactic arguments for the e* analysis go back to this work, and the overall approach is closer in spirit to the argument developed here than to the modifier approaches of the previous section.

5.3.1 McConnell-Ginet's Ad-Verb rule

McConnell-Ginet's (1982) starting point is that a treatment of adjuncts as functors fails to address important characteristics of adjuncts such as in (26):

(26a)   Linda spoke to Marcia.

(26b)   Linda spoke.

Intuitively, the PP in (26a) specifies the predicate: not only did Linda speak, but she also addressed Marcia in doing so. Conversely, speaking to someone entails speaking, so (26b) is entailed by (26a). To give adjuncts modifier semantics does not, McConnell-Ginet argues, express in sufficient clarity the entailment relation from (26a) to (26b), nor does it capture the intuition, noted above, that adjuncts such as the one in (26a) result in different extensional relations, and do not require an intensional, possible-world semantics. The alternative proposal developed by McConnell-Ginet models adverbs as arguments of verbs. It does not only cover lexical adverbs, but can be extended to include NP and PP adjuncts. The relevant basic features are, first, that VP-internal adverbs combine with verbs rather than with a VP, secondly, that adverbs typically have a dual function: they augment the order of the verb with which they combine and they specify the value(s) of the added argument place(s), and thirdly, that adverbs combine with verbs independently of verbal subcategorization (McConnell-Ginet 1982: 167). That is, for example, an optional PP combines with a verb by adding an argument position to the verb and specifying at the same time how it should be filled (e.g. by a 'location' if it is a locative adverbial). This process is freely available, independent of the subcategorization of the verb.

The formal statement of this approach makes use of multiple-order predicates, a possible translation of verbs like *speak*, which can be used as intransitive and as transitive verbs. The verb *speak* could be translated as 1/2-order predicate with the restriction in (27) (McConnell-Ginet 1982: 168), where 'Den' abbreviates the denotation of a predicate in particular situations:

(27)   if $\langle a, b \rangle \in \text{Den}(\textbf{speak})$, then $\{a\} \in \text{Den}(\textbf{speak})$

That is to say, if an ordered pair of constants, meaning, maybe, Anne and Berta, is in the extension of speak', then so is the first member of the pair, i.e. here, Anne. Under this interpretation, *speak* can be used with or without PP, and the inference from (28a) to (28b) is valid:

(28a)   Anne spoke to Berta.

(28b)   Anne spoke.

But rather than just translating some verbs as being of multiple order, McConnell-Ginet develops a formulation with which multiple-order verbs can be formed by adverbs, which 'augment' the verb. This is defined formally as follows (McConnell-Ginet 1982: 169):

(29)   *Admissible Augmentation*
           Let α be a verb in category X that translates into an *n*-order predicate denoting an *n*-ary relation $\mathfrak{R}$. Then α^+ is an Admissible Augmentation of α in categories X and X/Y only if α^+ translates into an $n/n + 1$-order predicate denoting $\mathfrak{R}^+ = \mathfrak{R} \cup \wp$, where $\wp \subseteq \mathfrak{R} \times$ Type Y. The augmented verb α^+ is admissible relative to $\xi \in$ Y only if $\wp \subseteq \mathfrak{R} \times \text{Den}(\xi) \neq \varnothing$.

The definition in (29) says that, for example, a binary predicate can be formed from a unary predicate if it can be augmented by a modifying expression such as an adverb. The denotation of this new predicate ($\mathfrak{R}^+$) is formed from the union of the denotation of the original, unaugmented verb ($\mathfrak{R}$) with the denotation obtained from the product of $\mathfrak{R}$ and the 'categorial range' (Type Y) of the modifier ($\wp$). The categorial range of manner adverbs, for example, is 'manner', i.e. the added argument is restricted relative both to the verb's meaning and to the 'kind' of modifier. A verb may be augmented by a modifier only if there is at least one member in the union of the denotation of verb and modifier ($\wp \neq \emptyset$). Thus for the example (28), above, rather than translating *speak* as a multiple-order predicate, it can be translated as a unary predicate, because by (29) it can become a multiple-order predicate if it is used with a modifier (here, the PP). The step from Anne spoke' (speak unary) to Anne spoke^{+}' (speak binary) is licensed (admissible) if there is somebody in the semantic model who Anne spoke to, as for example Berta. In this scenario, the denotation of the new predicate spoke^{+}' is both {Anne}, the denotation of the original verb, and {⟨Anne, Berta⟩}, an element of the product of verb and modifier denotations, where the categorial range of the modifier would be 'addressee'.

With this formulation of augmenting a verb, optional adverbial modification can be formulated as follows (McConnell-Ginet 1982: 169):[10]

(30) *Ad-Verb Rule*
      Let α be a lexical verb belonging to category X where $X \neq Y/\text{AD-V}$ and ξ be an expression belonging to category AD-V. Then expression $\alpha\xi$ belongs to category X. A translation of $\alpha\xi$ is defined if $\exists \alpha^{+}$, an admissible augmentation of α relative to ξ in categories X and X/AD-V. Then $\text{tr}(\alpha\xi) = \text{tr}(\alpha^{+})(\text{tr}(\xi))$.

With the rule in (30), any verb of any category (intransitive, transitive, etc.) can be augmented by an expression of category AD-V, that is, if it is an Ad-Verb, a type which includes those expressions which (can) function as optional arguments or adjuncts of a predicate. The combination of the verb and the Ad-Verb (e.g. by function–application) yields an expression of the same category as the original, unaugmented verb—both α and $\alpha\xi$ belong to category X (hence the rule is recursive). The interpretation of this rule (its translation) restricts its application, since a translation is only defined if there is an admissible augmentation (as defined above). If there is, then the interpretation of the complex

---

[10] There is a corresponding rule for obligatory adverbial modification, for cases like (McConnell-Ginet 1982: 166):

(i)   Liz resides in Kalamazoo.
(ii) *Liz resides.

This is irrelevant, since PPs are treated here as Ty(e) (in contrast to Ty(AD-V)), so that (i) does not need a special rule (other than lexical).

expression $\alpha\xi$ is defined as the translation of the augmented verb applied to the translation of the Ad-Verb.

To consider an example, if *speak* is an intransitive verb of type $Ty(e \rightarrow t)$ (i.e. $\langle e,t \rangle$ in Montagovian notation) denoting speak' and *to Linda* is an Ad-Verb of type $Ty(\text{AD-V})$ of 'addressee' Ad-Verbs, then an expression *speak to Linda* of type $Ty(e \rightarrow t)$ can be created. The interpretation of this new expression is the interpretation of *speak*, i.e. in terms of the lambda calculus $Fo(\lambda x \; speak'(x))$, plus the augmentation, so that α^+ here would be $Fo(\lambda x \; speak'(x) \; \& \; \lambda y \lambda x \; speak'\text{-addressee}'(y)(x))$, which combines with (*to*) *Linda* such that Linda' fills the second variable slot:

(31) $\quad \dfrac{(\lambda x \; speak'(x) \; \& \; \lambda y \lambda x \; speak'\text{-addressee}'(y)(x)) \; (\text{linda}')}{(\lambda x \; speak'(x) \; \& \; \lambda x \; speak'\text{-addressee}'(\text{linda}')(x))}$

Under this view, Ad-Verbs create an additional argument slot of the predicate which they subsequently fill. In this sense, the Ad-Verb and Augmentation rules describe a two-step process, creating and filling argument slots. Since the meaning of the augmented verb is built on, and incorporates the unaugmented verb, the inference from *Mary spoke to Linda* to *Mary spoke* is explicitly recorded in the semantics. By assuming different kinds of Ad-Verbs, the Augmentation rule ensures that only semantically 'suitable' Ad-Verbs can augment predicates.

McConnell-Ginet concludes that this characterization of Ad-Verbs overcomes the problems created by treating adverbials as functors. It takes account of the fact that Ad-Verbs modify their base verb, and that the meaning of the base verb is entailed by the augmented verb. The semantics is both compositional and extensional. Finally, the proposal draws on certain similarities between lexical adverbs and optional term phrases (NPs and PPs), and thus provides an analysis for both cases.

5.3.2 An extensional semantics for e*

The adverb rule and translation proposed by McConnell-Ginet are close in spirit to e*, since adjuncts are treated as arguments to verbs. Semantic interpretation is furthermore established incrementally, in tandem with the introduction of the adverb. The proposal is thus not difficult to exploit for underspecified verbs. Among the differences between McConnell-Ginet's proposal and the formalization of verbal underspecification is that McConnell-Ginet reserves a special semantic type for expressions which can augment verbs, Ad-Verbs, while adjuncts are simply $Ty(e)$ expressions for e*, where adjunction is analysed as underspecification of the verb. Underspecification, on the other hand, is not directly addressed by McConnell-Ginet. Secondly, McConnell-Ginet's rule assumes the complete parallel operation of syntactic and semantic rules, as implemented in Categorial Grammar ('bottom-up') derivations. Thus the two steps of adverbial modification, the creation and filling of an argument slot, are both expressed in the rule. In contrast, e^* models the incremental growth of a semantic tree, where the unfolding of tree structure is achieved by the structure-building actions of lexical items and computational rules, while the actual combination of functors and arguments by Elimination and Completion only takes place when the tree is complete. A formulation of McConnell-Ginet's Ad-Verb rule for e^*, expressing these two differences, is given in (32):

(32)   *Semantic Interpretation of e^**
        Let α be a lexical verb of $Ty(X \to (e^* \to t))$ and ξ be an expression of
        $Ty(e)$. Then α can be partially resolved to $Ty(X \to (e \to (e^* \to t)))$.
        A translation of $\alpha\xi$ is defined if $\exists \alpha^+$, an admissible augmentation
        of α relative to ξ with types $Ty(X \to t)$ and $Ty(X \to (e \to t))$. Then
        $tr(\alpha\xi) = tr(\alpha^+)(tr(\xi))$.

In (32), the typing reflects the e^* approach. The semantic interpretation, on the other hand, is as given in McConnell-Ginet, in that the translation depends on there being an admissible augmentation of the verb. This can be more conveniently expressed by incorporating the semantic requirement into the transition rule for e^*:[11]

(33)   *e^* Partial Resolution with Semantics*

$$\frac{\{_{n^*} \ldots Fo(\alpha), Ty(X \to (e^* \to t))\}, \{_{n0} \ldots Fo(\beta), Ty(e)\}}{\{_{n1^*} \ldots Fo(\alpha^+), Ty(X \to (e \to (e^* \to t)))\}, \{_{n0} \ldots Fo(\beta), Ty(e)\}}$$

        where $Fo(\alpha^+)$ is an admissible augmentation of $Fo(\alpha)$ relative to
        $Fo(\beta)$

Note that no reference needs to be made to the interpretation (translation) of the augmented verb, since it is covered by the general semantic rule of function–application which is in DS defined by the transition rule Elimin-

---

[11] The instruction for pointer movement in the original rule defined in Ch. 4 has been omitted here, since it would complicate the derivation without any benefit to the point to be made.

ation. This means that once the verb is augmented, its semantic interpretation is exactly like the interpretation of a normal predicate with respect to its argument. However, since (33) makes reference to admissible augmentations, this rule has to be part of the incremental semantics for e^* developed here. A modified version, with the categories replaced by types, is given below:

(34)   *Admissible augmentation for e^**
        Let α be a verb of $\text{Ty}(X \to (e^* \to t))$ that translates into an n-order predicate denoting an n-ary relation $\mathfrak{R}$. Then α^+ is an admissible augmentation of α with $\text{Ty}(X \to t)$ and $\text{Ty}(X \to (e \to t))$ only if α^+ translates into an $n/n + 1$-order predicate denoting $\mathfrak{R}^+ = \mathfrak{R} \cup \wp$, where $\wp \subseteq \mathfrak{R} \times \text{Ty}(e)$. The augmented verb α^+ is admissible relative to $\xi \in \text{Ty}(e)$ only if $\wp \subseteq \mathfrak{R} \times \text{Den}(\xi) \neq \varnothing$.

The rule interacts with the transition rule for e^*, so that the underspecification in e^* is partially resolved by expressions of $\text{Ty}(e)$ if the verb can be augmented with respect to that expression. With each step of application of the transition rule, i.e. with every new expression of $\text{Ty}(e)$, the predicate is extended with an additional argument slot, which is filled with the expression of $\text{Ty}(e)$ standardly under Completion.

5.3.3 Sample derivation

An example makes clear how the semantic rules work. Consider (35) and the derivation in (36):

(35)   Sue was singing with Mary in the shower.

(36a)   *Tree for* "Sue was singing

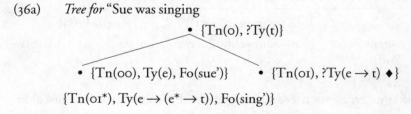

At this stage, *Sue* has been assigned its proper place in the tree, and a node with the requirement $?\text{Ty}(e \to t)$ has been built. The DU of *sing* is still unattached, pending further input. The lexical actions from the entry for *with* result in a new argument node which is annotated with a prepositional feature and a requirement $?\text{Ty}(e)$, which is fulfilled when *Mary* is introduced:

(36b)   *Tree for* "Sue was singing with Mary

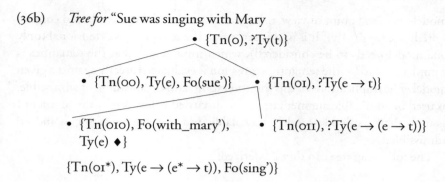

$\{Tn(o), ?Ty(t)\}$

$\{Tn(oo), Ty(e), Fo(sue')\}$ $\{Tn(oI), ?Ty(e \rightarrow t)\}$

$\{Tn(oIo), Fo(with\_mary'),$ $\{Tn(oII), ?Ty(e \rightarrow (e \rightarrow t))\}$
$Ty(e) \blacklozenge\}$

$\{Tn(oI^*), Ty(e \rightarrow (e^* \rightarrow t)), Fo(sing')\}$

The tree in (36b) provides a suitable input to e^* Partial Resolution, which now not only updates the underspecification of the location and the type value but also records the semantic operation of augmenting the predicate. An instantiation of the rule in this situation is given below:

(37)   *e^* Partial Resolution (instantiated as* sing with Mary*)*
$\{_{oI^*} \ldots Fo(sing'), Ty(e \rightarrow (e^* \rightarrow t))\}, \{_{oIo} \ldots Fo(with\_mary'), Ty(e)\}$

$\{_{oI^*} \ldots Fo(sing'^+), Ty(e \rightarrow (e \rightarrow (e^* \rightarrow t)))\},$
$\{_{oIo} \ldots Fo(with\_mary'), Ty(e)\}$

where $Fo(sing'^+)$ is an admissible augmentation of $Fo(sing')$ relative to $Fo(with\_mary')$.

According to the rule, the predicate is updated with respect to location, type value, and formula value. The operation on the formula value follows from the semantic rule for e^*, and can be expressed by lambda expressions. The step from $Fo(sing')$ to $Fo(sing'^+)$ thus corresponds to the step from (38a) to (38b):

(38a) $\{Tn(oI^*), Ty(e \rightarrow (e^* \rightarrow t)), Fo(\lambda x\ sing(x))\}$

(38b) $\{Tn(oII^*), Ty(e \rightarrow (e \rightarrow (e^* \rightarrow t))), Fo(\lambda y \lambda x\ (sing(x)\ \&\ sing^+(y)(x)))\}$

As can be seen from (38), the e^* semantic rule creates a new lambda term by introducing a new argument slot. Both the original lambda expression and the derived lambda expression represent the meaning of the new verb. This follows from the definition of augmentation, which states that the meaning of the new verb is the union of the extensions of the augmented and the unaugmented verb. The final requirement is that the expression of $Ty(e)$ which triggers the rule denotes something which can fill the new argument slot. From a model-theoretic point of view, this means here that the model should contain a predicate $sing^+(x)(y)$. It is in this sense that the semantics is extensional (only one model needs to be considered), which implies also that the semantics is completely static—the semantic expression is evaluated directly against a given model. The implications of this interpretation, and the meaning of admissible, as used in admissible augmentation, are discussed below, so for the moment I assume that a suitable model is available and the augmentation is indeed admissible.

The following tree can thus be derived:

(36c)   *Tree for* "Sue was singing with Mary

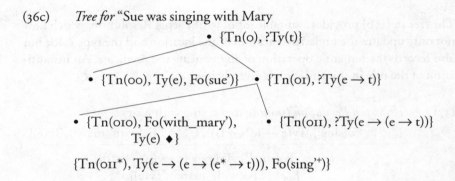

The introduction of the second adjunct, *in the shower*, develops the tree in a similar fashion, so that after the relevant actions the adjunct is integrated at an argument node. This situation then provides the input to another application of e* Partial Resolution to result in the following tree:

(36d)   *Tree for* "Sue was singing with Mary in the shower

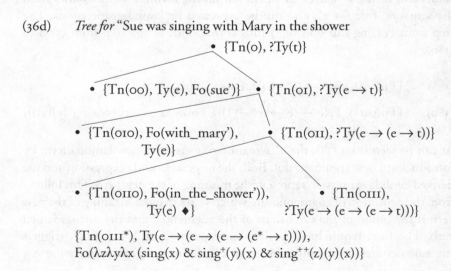

This step is formally identical to the preceding one. The predicate has now been augmented twice so that the formula value includes three different predicates of three different arities. In the absence of further lexical input, Merge applies and the unfixed node can be incorporated into the tree. The application of Completion and Elimination then yields the following formula values:

(36e)   *Tree for* "Sue was singing with Mary in the shower"

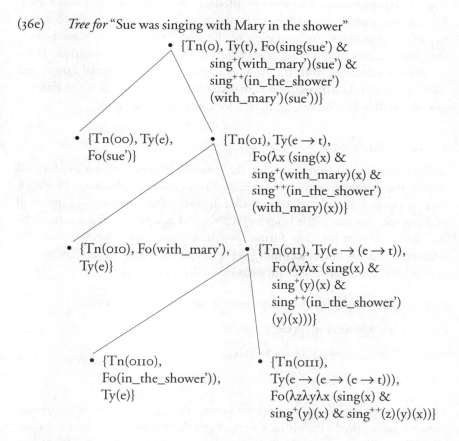

This sample derivation shows how the rule for e* with semantics works, and that it results in an array of predicates with different arities, following the definition of augmentation. This treatment is incremental, in that the predicate is augmented at every introduction of a Ty(e) expression, compositional, in that syntactic and semantic rules are defined in tandem, and extensional, in that the resulting expressions can be evaluated in a first-order model by relating the ordered tuples denoted by the augmented verbs to the extensions of the relevant predicates—which, however, implies that all relevant predicates have to be in the model.

5.3.4 Discussion

Although the interpretation of underspecified verbs along the lines of the Ad-Verb rule comes much closer to the original intention and motivation of the approach advocated here, there are a number of problems connected with it. One of them is the syntactic one that, because augmentation is defined as a step-by-step process developing one predicate from the other, it is not clear how the rule would cope with head-final structures, which, as discussed above, require an instantaneous resolution of the underspecification. More important, however, are the problems associated with semantic interpretation. These are mainly associated with the notions of entailment, categorial range, and admissibility, and ultimately show that the Ad-Verb approach is too static to provide an illuminating interpretation for underspecified verbs.

5.3.4.1 *Entailments*

According to the Ad-Verb approach, the semantic interpretation of augmented verbs is the set of their entailments, as seen from the example above. However, there is a technical problem, namely that the formalization does not capture all relevant entailments, while from a psychological perspective, there seem to be too many entailments. The former problem results from the way recursive augmentations are built. According to the definition given, the inferences from (37) to (38a), (38b), and (38c) are encoded in the semantics:

(37)   Sue was singing on her birthday with Mary in the shower.

(38a)   Sue was singing on her birthday with Mary.

(38b)   Sue was singing on her birthday.

(38c)   Sue was singing.

However, the rule as it stands does not express the augmentation of the unaugmented, initial predicate with the second and third adjunct, or the augmentation of the initially augmented predicate with the third adjunct. This means that the following inferences are not encoded in the semantic representation of a sentence like (37):

(39a)   Sue was singing with Mary.

(39b)   Sue was singing in the shower.

(39c)   Sue was singing with Mary in the shower.

(39d)   Sue was singing on her birthday in the shower.

Since from (37) the inferences in (39) are as valid as those in (38), there is no reason for not including them in the semantics. But it is not clear whether the rule could be modified to achieve this, since it would imply that already established augmentations have to be undone in order to recover the initial unaugmented verb. Even if such a rule could be formulated, it would presumably complicate even further the interpretation process and the final semantic representation. This leads to the second point. While the semantic representation is fine as a statement of the semantics understood as a set of entailments, its psychological usefulness is limited, since it is unlikely that a hearer hearing (37) really entertains all the possible entailments resulting from the semantics of augmentation. While the role of pragmatics could be thought of as selecting from the set of entailments provided by the semantics, the perspective adopted here views the hearer as more active in the establishment of utterance meaning. In particular, the hearer is, with recourse to pragmatic knowledge, involved in the establishment of the proposition expressed by the utterance, which then can be used to derive those entailments which can reasonably be assumed to have been communicated to the hearer by the speaker, as governed, for example, by the presumption of optimal relevance. As discussed in more detail below, this view implies, in contrast to the semantic approaches discussed here, the existence of a level mental representation of the semantic form of the utterance. A semantic analysis which results in a list of entailments is not very compatible with this view, and there is thus pragmatic motivation to provide a different treatment.

5.3.4.2 *Categorial range*

Another problem with the Ad-Verb analysis is the selection and restriction of new arguments, which is achieved by restrictions on their categorial range and their admissibility. In contrast to the e* approach, where subcategorized arguments and adjuncts are of the same semantic type Ty(e), the optional argument in the Ad-Verb approach is, as is the case in Dowty's approach, of a special category. This means that PPs of the type Ad-V not only license a new argument node (as do prepositions for e*) but also restrict the new node according to semantic (or thematic) type. The semantic rule would thus not just increase the arity of the predicate, but also ensure that the augmentation is justified with respect to the categorial range of the expression with which the predicate is augmented.

This analysis implies that both McConnell-Ginet and Dowty assume that PPs, whether as functors or as arguments, can be analysed as specifying lexically in which thematic relation they stand to the expression they modify. According to this view, PPs and adverbs come with some information as to whether they relate to time, location, manner, etc. For example, temporal adverbs for Dowty are members of a special category (TmAV), although no categories are proposed for other ways of modifying.[12] McConnell-Ginet assumes that expressions in the category Ad-V provide information about whether they refer to manner, 'addressee', etc. Although this is not made precise, it is inherent in the 'two-step' analysis of adverbial modification, where the additional argument slot is annotated with an appropriate label, and a given verb–Ad-Verb expression is admissible if the modifier denotes a member of this particular type of modification. As discussed in Chapter 3, thematic roles are not part of the syntactic architecture assumed here. In addition to the reasons already discussed, there is another relevant point in the present context, relating to the previous point about entailments: if thematic roles are thought of as a shorthand for recurrent entailments, these entailments are, under the assumptions about representationalism here, derived from a representation of the propositional form of the utterance, but not from the natural language string directly. Again, this can be regarded as motivation for exploring an alternative account of adjunction.

5.3.4.3 *Admissibility*

The final and most important problem concerns the notion of admissibility. According to the definition given, a verb may only be augmented if the ordered set of terms denoted by the new verb has a denotation in the model. Admissibility is thus restricted by the requirement that the augmented predicate can be assigned a denotation in a given model, i.e. that a predicate with the appropriate arity is defined. So, for example, for the interpretation of the example sentence in the derivation above, a corresponding ternary predicate $sing\langle x, y, z\rangle$ has to be defined in the model, otherwise the augmentation is not allowed, and no semantic interpretation can be assigned to the string. This implies that for a model-theoretic interpretation, predicates of varying arity have to be defined in the model against which the string is evaluated, with any arity they may have. Since underspecified verbs are defined as having an infinite number of arguments, a corresponding model would have to be open-ended with respect to the predicates it contains, and it would thus not be possible to define a model in advance. Since no model can be given, a model-theoretic interpretation for

---

[12] The prominent place of temporal modification in Dowty (1979) presumably reflects partly the fact that tense, together with modality, is the best worked-out case of possible-world semantics, whereas there is no correspondingly developed possible-world semantics of places, instruments, or 'accompaniment'.

underspecified verbs is impossible, and thus does not provide a possible analysis for them.[13]

The main problem of semantic approaches to underspecified verbs is thus that they assume that the arity of predicates is fixed in advance, in direct contrast to the e* approach, which models the intuition that a predicate's arity is not fixed. This, and the related assumption that the interpretation of a natural language expression is assigned directly, without mediation of an intermediate level of representation, leads to the problems set out here, and provides the motivation for seeking an alternative analysis. As will be shown below, the intuition behind underspecified verbs and their most interesting feature, their context-specific nature, are better approached from a richer theory of cognition.

5.4 A PRAGMATIC APPROACH TO VERBAL UNDERSPECIFICATION

The arguments presented in this study have so far been centred around different aspects of linguistic knowledge and its representation in the literature (Kempson 1988). The formalization of verbal underspecification as underspecified syntactic type e* was based mainly on syntactic evidence, within a restrictive model of tree building, corresponding conceptually to the generative position to specify the grammar of a language by a set of psychologically plausible principles or rules.[14] The discussion in this chapter then highlighted the idea that natural language strings are systematically related to an interpretation, an assumption characteristic of formal grammar approaches following Montague (1974). However, the model-theoretic approaches discussed up to now failed to provide an analysis of the interpretation of underspecified verbs, partly because of the assumption that predicates of varying arity are defined a priori in a given model, which would have to include a non-finite array of predicates like sing'(x), sing'(x,y), sing'(x,y,z), etc., and partly because of the assumption that natural language expressions are mapped directly onto some model-theoretic interpretation.

[13] One way to circumvent this problem is outlined in Kibble et al. (1997), where it is proposed to associate predicates with a thematic template comprising the presumed maximum number of adjunct 'slots' which are filled by an appropriate adjunct or by 'existential closure'. As pointed out in that paper, this solution is not without problems, and does not reflect the intuition behind underspecified verbs.

[14] Psychologically plausible can be further specified here, for example to mean that the grammar should reflect the fact that language is acquired, rather than learnt, or, as more pressingly advocated here, that language is used by hearers to arrive at an interpretation.

A different assumption is introduced now: that knowledge of language, including syntactic and (truth-conditional) semantic aspects, is embedded in a representational theory of mind, an assumption which links DS to Fodorian (1981) cognitive philosophy and to the cognitive psychology developed in relevance theory (Sperber and Wilson 1995). In particular, the relevance-theoretic distinction between 'logical form' and 'propositional form' and its interpretation in the DS model are discussed in this section. Against the background of this distinction, I introduce the notion of mental concept and the process of concept formation. The interpretation of e* can with the aid of these notions be analysed as an instruction to concept formation, which includes the enrichment of the predicate and plays a role in context selection. This pragmatic approach to the interpretation of underspecified verbs overcomes the problems encountered by the model-theoretic approaches and embeds verbal underspecification in a larger theory of communication and cognition. After the approach is introduced, its implications and consequences are discussed at the end of the section.

5.4.1 Logical forms and pragmatic enrichment

As has been discussed in Chapter 2, relevance theory assumes that the interpretation of natural language sentences is established in conceptual structure. The interpretation of an utterance includes its associated propositional form, a mental representation, which is established with recourse to pragmatic, conceptual reasoning. As was pointed out earlier, pragmatic processes in utterance interpretation include reference assignment, disambiguation, and conceptual enrichment. One reason for this representational assumption is the indexicality of a number of natural language expressions. Most prominently, pronouns cannot be evaluated per se in a model, but their denotational content needs to be fixed by a value provided from the linguistic or non-linguistic context. Secondly, ambiguous lexical items are disambiguated in context. These two processes, reference assignment and disambiguation, are standardly assumed to be pragmatic in nature, yet to apply before a natural language string can be truth-theoretically evaluated (cf. Carston 1988, 2000). In relevance-theoretic terms, the logical form, i.e. the output of the grammar, needs to be pragmatically developed into a propositional form, which is the representation capable of truth-theoretic evaluation (Sperber and Wilson 1995).

But just reference assignment and disambiguation do not seem to be quite enough. Carston (1988) takes the English conjunction *and* as an example and shows that pragmatic enrichment plays an equally necessary role in establishing the propositional form of an utterance. It is uncontentious that *and* on occasion means more than is denoted by the corresponding logical connective. For example, in (40) *and* has a reading where the second action follows the first (and is probably also caused by it):

(40)   She became an alcoholic and her husband left her.

The question for the temporal interpretation of *and* in (40) is whether this meaning is an implicature, i.e. an inference from the literal, truth-conditional meaning of *and*, which is independent of this inference, or whether the temporal meaning contributes to the truth conditions of (40). Carston (1988) argues that the latter is the case. Technically, the temporal meaning of *and* in (40) is an explicature, a case of pragmatic enrichment, which has to be derived in order to establish the propositional form of (40). That this is so can be seen from the interaction of explicatures with logical operators such as negation and disjunction (Carston 1988: 172–3):

(41)   It is not the case that she became an alcoholic and her husband left her, but rather that her husband left her and she became an alcoholic.

(42)   Either she became an alcoholic and her husband left her or he left her and she became an alcoholic; I'm not sure which.

If the temporal/causal meaning of *and* was merely an implicature, then (41) should express a contradiction (of the form ($\neg$(P & Q) & (Q & P))), and (42) a tautology (of the form ((P & Q) v (Q & P))), which is intuitively not true. In contrast, the meaning of (41) and (42) can be adequately explained if it is assumed that the temporal/causal meanings of *and* are explicatures which do contribute to the propositional form, since under this view it is those enriched propositional forms which can be meaningfully negated/disjointed in (41) and (42). Enrichment is thus, in addition to reference assignment and disambiguation, a pragmatic process which bridges the gap from logical form to propositional form.

Carston further argues that the proper theory to express this observation is relevance theory. Given the overall psychological perspective of relevance theory, enrichment is viewed as a psychological process, in particular a non-demonstrative inferential process performed by the hearer and guided by the communicative principle of relevance. This ensures that there is both a lower and an upper limit for the derivation of explicatures in enrichment. The hearer is expected and entitled to derive as many explicatures as is justified given processing costs. In effect, the hearer infers enough to get a truth-evaluable relevant propositional form and then stops.

Relevance theory is intrinsically connected to the Fodorian concepts of mental representations and the language of thought (Fodor 1975, 1981). In the Fodorian conception of the mind, the linguistic module is an input module which derives uninterpreted logico-syntactic structures. These structures provide the input to the general reasoning faculty which 'translates' logical forms into the language of thought. Cognitive effects, the result of processing an utterance, are computed in the language of thought. They include the establishment of new conclusions from interacting assumptions, the derivation of contradictions and the subsequent abandoning of previously held assumptions, and the confirmation of existing assumptions (Carston 1988: 168). The language of thought is thus inferential. Furthermore, given that truth conditions cannot be checked against a logical form, but only against an enriched propositional form, there is no direct relation between natural language and objects in the world. Rather, this relation holds between objects in the world and propositions, i.e. mental representations in the language of thought.

The DS perspective on mental representations is conceptually very similar to the relevance theory stance, but differs in detail. The difference concerns the notions of modularity and encapsulation. Relevance theory is, at least in principle, committed to the Chomskian view of the language faculty as an encapsulated module (cf. Fodor 1981, Chomsky 1995). I take this here to mean (1) that the language faculty can be characterized as a computational system with rules and operations specific to language, not found elsewhere in the mind (in that sense, it is a proper module), and (2) that it can exclusively be so specified, i.e. not only are there language-specific rules but also no other mental specifications (i.e. rules, operations, format of representations) have access to the language faculty—the only interaction between the language faculty and other mental faculties obtains at (syntactically) designated interface levels (in that sense, it is encapsulated). In contrast, in DS, the language faculty is not encapsulated, i.e. (1) holds, while (2) does not. In particular, pragmatic reasoning—non-demonstrative inference—applies during the process of tree construction (Kempson 1996). The output of the phonological parser is taken to build propositional forms directly, by an interaction of general reasoning and structure-building rules. Although the language faculty can still be viewed as a Fodorian module (the rules are module-specific), it cannot be characterized as encapsulated (there is no designated output, or interface level).[15]

The view that structure building and pragmatic interpretation interact freely in utterance interpretation is motivated by the problem of anaphoric

---

[15] Cf. Kay (1995), who advances a similar argument, but pitched against modularity per se, without distinguishing between modularity and encapsulation.

interpretation. A unified analysis of pronominal interpretation requires, according to the DS position, both a representational conception of natural language and the interaction of structure building processes and pragmatics (Kempson 1996, Kempson et al. 1999, Kempson et al. 2001).[16] The problem is that the denotational content of pronominal expressions, in addition to their general context dependency, varies between different readings, i.e. apparently different discrete semantic requirements. Cases in point include bound-variable (43) and E-type readings (44), cross-sentential cross-reference (45), and bridging cross-reference (46) (Kempson et al. 2001: 10):

(43)   Every girl worries that she might get pregnant.

(44)   Most girls passed with distinction. They had worked very hard.

(45)   Sue came in. She was pregnant.

(46)   The Smiths are very nice. He is a doctor.

Furthermore, pronouns can be interpreted as discourse-based anaphorical. This involves the establishment of a relevant context in which the pronoun can be uniquely identified. However, a purely semantic account of context selection (as in Situation Semantics, Barwise and Perry 1983) fails to identify the intended referent in a discourse situation with, for example, two boys and two dogs, with one of the boys holding one of the dogs too tightly (Kempson et al. 2001: 13):

(47)   He's holding it too tightly.

The problem can be overcome once a level of syntactic representation is assumed, at which pronominal expressions are projected and interpreted with reference to pragmatic reasoning. This is perhaps even more clear with cases of indirect reference, as illustrated in the following example (Kempson et al. 2001: 14):

(48)   John had a heart attack right outside the hospital, and they refused to treat him without an insurance card.

There is no appropriate antecedent for the pronominal expression in the second clause. The interpretation of *they* here involves the inferential steps that doctors work in hospitals, and that doctors treat heart attacks.

---

[16] I only give a brief summary of the argument here. For full discussion and more examples, see the references cited in the main text. Note also that pronominal construal is only the paradigm case, but that the same problem of context dependency extends to definite NPs and demonstratives.

The conclusion from these and related data is, according to Kempson et al., that a purely semantic account of pronominal interpretation—be it situations, dynamic binding (Groenendijk and Stokhof 1991, Chierchia 1995), or discourse representation (Kamp and Reyle 1993)[17]—fails to provide a unified characterization of anaphoric expressions. In addition, semantic accounts fail by the nature of the enterprise to address questions of syntactic restrictions on pronouns, such as resumptive pronouns and island constraints. The DS solution to this problem is to postulate a representational level of structure building where interpretation is subject to considerations of relevance. The argument which will be developed in the remainder of this chapter provides another piece of evidence for this view. It is perhaps an even more powerful argument, since I propose that, because the resolution of verbal underspecification can only be achieved with recourse to pragmatic enrichment, no logical form can be established in principle without, or prior to, pragmatic processes taking place. The syntax–pragmatics interface seen from this perspective is not an output structure of the linguistic module, but rather is characterized by the concerted interaction of syntax and pragmatics in establishing inferential effects.

5.4.2 From enrichment to concepts

A central consequence of the relevance conception of communication is that inferential reasoning plays a pervasive role in utterance interpretation, and that a code model is insufficient for the explanation of natural language meaning. Correspondingly, pragmatic enrichment in the development of the proposition expressed is the rule rather than the exception in communication. Enrichment does not only apply to 'logical' words such as *and*. Another example is (49) (Carston 1988: 158):

(49)   She gave him her key and he opened the door.

The utterance in (49) is to be understood such that whoever *he* is used the key *she* (whoever *she* is) gave him to open the door. To derive the proposition expressed by (49), the hearer has to fill in the pronouns with some suitable representations and enrich *and* in the manner outlined above so as to get a stronger temporal reading. On the assumption that denials bear on what has

---

[17] DRT, in contrast to the two other approaches, does postulate a level of discourse representation, and is thus closest to DS. However, in DRT this intermediate level is purely semantic and does not incorporate syntactic structure, which is assumed to be independent (the relation being established by translation rules).

been explicated (the propositional form) and not what has been implicated, (50) and (51) show again that the temporal reading of *and* is an explicature (Carston 1988: 172):

(50)   No. He opened the door before she gave him the key.

(51)   No. He opened the door and then she gave him the key.

The third process of enrichment, the hearer has to 'fill in' that it was the key she gave him that he used to open the door, to derive a propositional form like (52):

(52)   [Karen] gave [Keith] [Karen's] key and [then] [Keith] opened the door [with Karen's key]

The relevant bit here is the PP, which is filled in as an explicature. That it is not just an implicature can be seen from the denials in (53) and (54), in analogy with Carston's examples in (50) and (51):

(53)   No. He had his own key all the way through.

(54)   No. It wasn't locked.

What is being denied in these examples is not that Karen gave her key to Keith, but that Keith used that key to open the door—(53) says that he used his own key, (54) says that he didn't use any key at all.

But is the representation in (52) the right way to think about these things? The difference between the *and* case and the *with the key* case is that the former is an enrichment of the lexical meaning of the word *and*, whereas in (52) what is enriched is a formal ('logical') structure. Of course, if we wanted to *encode* the explicature communicated by (49), we would use a PP like the one filled in in (52). But are these two processes independent of each other? On the analogy with the enrichment of *and*, the target of the enrichment in (49) seems at least partly to be the meaning of *open*. In order to state that more clearly, we need the notion of concept.

5.4.2.1 *Fodorian concepts*

Another notion of the Fodorian theory of mind is 'concept' (see esp. Fodor 1998). It is this use of concept which is what is meant by saying that DS formula values are—or, more precisely, address—concepts. For Fodor, concepts are atomic elements of the language of thought, which combine and over which inferences can be stated. Their main purpose within the Fodorian system is to develop an analysis of lexical meaning, which is, for Fodor, minimal. Words address concepts and concepts combine compositionally at the level of the language of thought. Fodor's point is that there is no lexical semantics; that is, there is no meaningful level of analysis where it can be stated that *kill* 'means' cause to die, or that *bachelor* 'means' unmarried man.[18] For Fodor, the meaning of *kill* is that it addresses the mental concept kill'. The inferences from (55) to (56) or (57) are inferences over propositions at the language of thought, not linguistic or conceptual inferences:

(55)   John killed Bill.

(56)   John caused Bill to be dead.

(57)   Bill is dead.

The reason for not attributing any 'inferential roles' to lexical items and there-fore, according to Fodor, to concepts, is that it is impossible (so Fodor argues) to distinguish exactly which inferential properties are constitutive of word meaning and which are merely encyclopedic facts; or, in other words, which inferences are 'analytic' (hence 'semantic') and which are 'synthetic' (hence 'world knowledge'). From this perspective, any attempt to sort out invariable or necessary parts of word meaning so as to put them into a lexical entry is futile. Furthermore, even if it were possible to find all relevant entailments for a given lexical item and define a word by them (e.g. again *kill* as really meaning something like 'cause to die', and nothing else), the consequence would be that there would only be a word *kill*, but no concept or other mental representation of kill', which would make it impossible to think about killing. In order to avoid this consequence, all words for which entailments can be stated neces-sarily need to have an associated concept. Thus, the only meaning component of the lexical entry for *kill* is that it addresses the concept kill'.[19]

In DS, lexical semantic information is expressed as the formula value, while all other information found in lexical items, for example types, control, pointer movement, is purely syntactic. However, in contrast to Fodor, DS assumes with relevance theory that the mapping between linguistic form (words) and

[18] Fodor's argument is thus directed against the lexical decomposition approach in Generative Semantics, but also against 'structural' linguistic analyses of lexical items as meaning com-ponents (see e.g. Lyons 1977).

[19] There is in addition psycholinguistic evidence specifically against deriving *kill* from 'cause to die' reported in Fodor (1973).

mental representations (concepts) is neither direct nor one-to-one; rather, there is a gap between the two which has to be bridged if words are to be used to address concepts. Fodor's criticism of inferential roles is, from this perspective, valid for lexical items but not for concepts. The broadly Fodorian view of concepts espoused by DS and the different conception of natural language content are discussed in the next section.

5.4.2.2 *Relevance theory concepts*

Recent work in relevance theory has addressed the idea of concepts, and the role concepts play in utterance interpretation (Carston 1996, 2000; Sperber and Wilson 1997). Concepts can be thought of as storage points for information. Since concepts are entities of the language of thought, and since operations at the level of the language of thought are inferential, concepts have to interact with assumptions, i.e. propositions (Sperber and Wilson 1997). Concepts thus aid in accessing 'chunks of knowledge'. But does the identification of a set of assumptions as a mental concept depend on the existence of a lexical word for it? Sperber and Wilson (1997) argue that this cannot be correct. While lexical decomposition results in a situation where there are fewer concepts than words, Fodor argues that there is a concept for every (lexical) word. Sperber and Wilson take this line of thought further and propose that there are many more mental concepts than natural language words. The claim is trivially true, Sperber and Wilson argue, in the case of unstable and ineffable concepts—there are far more perceptual stimuli which we can discriminate and yet for which we do not have a word. Similarly, there is a good possibility that we form individual idiosyncratic concepts, for example for a particular kind of pain which annoyingly recurs, without having a word for them. Yet in a more interesting sense the claim is also true for stable, effable concepts. In fact, according to Sperber and Wilson, this follows from the relevance theory assumption that communication involves not only decoding but inference in the construction of meaning.

One of the examples discussed in Sperber and Wilson (1997: 116) is the use of *tired* in the following dialogue:

(58)   Peter: Do you want to go to the cinema?
        Mary: I'm tired.

Since Mary has committed an act of ostensive communication, and furthermore Peter is entitled to assume that her utterance has some bearing on his question, he is invited to use his inferential abilities to derive a relevant answer. He might go through the following steps of reasoning (Sperber and Wilson 1997: 116):

(59a)   Mary is tired.

(59b)   Mary's being tired is a sufficient reason for her not to want to go to the cinema.

(59c)   Mary doesn't want to go to the cinema because she is tired.

Peter uses (59b) as an implicit premise to derive (59c) as an implicit conclusion. It appears that the explicit content in (59a) is complemented by (59b) and (59c) at the implicit level. However, as Sperber and Wilson (1997: 117) point out, that is not quite correct—Peter cannot soundly infer (59b) and (59c) from the 'explicit' content that Mary is tired, because the fact that Mary is tired is not in itself strong enough to warrant the inferential process. Rather, the process of implicit inference must be accompanied by a process of enrichment at the level of explicature. In order to derive (59c) from (59a) and (59b), Peter has to enrich the concept of Mary's tiredness: just being tired as such is not enough. Peter can assume that Mary wanted to convey that she is tired enough not to want to go the cinema. This is of course a much more specific concept than just being tired, but it is the one which is needed to derive the relevant interpretation of Mary's answer. Sperber and Wilson describe the underlying reasoning process as one of parallel adjustment: 'expectations of relevance warrant the derivation of specific implicatures, for which the explicit content must be adequately enriched' (1997: 117). In this sense, there are many more concepts than words, since in general concepts result from a process of enrichment on a given occasion. Complementarily, given the pervasiveness of enrichment in utterance interpretation, the literal direct map from a word to a concept is a rather rare event, a borderline case of the general process where concepts result from contextual fixing.

The relevance theory characterization of concepts thus differs from the Fodorian conception in that words are taken to be only loosely associated with concepts. The establishment of the actual concepts on which the interpretation of the utterance is built is subject to pragmatic reasoning. But after the process of enrichment, concepts do play a crucial part in inference, and can be described with reference to their inferential roles. Thus, Fodor's argument against inferential roles is correct for lexical items, which provide the hearer with an instruction to build a concept, but not for concepts as constituents of the language of thought. Mental concepts do have inferential roles, but they cannot be stated in the lexicon since words do not in general address concepts directly. As can be seen from the example discussed here, it is in fact exactly inferential roles which are essential for the process of constructing the occasion specific concept, say **tired**$_{21}$ from the word *tired*, since the process is driven by the derivation of implicatures, which are inferences.[20] With this analysis of words and concepts in mind, I now return to the interpretation of underspecified verbs.

5.4.3 Concepts addressed by underspecified verbs

With the analysis of concepts discussed in the preceding section, the role of underspecified verbs in interpretation can be characterized more precisely. Consider again the case where the instrument is derived by enrichment (repeated here as (60)):

(60)   She gave him her key and he opened the door.

I assume that the context for (60) is rich enough for the pronominal expressions to be interpreted, in particular that the people talked about are Keith and Karen. The second clause in (60) then has a representation like (61) before completion:

(61)   *Tree for* ". . . he opened the door

$$\{Tn(o), ?Ty(t)\}$$

$$\{Tn(oo), Ty(e), Fo(keith')\} \quad \{Tn(oi), ?Ty(e \rightarrow t)\}$$

$$\{Tn(oio), Fo(the\_door'), \quad \{Tn(oii), ?Ty(e \rightarrow (e \rightarrow t))\}$$
$$Ty(e)\}$$

$$\{Tn(oii^*), Ty(e \rightarrow (e \rightarrow (e^* \rightarrow t))), Fo(open')\}$$

The tree in (61) is a semantic tree. More specifically, the tree is a representation of the process of how the hearer establishes the proposition expressed—there is, as argued above, no 'logical form'. So if 'with her key' is an explicature, i.e. part of the proposition expressed, it should be assigned a place in the semantic tree:[21]

---

[20] From now on I use bold typeface to indicate particular, occasion specific concepts, as opposed to lexical concepts or instructions to access or build concepts.

[21] The genitive here remains unanalysed.

(62)   *Tree for* "... he opened the door

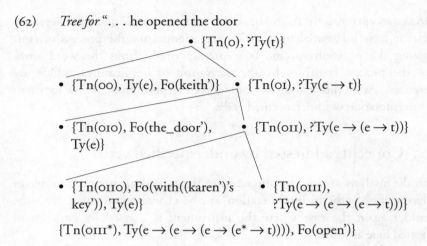

{Tn(0111*), Ty(e → (e → (e → (e* → t)))), Fo(open')}

Assuming a context where the hearer derives an interpretation of (60), consistent with the expectation of optimal relevance, which includes the implicatures 'Keith didn't have a key for the door', and 'the door was locked', the concept addressed by *open* has to be enriched in the manner indicated in (62), namely as including the information that the opening involved the use of Karen's key. Given that we know that concepts are enriched, and that we want to model a process of enrichment, what (62) shows is that the concept open' is enriched to **opening_(that_particular)_door'** with information from the concept addressed by the object, and further to **opening_(that_particular)_door_with_(that_particular)_key'** by building the explicature into the complex concept. Too many concepts? Well, no: given that there are infinitely more concepts than words, and that concepts are the only entities we want to postulate at the language of thought, all these concepts play a role in the interpretation of (60). Upon hearing (60) the hearer is entitled to derive an occasion-specific, possibly (in fact probably) complex concept strong enough to be used to derive sound inferences. If necessary for the derivation of implicatures, the final complex concept is established, and it is this complex concept which is being negated in (53) and (54) above.

But now that we know what a 'PP' does which is *not* there, i.e. help in concept formation, it is easy to reconstruct what a PP does which *is* in fact there: it is an instruction for concept formation.[22] The syntactic optionality of PPs (and NPs) behaving otherwise as arguments, which I have modelled as e*, the intuition that VP-modifiers behave semantically as modifying the verb, which

---

[22] The reason for starting with 'unencoded' as opposed to encoded NPs/PPs is that these cases are more extensively discussed in the relevance theory literature than the syntax and pragmatics of the verb phrase.

in McConnell-Ginet (1982) is modelled as admissible augmentation, the 'unexpressed PP' as explicature—it all falls into place once the analysis includes complex concepts to be constructed anew on each occasion of use. The picture that emerges is that verbs not only provide an instruction for concept formation in the way all other formula values do, but, in addition to this general underspecification, verbs also explicitly encode that the particular concept to be constructed depends on any further information provided by the speaker.[23] Optional expressions of $Ty(e)$ in the VP, i.e. those introduced via e^*, function as constraints on the general instruction of concept formation. Given the syntax and semantics of e^*, it follows that the constructed eventual concept which is built into the proposition expressed is indeed of varying arity, as outlined in the preceding chapter. On the further assumption that concepts are storage points for sets of assumptions, $Ty(e)$ expressions can be seen as providing filters on context selection. They aid in constructing the relevant contextual assumptions associated with the eventual constructed concept.

5.4.4 Processes of concept formation

The process of concept formation I have invoked in the preceding section is, as already indicated, based on work in relevance theory. In the following two sections I discuss in more detail the process of enrichment as it has been formulated in relevance theory. First, I present another example (from Wilson and Sperber 1999) of how enrichment interacts with inferential effects, and secondly I discuss (based on Carston 1996) how the process of enrichment can be characterized as interacting with encyclopedic information.

5.4.4.1 *Concept formation with* eat

Wilson and Sperber (1999) discuss enrichment in the context of truthfulness, in particular with respect to the question of the role of the 'literal truth' of (the proposition expressed by) an utterance in communication. They argue that there is no need for notions like truthfulness or literal truth in

---

[23] I don't want to claim that this encoding is exclusive to verbs. I am concentrating on verbs here, since verbal underspecification is the topic of this study. A natural extension of this work would be to consider other construction types. As just one example, a correspondingly underspecified type for nouns, e.g. $Ty(e^* \rightarrow cn)$, might fruitfully be employed for adjectival or genitive modification in the noun phrase, particularly given similar processes of enrichment as for example in 'bridging' cases:

   (i)   I was trying to get out of the car but the door was locked.

Enrichment in (i) is needed to construct the car's door from *door* in the second clause. In fact, the case of *key* in the example discussed above is similar.

communication (as for example expressed by Grice's maxim of quality), but rather that whatever notions of truthfulness would be required can be better explained by the principle of relevance. Wilson and Sperber first point out that even for clear cases of violation of truthfulness in communication, for example in metaphor or fiction, it is not entirely clear how the non-truthful meaning can be recovered from any postulated literal true meaning. Furthermore, literally false information is much more common than just these obvious cases. Notably loose talk cannot be analysed as any overt suspension or flouting of truthfulness, yet what is said in loose talk is literally false. The solution to this problem, according to Wilson and Sperber, is to substitute the problematic notions of literalness and truthfulness by the well-defined relevance-theoretic notions of explicature and relevance respectively. I am here particularly interested in literalness and explicature,[24] which relates to the points raised already above, since, according to Wilson and Sperber (1999), there is no significant level of literalness in utterance interpretation, because all interpretation involves a process of meaning construction. What is of particular interest is that two examples are discussed in detail. The first one involves the utterance *Holland is flat* in the given context of a planned cycling holiday. The utterance is false if *flat* is taken literally, but in the context the hearer can enrich the concept flat' to mean something like 'good terrain for cycling since there are no steep hills'. This example, similar to the example involving *and* discussed above, involves the enriching of a concept addressed by a single word, albeit a lexical rather than a 'logical' word.

The second example discussed in Wilson and Sperber (1999) is even more relevant in the present context, since it involves a verb. The context of the example is a situation where Lisa visits her neighbours the Joneses, who are just about to have supper. The following dialogue ensues (Wilson and Sperber 1999: 15):

(63)   Alan Jones: Do you want to join us for supper?
        Lisa: No, thanks. I've eaten.

Lisa's answer *I've eaten* could here be analysed to mean literally something like 'Lisa has eaten something at some point in time within a time span ending at

---

[24] The argument concerning the point of truthfulness runs in broad outline as follows. Wilson and Sperber note Grice's statement (1989: 371) that 'false information is not an inferior kind of information; it is just not information'. Since hearers have justified expectations of the relevance of an utterance, and since relevance is (can be) achieved by improvement of knowledge, hearers have justified expectations of relevant information, which is, by being information, true information. Hence the notion of truthfulness can (could) be defined by relevance, which is the more (and only) basic notion.

the time of utterance'. But clearly Lisa means something more specific than that, namely that she has eaten that evening, and that she has eaten something which might reasonably be regarded as being equivalent to supper. Wilson and Sperber (1999: 17) sketch how Alan might derive an interpretation of Lisa's utterance which achieves adequate contextual effects. The process is sketched as a table, with the interpretive hypotheses he builds given on the left and the basis for these hypotheses on the right, which I represent in the format given in Wilson and Sperber (1999: 17):

(64a)	Lisa has said to Alan 'I have eaten'	Decoding of Lisa's utterance
(64b)	Lisa's utterance is optimally relevant to Alan	Expectation raised by the recognition of Lisa's utterance as a communicative act, and the acceptance of the presumption of relevance it automatically conveys
(64c)	Lisa's utterance achieves relevance by explaining her immediately preceding refusal of Alan's invitation to supper	Expectation raised by (64b) and by the fact that such an explanation would be most relevant at this juncture
(64d)	Having eaten supper on a given evening is a reason for refusing an invitation to have supper that evening	First assumption to come to Alan's mind which, together with other appropriate premises, could satisfy expectation (64c). Accepted as an implicit premise of Lisa's utterance
(64e)	Lisa has eaten supper this evening	First enriched interpretation of Lisa's utterance as decoded in (64a) to come to Alan's mind which, together with (64d), could lead to the satisfaction of (64c). Accepted as Lisa's explicit meaning
(64f)	Lisa does not want to eat supper with us because she has eaten supper this evening	Inferred from (64d) and (64e), satisfying (64c) and accepted as an implicit conclusion of Lisa's utterance

Wilson and Sperber point out that their representation of Alan's thought process in (64) is of course only an approximation: his hypotheses are formulated in the language of thought, so that the English sentences in (64) are just rough paraphrases. Furthermore, the thought processes are not necessarily in the sequence given in (64); rather, interpretation is carried out on-line, starting before the utterance is over, and 'interpretive hypotheses about the explicit and implicit content are developed in parallel, and stabilise when they are mutually adjusted, and jointly adjusted with expectations of relevance' (1999: 17). Given these assumptions, what (64) shows, then, is how by using interpretive hypotheses, Alan derives both the explicit meaning of Lisa's utterance (in (64e)) and the implicit conclusion (64f). Further 'weak' implicatures can be derived from (64f) and further world knowledge, the example given by Wilson and Sperber being 'Lisa might accept an invitation to supper another time'. However, the purely encoded part of the utterance in (64a) is not in itself taken to be the meaning of the utterance at any stage in the interpretation process. One of the claims in Wilson and Sperber (1999) is that, given that pragmatic enrichment is always involved in utterance interpretation, there is no justification for postulating underlying hidden constituents in the encoded part of the utterance; the step from (64a) to (64f) is an inferential process which narrows down the time span encoded by the present perfect, and which provides 'supper' as the relevant 'object' of eating. Therefore, the encoded part of the utterance does not provide any restrictor variable for the temporal interpretation, nor an empty variable in object position. The process of enrichment runs purely on the concepts activated by the words in the string: Alan is 'using the concept of eating, which Lisa's words have activated in his mind, and narrowing it down to the concept of eating supper, which helps him to construct a relevant-as-expected interpretation of Lisa's utterance' (p. 19). The same reasoning applies to other possible hidden constituents, as for example in (65) and (66) (p. 19):

(65)   'I've often been to their parties, but I've never eaten anything' [there]

(66)   'I must wash my hands: I've eaten' [using my hands (rather than, say, being spoon-fed)]

The locative and instrument/manner interpretations indicated in the square brackets are pragmatically derived. There is no motivation for postulating an underlying thematic slot (see also Carston 2000).

The example discussed here shows more clearly than the enrichment of 'and' or 'flat', that the enrichment of concepts in context interacts with verbal subcategorization, since in the case of *eat*, similar to the example with *open*, the enrichment involves the postulation of an optional NP. Syntactically and semantically, *eat* in this example can presumably be treated as intransitive, even if this means that the denotation of the verb is not truth-theoretically interpretable only by decoding.[25] Taken literally, eat' in this example would then be undefined, but the force of Wilson and Sperber's argument is that literalness cannot be properly defined in the first place: 'However, we have argued that a notion of literalness has no role to play in a theory of language use. All utterances involve a process of meaning construction' (p. 29). In this example, the enrichment is conceptually mandatory in order for the hearer to arrive at the proposition expressed, as it involves the enrichment of the concept eat' to **eating_supper'**, or in fact to **eating_supper_this_evening'**.

Given the interpretation of e* so far, the analysis of this example from the perspective adopted here differs slightly from the analysis given by Wilson and Sperber. While I agree with the view that the enrichment is pragmatic and, in this particular example, mandatory, DS assumptions about syntax and semantic representations lead to a different analysis of the structural representations involved in the enrichment process. For me, the particular enrichment of eating discussed here is an e* case, where enrichment interacts directly with the logical tree derived from the words in the utterance. Recall again that DS trees represent vehicles for interpretation, which are subject to pragmatic processes in general, and might encode the need for, or the possibility of, further enrichment. Since underspecified verbs do indeed explicitly encode the possibility of further enrichment, and since the final concept derived in the proposition expressed in this example is the specific ternary predicate **eat$_{27}$'** (with a randomly chosen numerical index for ease of reference), the enriched constituents are part of the process of eliminating the inherent underspecification, as would be corresponding overt NPs.[26] Thus, with e*, the semantic tree derived for Lisa's uttering *I've eaten* corresponds to the enriched representation in (64e):

(67)   *Tree for* "I've eaten"

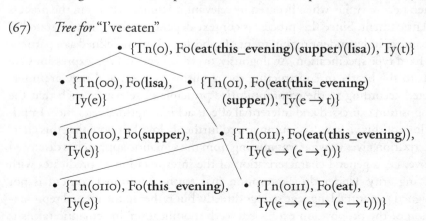

[25] On the assumption that there is only the binary predicate 'eat' in the model.

[26] The only difference between overtly expressed and inferred Ty(e) expression being the degree of responsibility taken respectively by speaker and hearer (see Carston 1996), further discussed below.

The boldface font for formula values in (67) is meant to indicate that these are properly enriched and constructed concepts, rather than instructions for concept formation. It should be borne in mind that these are occasion-specific concepts, so that Fo(**eat**) does not mean *the* concept of eating, but rather *this particular* concept of eating which I have earlier labelled **eat**$_{27}$'.

The tree in (67) reflects the two observations that hearers build semantic trees directly, without S-structure or LF, and that the tree in (67) is the first enriched interpretation of Lisa's utterance and thus her explicit meaning, as argued by Wilson and Sperber. It also naturally models Wilson and Sperber's argument that literal meaning has no place in utterance interpretation, since all structures prior to the tree in (67) are explicitly incomplete structures (by virtue of e*) and thus there is no way to model literal meaning, which is as it should be. Furthermore, in addition to Wilson and Sperber's argument, there is also no relevant level of LF, since no complete structural representation is available independent of interpretive processes. Note that any differences between the view proposed here and Wilson and Sperber's view is not about pragmatics or enrichment, but about the nature of syntax, since here the link between structure building and pragmatically determined interpretation is made explicit, while the relation is less explicit in relevance theory. I agree with Wilson and Sperber that there is no need for hidden constituents in the syntax, such as the thematic slots mentioned with respect to examples (65) and (66) above. It is precisely because I model verbal subcategorization as both underspecified and available for pragmatic enrichment that any ('hidden') thematic requirements from the verb are unnecessary. Further information, for example regarding objects, means, location, or accompaniment, can and will be expressed if and when necessary, i.e. when licensed by relevant inferential effects in the process of enrichment. Since this process is context-dependent, it cannot be stated as a context-independent requirement of subcategorization defined as a particular fixed type specification. Analogously, overtly encoded Ty(e) expressions are aids to the hearer in constructing the requisite concept, and they are interpreted according to the communicative principle of relevance such that the proposition expressed and inferential effects achieve optimal relevance. Implications of this view will be summarized further below, but note that this characterization gives us what was missing from the semantic approaches discussed above, i.e. a general characterization of the interpretation of predicates with varying arity. Under the assumption that truth-conditional content is not assigned to natural language strings directly, but rather to the mental representation of the proposition expressed, 'verb modification' in semantic terms is concept construction in the view developed here, and is, as a case of enrichment, subject to the principle of relevance. Processes of enrichment are, then, of very high importance for the on-line construction of argument structure, and the following section examines possible enrichment processes more closely.

5.4.4.2 *Concept formation and encyclopedic information*

Carston (1996) discusses the relationship between two processes of contextual concept formation, enrichment, and loosening. Enrichment cases include the example discussed in the preceding section, where the lexically encoded meaning of eating is enriched to eating supper. Enrichment is characterized by the fact that the enriched concept entails the lexical concept: the set of attributes of the enriched concept includes the attributes of the lexical concept.[27] With loosening, on the other hand, the relation between the constructed concept and the lexical concept is not as clear. In some cases loosening is the opposite of enrichment, in that the attributes of the constructed concept constitute a subset of those of the lexical concept. An example for this is bald' in (68):

(68)   I love bald men.

Assuming that the lexical concept bald' refers to total hairlessness, the constructed concept includes all men in such condition, but also men with (sufficiently) little hair. In other cases, however, the constructed concept may exclude some attributes of the lexical concept. In the case of flat' in *Holland is flat*, mentioned above, the lexical meaning of *flat* is not fully included in the new concept. Another example is the case of metaphoric use in (69) (Carston 1996: 73):

(69)   Bill is a bulldozer.

The constructed metaphorical concept **bulldozer'** in (69) includes among others, and in contrast to the lexical concept, the attribute human', so that not all attributes of the loosened concept are also attributes of the lexical concept, i.e. there is no subset relation as with the enrichment cases.

Carston (1996) argues that despite this difference, both enrichment and loosening can contribute to the proposition expressed: that both processes are potentially necessary to arrive at an interpretation of the speaker's intended meaning.

With enrichment, as stated above, the constructed concept includes the attributes of the lexical concept. One of the examples discussed by Carston is

---

[27] Cf. also the discussion of the semantics of e*, in particular McConnell-Ginet's intuition that an augmented verb retains the extension of the unmodified verb.

the concept **bachelor'** constructed from the utterance in (70), in a context where the speaker has made it clear that she wants to settle down and have children (1996: 63):

(70)   I want to meet some bachelors.

The ad hoc concept constructed in (70) would include young, beautiful, eligible, unmarried men, but not, for example, the pope. So, everything which qualifies as a constructed **bachelor'** is also a lexical bachelor', but not vice versa.

Taking both loosening and enrichment to be potentially relevant for establishing the proposition expressed offers new perspectives on how these processes can be characterized. One important question in this context is whether enrichment necessarily involves the construction of an ad hoc concept in the sense of an operation on the attributes of the lexical concept. On the analogy of metaphor, a case of loosening, the answer is no. Carston discusses the ('standard') relevance theory account of the metonymic and metaphoric predications in (71) and (72):

(71)   Maria is a divine voice.

(72)   Maria is a nightingale.

In these cases, it is not necessary to construct a new ad hoc concept: 'the properties whose predication of Maria the speaker endorses can be accessed directly from stored information concerning divine voices and nightingales [. . .]. An array of implicatures is thereby constructed and a fully propositional form at the explicit level need never be entertained' (Carston 1996: 83). On the analogy of loosening and enrichment, there is the possibility that some enrichment cases could be analysed in a similar fashion. For example 'an utterance of "John's a bachelor" in the context of a discussion of Mary's desire to get married could implicate that John is heterosexual, youngish, eligible for marriage, etc, without the setting up of a new address/label for the narrowed ad hoc concept *bachelor'* ' (1996: 83). This is because bachelor' has a rich encyclopedic entry including a number of assumptions which cluster together to delimit a stereotype. This would lead to the possibility that only some cases of enrichment need to be built into the propositional form, while others, like the *bachelor* case, do not have to be built in, since 'the intended interpretation can be derived without them (by an encyclopedic sorting process)' (Carston 1996: 84). However, invoking encyclopedic entries does not necessarily imply that no concept is being built. By assuming that explicatures, like implicatures, can be communicated more or less strongly, the building of ad hoc concepts becomes part of the hearer's responsibility:

Just exactly what concept is the hearer of [. . .] 'Bill is a bulldozer' expected to construct out of the lexical concept *bulldozer*? The construction process is constrained by the information stored in the individual hearer's encyclopedic entry for *bulldozer* and by his bid for an interpretation consistent with optimal relevance. But this leaves a degree of leeway so that the ad hoc concept actually constructed is to that degree the hearer's responsibility. . . . Explicatures are communicated with varying degrees of strength; a conceptual range is endorsed by the speaker without any specific concept in that range being given full endorsement. . . . (Carston 1996: 87).

The process here sketches concept formation as an interplay between encyclopedic information and expectations of relevance. The choice of encyclopedic information is occasion-specific and hearer-dependent, and thus falls within the range of meaning construction discussed in the preceding section. Before discussing Carston's position with respect to the argument developed here, it should be noted that she includes cases of verb meaning in the range of enrichment processes. Although not discussed in detail, the following example is found (Carston 1996: 63):

(73)   Mary cut the cake.

The enrichment here is of the concept addressed by *cut*: 'In the case of [(73), LM], it is not any old severing of the fibres of the cake that would be communicated in most contexts but rather a particular mode of cutting; comparison with different objects of cutting makes this apparent, for instance *grass*, *hair*, *cloth*, *flesh*, etc.' (1996: 63). That is, the meaning of *cut* is subject to the same principles of meaning construal as is the meaning of *bachelor*.[28]

The main point of interest in the preceding discussion is that Carston postulates a clear link between enrichment and encyclopedic sorting. The inclusion of encyclopedic entries into the characterization of the interpretation of underspecified verbs opens up the possibility of operating with richer meaning representations in analysing the process of incremental adjustment of explicatures.

Intuitively, the argument I explore here is that, for example, *cut* provides the hearer with an instruction to access a number of assumptions stored under the encyclopedic entry cut' (where cut' is an expression of the language of thought), as in (74):

---

[28] Similarly, Sperber and Wilson (1997: 109) mention examples with *open*, contrasting *open the bottle* with *open the washing machine*, and comment: 'It seems reasonable to conclude that a word like "open" is often used to convey a concept that is encoded neither by the word itself nor by the verb phrase "open X".'

(74a)   Mary cut

At this stage, very little can be constructed, but certain assumptions are 'activated', maybe 'Mary spent some time cutting', 'Mary was awake and probably reasonably concentrated', 'Mary used an instrument suitable for cutting', 'Mary was in danger'. All of these assumptions are more or less tentative, although the context (i.e. the expectation of deriving contextual effects) even here favours some assumptions over others, say, knowing that Mary is a two-year-old child, rather than a grown-up neighbour. Furthermore, assumptions activated by a concept are more or less relevant for determining truth conditions, which is good, since it is not obvious that (74a) has truth conditions. In any case, what I want to avoid here is any detachment between analytic and synthetic truth, since making concepts a set of world knowledge assumptions means that the set can be construed rather liberally. The next piece of information, the concept addressed by *the cake*, does in principle the same thing: it provides access to a number of assumptions, things (we think) we know about cakes, possibly 'cakes are sweet', 'cakes are expensive', 'I don't like cake', 'cakes cause tooth ache':

(74b)   Mary cut the cake

However, the activated assumptions from *Mary cut* serve as context for the assumptions addressed by *the cake*, so they are here selected according to the principle of relevance with reference to contextual effects derivable from combining them. In a given context, the enrichment of cake' may favour the assumptions that Mary cut a real cake, rather than a blow-up toy one, or that it was ready to serve, rather than deep-frozen. However, the concept addressed also has an effect on the concept addressed by the verb, i.e. here, it provides further information about which assumptions activated by *cut* are being communicated. Of the ones listed above, 'Mary was in danger' is probably out, while 'Mary was reasonably concentrated' might be maintained. Furthermore, Mary probably used a knife (in particular a knife suitable for cutting cake with) rather than a lawnmower. Of course, without any particular context, this assumption is rather weak, but on the assumption that it is potentially communicated, it should be part of the activated assumptions. In particular, I propose that this assumption is part of the assumptions addressed by the constructed concept **cut**', i.e. it is part of the enrichment process of *cut*. In this way, the difference between (75a) and (75b) can be characterized as a difference in speaker commitment:

(75a)   Mary cut the cake.

(75b)   Mary cut the cake with a knife.

In both cases, the enriched concept of **cut**' includes an assumption that Mary used a knife suitable to cut cakes with.[29] However, in (75b), this assumption is explicitly communicated so that the hearer is completely justified in taking this assumption both to be meant by the speaker and to be relevant, while in (75a), the responsibility of the hearer is much greater; there is no guarantee that the assumption is relevant (and in most contexts it is probably not), nor a guarantee that it is meant. However, the speaker can consider that the assumption is arrived at (if it is arrived at at all) by 'default'. In other words, if it is not meant, it should be explicitly cancelled:

(76)   Jamie: Where's the cake?
       Fran: Mary has just cut it!
       Jamie: Can I have a piece then, please?
       Fran: No. She cut it with the lawnmower!

In (76), Jamie can safely assume that Mary cut the cake with a suitable knife, that the cake still exists, and that it is sliced nicely into pieces. However, all these inferential effects are cancelled after Fran's second use of *cut*, this time differently enriched. Under the view proposed here, this results from the hearer's responsibility in meaning construction and the speaker's different means of communicating assumptions. Of course, Fran's just saying that Mary cut the cake is not optimally relevant; she should have foreseen that Jamie will run into unjustified cognitive effort (involving a lot of belief revision). But the important and general point is that the lack of relevance results from the particular concept formation, not from, say, untruthfulness.[30]

There are, then, two aspects of the interpretation of underspecified verbs. While part of the interpretation process results in the construction of a specific concept to be built into the proposition expressed, the second part plays a role in context selection. In particular, an underspecified verb accesses a set, or maybe a number of sets, of (encylopedic) assumptions stored in long-term memory, which may cluster together as prototypes, or 'defaults'. However, since the instruction to create 'verbal' concepts[31] explicitly encodes the possibility that further modifying information might be provided, the access is tentative, in that, abstracting away from other contextual information, no

[29]   Which also involves an enrichment of knife' in (75b).

[30]   Which would amount to saying that one can't cut cakes with lawnmowers, but given that one can cut with lawnmowers in general (e.g. grass), this would mean that there are two words *cut*, one for cakes, one for grass, i.e. a rather unwarranted postulation of ambiguity.

[31]   That is, a particular species of predicate. Again, the restriction to verbs here is probably too narrow.

assumption is actually maintained as part of the interpretation. The introduction of Ty(e) expressions under e* then provides further assumptions, which act as a filter on the assumptions provided by the instruction from the verb. Since increasing Ty(e) expressions is always a process of enrichment,[32] the process of filtering can be viewed as monotonic, since with each step of enrichment involving the introduction of Ty(e) expressions, a subset of assumptions is selected. The interpretation of underspecified verbs then involves both the enrichment of the concept addressed and its place in the proposition expressed, including the eventual concept's arity, and the selection of assumptions accessed during this process in interaction with other contextual information. Both processes are driven by relevance considerations and involve non-demonstrative inference. However, the possibility of enrichment is explicitly encoded in the syntactic information provided by the verb.

5.4.5 Sample derivation

After discussing the syntax and semantics of e*, I have in the preceding sections discussed the role of relevance in utterance interpretation, and introduced the notions of concept and propositional form. The DS position with respect to these notions is that hearers construct semantic, i.e. propositional representations directly, and that pragmatic processes may apply at any stage in the process of tree building. This includes the process of pragmatic enrichment, which plays a pervasive role in the establishment of the particular concepts used to build the propositional form, since lexical words merely project a requirement to construct concepts. Against this background, I have discussed cases of enrichment involving concepts addressed by verbs, and have argued that constituents in the verb phrase introduced by lexical items help to construct the concept addressed by it. The process of enrichment relevant for e* determines the role of the concept in the propositional form, and provides filters for context selection. The process is here shown in more detail, with the help of a sample derivation.

In a context where I am just coming home from the shops on a Saturday morning expecting my parents-in-law to come over for lunch later on, my wife informs me about the whereabouts of our seventeen-year-old son Trevor:

(77)   Trevor is baking in the kitchen.

The relevant tree structure after the introduction of *bake* is as follows:

---

[32] As assumed both in relevance theory (e.g. Carston 1996: 62–3) and by McConell-Ginet (1982), as discussed above.

(78a)   *Tree for* "Trevor is baking

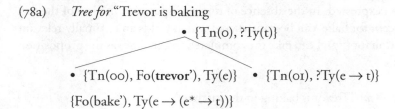

Since the identity of Trevor is salient, the formula value introduced by Trevor, Fo(trevor'), can be resolved immediately to Fo(**trevor'**). The lexical specification of *bake* introduces the underspecified type specification and the instruction to construct a relevant concept. A set of assumptions is latently activated, and tentative interpretive hypotheses can be built with respect to the constructed concept **trevor'**. Note that I have not analysed *bake* here as lexically transitive, introducing an object node. Nor is it necessary in this example to enrich such a node. Given the context, the inferential effects I derive from (77) concern my need to use the kitchen for sorting the shopping and preparing lunch. But I also know that if Trevor is baking, it probably involves the use of some utensils and some foodstuff, resulting in a fair mess. From this I can start to worry whether I have enough time to clean the kitchen, whether I can find everything I need, whether I can even put my shopping bags somewhere. The question what it is that Trevor is baking, or intends to bake (note that the continuous present leaves the progression of the event open), is irrelevant in this context. However, the next Ty(e) expression is necessary to derive these inferential effects:

(78b)   *Tree for* "Trevor is baking in the kitchen

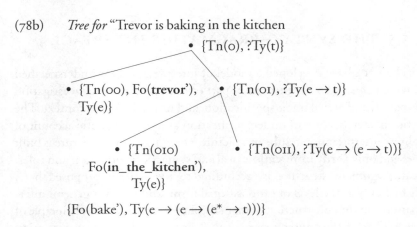

The introduction of the PP leads to the partial resolution of the underspecified type licensed by relevance, namely by the fact that in order to achieve optimal relevance, the information from Fo(in_the_kitchen') has to be built into the proposition expressed. In the absence of further input, and in view of the fact that a concept for bake' can be constructed which yields an optimally relevant interpretation for (77), I can take the completed tree in (78c) as the proposition expressed:

(78c)　*Tree for* "Trevor is baking in the kitchen"

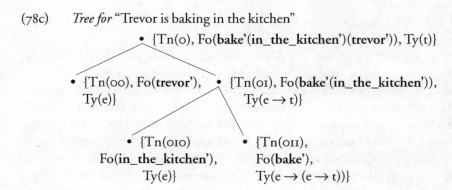

The process of enrichment of Fo(bake') affects both the arity of the eventual concept and the particular assumptions taken to be communicated by the eventual concept **bake'**, which in this case do not include the object of baking, but only those assumptions which are needed to derive the relevant contextual implications, including that the kitchen is dirty. As this derivation shows, in the interpretation of e*, syntactic, semantic, and pragmatic factors conspire in the establishment of the proposition expressed.

5.5 THE SYNTAX–PRAGMATICS INTERFACE

In this chapter I have developed a model of interpretation for underspecified verbs, which concludes the theoretical part of this study, i.e. the investigation of adjunction and verbal underspecification, and its resolution in context. The syntactic characterization of underspecification and the pragmatic account of verb phrase interpretation results in a picture where argument structure is built on-line, and only partly from static lexical and syntactic information and rules. Predicate–argument structure is, according to the analysis proposed here, established only at the level of propositional form, and involves general inference patterns in the construction of mental concepts guided by the principle of relevance. One of the consequences of this view of verbal subcategorization and the establishment of predicate–argument structure for the syntax–pragmatics interface is to abandon the notion of LF as a syntactically defined output level of a putative linguistic component. In a manner similar to the relevance theory abandonment of truth-conditions as a division between semantics and pragmatics, no level of LF can be taken as demarcation of syntax and pragmatics, since pragmatic enrichment and explicatures are needed to establish the very logical structure which could qualify as LF. There is thus no clear division between the linguistic module and general reasoning. Rather, general reasoning has a role to play in any aspect of utterance interpretation. In a sense, then, there is no syntax–pragmatics interface, since no level of representation can be postulated which defines the boundary of grammar-internal processes and general pragmatic processes. The interaction between lexicon, syntax, and pragmatics is more fine-grained and complex, and is characterized by the hearer's overall goal to establish an interpretation of the communicative behaviour of the speaker, where linguistic form provides central pieces of evidence but can be only used when embedded into the larger cognitive setting of communication.

The pragmatic approach to verb meaning also sheds light on the fact that underspecified verbs result in different representations for sentences which only differ in the order of adjuncts, as noted at the outset of the chapter. While these sentences are truth-conditionally identical, they differ with respect to pragmatic parameters such as emphasis and information structure, and it is these differences which are plausibly expressed in the different orders.

Compared to the semantic approach based on McConnell-Ginet (1982) sketched earlier in this chapter, the pragmatic approach is more natural in accounting for the freedom with which natural language predicates can take adjuncts to express more subtle meaning differences. By developing a relation between verbal underspecification, adjunction, and concept formation, the e* approach makes explicit the link between the 'licensing' of adjuncts in the VP and general processes of enrichment, while this relation is only implicitly referred to by the notion of admissibility in the augmentation approach. The contrast between the solution here and the approach of giving adjuncts modifier semantics is of course much bigger, since here adjuncts receive argument status not only in the syntax but also in the semantic representation, with the added advantage that the relation between syntax, i.e. here the process of tree building, and semantics is transparently parallel.

In the following chapter, the analysis of verbal underspecification is not developed further, but rather applied to a new range of data, namely applied verbs in Swahili, which are particularly interesting since they involve instances of valency changing. The analysis developed here shows how applied verbs are intrinsically related to concept formation.

6

Applied Verbs in Swahili

6.1 INTRODUCTION

In the preceding chapter, I have discussed how underspecified verbs contribute to the establishment of the proposition expressed in the process of utterance interpretation, and concluded that underspecified verbs encode lexically the possibility for conceptual enrichment. Underspecified verbs address a concept which accesses a set of assumptions. The introduction of optional Ty(e) expressions provides an aid in filtering the assumptions tentatively accessed and in strengthening the concept addressed by the verb. Concept formation is thus related to complementation, in that the eventual arity of the particular constructed predicate is established, and that possibly additional Ty(e) expressions are incorporated into the predicate. The construction of an occasion-specific concept from a lexical concept may thus imply a change in valency, but it does not do so necessarily.

In this section, I review this analysis in the light of new data, which show clearly the link between complementation and valency changing on the one hand and concept strengthening on the other. I develop an analysis of applied verbs in Swahili which shows that applied verbs provide an instruction to construct an occasion-specific concept, in particular a concept that is stronger than one which could have been constructed from the related base verb. In other words, applied verbs instruct the hearer to derive additional contextual effects from the proposition expressed. The argument developed thus crucially involves the hypothesis developed so far, and results in the formulation of an alternative to analyses of applied verbs reported in the literature.

6.2 APPLIED VERBS IN SWAHILI

Applied, or applicative, verbs are a characteristic of most Bantu languages. They result from a system of verbal extensions which also includes causative, passive, and neutro-passive forms, amongst others. Traditionally, the applicative extension has been analysed as extending the valency of the base verb so that a new object can be introduced. The effect can be seen in the examples from Swahili in (1):[1]

(1a)   *A-li-andik-a*   *barua*
        SCDI-PAST-write-FV   letter
        'S/he wrote a letter'

(1b)   *A-li-mw-andik-i-a*   *shangazi*   *barua*
        SCDI-PAST-OCDI-write-APPL-FV   aunt   letter
        'S/he wrote a letter to the aunt'

As can be seen in (1a), the verb *andika*, 'write' is used with one object in its transitive use, but appears with two objects in its applied form in (1b). The examples given in (1) illustrate the prototypical use of applied verbs, namely the introduction of a beneficiary object. Applied verbs can be formed from transitive verbs as in (1) as well as from intransitive verbs as in (2):

(2a)   *A-li-tembe-a*
        SCDI-PAST-walk-FV
        'S/he had a walk'

(2b)   *A-li-m-tembel-e-a*   *rafiki*   *yake*
        SCDI-PAST-OCDI-walk-APPL-FV   friend   her/his
        'S/he was visiting her/his friend'

The intransitive verb *tembea*, 'walk, promenade, stroll' in its applied form can be used with a direct object to mean 'visit'.

     The thematic functions of applied verbs include, as well as beneficiary, instrument, and place:[2]

---

[1] All data in this chapter have been collected over a number of years in Hamburg, London, and Zanzibar. The following less familiar morphological tags are used: SCDI = subject concord class 1; OCDI = object concord class 1; SITU = situational tense; APPL = applicative morpheme; FV = final vowel; the morphological analysis follows Schadeberg (1992).

[2] Speakers strongly prefer instrument applicatives to locative applicatives, part of the reason for which I try to explain in the analysis proposed here.

(3)   *A-li-andik-i-a*   *barua*   *kalamu*
      SCDI-PAST-write-APPL-FV   letter   pen
      'S/he wrote a letter with a pen'

(4)   *A-li-andik-i-a*   *barua*   *meza*
      SCDI-PAST-write-APPL-FV   letter   table
      'S/he wrote a letter on the table'

However, although the examples in (3) and (4) involve applied verbs, I will argue below that there is a difference in the structure projected from (1) and (2) on the one hand and (3) and (4) on the other.

Applied verbs are thus morphologically marked verbs which are related to corresponding base forms by a process which traditionally has been described as an increase in valency. A brief summary of previous analyses of applied verbs is given in the next section.

6.3 PREVIOUS ANALYSES

Analyses of Bantu applicative constructions have been proposed from several theoretical perspectives. The vast majority of these are concerned with benefactive applicatives and the analysis of cross-linguistic extraction patterns. I am here concentrating on one language, by discussing a variety of uses of the applied verb in Swahili, so that the emphasis is different than in most previous analyses. I thus discuss previous work only briefly.

Bresnan and Moshi (1993) and Alsina and Mchombo (1993) provide an analysis of applicative constructions, based on data from Chichewa and Kichaga, in the framework of Lexical Functional Grammar. Part of the analysis is concerned with establishing universal hierarchies of thematic roles, while the main point is to establish the correct linking relationships between elements of the LFG levels of representation, function, and argument structure (f-structure, a-structure). The analysis is lexical, since it is argued that lexical operations change subcategorization information.

Within the Government and Binding/Minimalist Program (GB/MP) framework analyses have been proposed by among others Baker (1988), Marantz (1993), and Nakamura (1997). The analyses share the idea that applicative constructions involve movement, in particular of the head of an additional constituent (i.e. an 'abstract' preposition) to the head of the verb. Variations of this analysis include incorporation, adjunction, and feature checking. The data discussed are mostly from Chichewa, or from Kimenyi's (1980) work on Kinyarwanda. Although thematic roles are often employed in

GB/MP analyses, Marantz (1993) proposes that deep structure (D-structure) is sensitive to richer semantic event structure, so that syntactic projections reflect how speakers construe particular situations.

Shibatani (1996) develops an analysis of cross-linguistic applicative constructions, including data from Chichewa (i.e. from Alsina and Mchombo 1993), which is formulated in Construction Grammar and is based on the idea that applicative constructions are formed by projecting transitive verbs onto a prototypical 'give' construction, which is a language-particular lexical schema which encodes both semantic and syntactic information. Applied verbs can be formed in a given language according to how similar, in the relevant sense, the respective base verbs are to the 'give' construction. Construction grammar is similar to DS in that lexical instructions project rich syntactic structure, but DS does not employ grammatical prototypes or schemata.

A few more recent analyses are closer to the approach taken here, since they assume that there is more to applied verbs than (pure) valency changing. Matsinhe (1994), Rapold (1997), and Mabugu and Cann (2001) all develop various ways in which applied verbs can be related to non-syntactic parameters. Although none of these authors links the analysis of applied verbs to pragmatic processes of concept formation, these approaches are most closely related to what I am going to propose below.

In summary, both syntactic and lexical analyses of applied verbs have been proposed from several perspectives. Despite differences in formalization and basic assumptions, the majority of previous formal analyses of applied verbs in Bantu agree on the fact that applicative constructions imply an increase in valency vis-à-vis the base verb. In addition, the majority of analyses proposed are illustrated with data originally presented in the LFG or Relational Grammar literature.[3]

6.4 PRELIMINARY ASSUMPTIONS

As discussed above, previous analyses of the applied verbs in Bantu languages have concentrated largely on examples of the applied verb where a benefactive object is introduced. Furthermore, most analyses assume that the applied function expresses a change in valency, and try to capture the syntactic aspect of this. In this section I discuss and justify some assumptions I make about Swahili verbs, about the representation of the applicative morpheme, and

[3] In addition, traditional grammar analyses are available for many Bantu languages. For Swahili, see e.g. Sacleux (1909), Ashton (1947).

about the status of lexicalized forms of applied verbs, which will be used in the analysis presented in the following section.

6.4.1 Swahili as e* language

In this section I present evidence for assuming that the e* analysis developed in the preceding chapters holds for Swahili. This means that verbs encode lexically an underspecified type, and that optional Ty(e) expressions have to be licensed by a preposition or by a locative case marker, in addition to a few cases of adverbial nouns (e.g. *jana*, 'yesterday', *usiku*, 'at night').

In general, optional Ty(e) expressions have to be licensed:

(5a)   *A-li-fik-a*   *usiku pamoja na   Sudi*
        SCDI-PAST-arrive-FV night with and   Sudi
        'S/he arrived with Sudi at night'

(5b)   **Alifika   usiku   Sudi*
        (in the relevant reading; fine as 'Sudi arrived at night')

(6a)   *A-li-andik-a*   *barua kwa   kalamu nyekundu*
        SCDI-PAST-write-FV letter with pen   red
        'S/he wrote a letter with a red pen'

(6b)   **Aliandika barua kalamu nyekundu*

(7a)   *A-li-nunu-a*   *vitabu kwa   bei   rahisi   soko-ni*
        SCDI-PAST-buy-FV   books with price easy   market-LOC
        'S/he bought books cheaply at the market'

(7b)   **Alinunua vitabu bei rahisisi soko*

The example in (5a) shows the modification of the predicate with *usiku*, which is self-licensing, and *Sudi*, which is licensed by the complex preposition *pamoja na*. In (6a) *kalamu nyekundu* is licensed by *kwa*, which also licenses *bei rahisi* in (7a). *Soko* in (7a) is licensed by the locative suffix *-ni*.[4] I thus assume that verbs in Swahili are underspecified, and that optional Ty(e) expressions need to be licensed.

A lexical entry for *andika*, 'write' thus looks like:

---

[4] All of the forms which license Ty(e) expressions are historically nominal; *kwa* and, more transparently, *pamoja* show locative noun class agreement. The suffix *-ni* is argued by Samsom and Schadeberg (1994) to result from a grammaticalization process with *ini*, 'liver', as source.

(8)　*Lexical Entry for* andik

　　IF　　　$?Ty(e \rightarrow t)$

　　THEN　$make(\langle\downarrow*\rangle)$, $put(Fo(andik'), Ty(e \rightarrow (e \rightarrow (e* \rightarrow t))))$,
　　　　　　$go(\langle\uparrow*\rangle\ ?Ty(e \rightarrow t))$,
　　　　　　$put(?\langle\downarrow_1\rangle\ Ty(e \rightarrow (e \rightarrow t)))$,
　　　　　　$make(\langle\downarrow_0\rangle)$, $put(Ty(e))$

　　ELSE　 abort

The lexical entry specifies the actions of a transitive $e*$ verb, as outlined in Chapter 4. The formula value gives Fo(andik'), rather than *andika*, since the final -*a* is part of the inflectional morphology.[5]

The corresponding tree structure after the actions specified in the lexical entry for *andika* have been performed is given below:

(9)　*Tree for* "A-li-andik

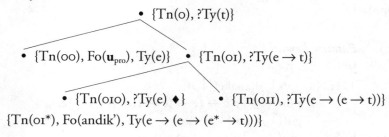

$\{Tn(o), ?Ty(t)\}$

$\{Tn(oo), Fo(\mathbf{u}_{pro}), Ty(e)\}$　$\{Tn(oi), ?Ty(e \rightarrow t)\}$

$\{Tn(oio), ?Ty(e)\ \blacklozenge\}$　$\{Tn(oii), ?Ty(e \rightarrow (e \rightarrow t))\}$

$\{Tn(oi*), Fo(andik'), Ty(e \rightarrow (e \rightarrow (e* \rightarrow t)))\}$

As expected, the verb is unfixed, and the current node is $Tn(oio)$. Note that the formula value of the DU at $Tn(oo)$ is $Fo(\mathbf{u}_{pro})$, indicating that the subject marker in Swahili is pronominal; no overt subject NP need to be encoded. However, if a postposed subject is scanned, the two formula values may be combined by Merge, so that a lexical subject will occupy the subject node.[6] The contribution of the final vowel -*a* relates to tense, mood, and polarity, and I ignore it throughout. The scanning of a $Ty(e)$ expression in this situation leads to the fulfilment of the requirement $?Ty(e)$ holding at $Tn(oio)$ and, in the absence of further lexical input, the tree can be completed by applications of Merge, Completion, and Elimination.

I assume that the assumptions made here are correct throughout this chapter. In the next section, I develop a possible analysis of applied verbs within the general outline given here, which follows the assumptions made in

---

[5]　I continue to use the citation form with an -*a* suffix in the running text.

[6]　See Bresnan and Mchombo (1986, 1987) for an analysis of Bantu subject and object markers as pronouns.

previous analyses of applied verbs. An alternative proposal is developed in section 6.4.3.

6.4.2 A syntactic analysis of the applicative morpheme

In order to show how a syntactic analysis of applied verbs can be modelled in DS with underspecified verbs, I first sketch such an analysis, and then provide a lexical analysis which I show is superior to a syntactic analysis in several ways. Here I assume first that the applicative morpheme has its own lexical entry, and that it functions to introduce a new node. Such a putative analysis of applied verbs implies that the applicative morpheme functions in a way similar to prepositions and locative morphemes, in that it licenses the introduction of an additional Ty(e) expression.

The following lexical entry for the applicative morpheme -*IL*- reflects this approach:[7]

(10)   *Putative Lexical Entry for* -IL-:
   IF   ?Ty(e)
   THEN $go(\langle\uparrow_o\rangle)$, $make(\langle\downarrow_1\rangle)$,
           $put(?\langle\downarrow_1\rangle Ty(e \rightarrow (e \rightarrow (e \rightarrow t))))$, $?\langle\downarrow_o\rangle Ty(e))$,
           $go(\langle\uparrow_1\rangle)$, $go(\langle\downarrow_o\rangle)$
   ELSE $put(?\langle\downarrow_1\rangle Ty(e \rightarrow (e \rightarrow t)))$,
           $make(\langle\downarrow_o\rangle)$, $put(?Ty(e))$

The entry distinguishes two cases; if the applicative morpheme follows a transitive verb, the condition will be ?Ty(e) (i.e. the pointer will be at the object node built from lexical instructions of the verb), as shown in the tree above, and the actions in the THEN clause will be performed. If, on the other hand, -*IL*- follows an intransitive verb, the actions under the ELSE statement will be performed (in effect the pointer will still be at the ?Ty(e → t) node). Since the morpheme has a fixed position in the morphological verbal template, it always follows the verbal base, so that if there is no task ?Ty(e), the applicative morpheme is preceded by an intransitive verb. Ditransitive verbs cannot take the applicative morpheme. Note here another advantage of underspecified verbs: without e*, intransitive verbs would fulfil the requirement ?Ty(e → t)

[7] The surface form of the applicative morpheme is subject to phonological processes, one of which is discussed in more detail below; in the abstract form -*IL*-, -*I*- indicates a vowel subject to vowel harmony, while -*L*- indicates an underlying consonant /l/ which surfaces when followed by a historically high vowel; see Schadeberg (1992).

directly, so that the applicative morpheme could no longer build new argument nodes.

With this lexical definition of the applicative morpheme, the tree in (9) could be continued as (11):

(11)   *Tree for* "A-li-andik-i . . .

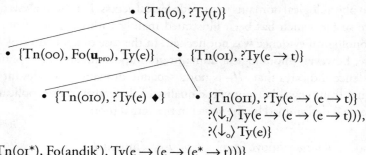

$\{Tn(o), ?Ty(t)\}$

$\{Tn(oo), Fo(\mathbf{u}_{pro}), Ty(e)\}$ $\{Tn(o1), ?Ty(e \rightarrow t)\}$

$\{Tn(o1o), ?Ty(e) \blacklozenge\}$ $\{Tn(o11), ?Ty(e \rightarrow (e \rightarrow t))$
$?\langle\downarrow_1\rangle Ty(e \rightarrow (e \rightarrow (e \rightarrow t))),$
$?\langle\downarrow_o\rangle Ty(e)\}$

$\{Tn(o1^*), Fo(andik'), Ty(e \rightarrow (e \rightarrow (e^* \rightarrow t)))\}$

The introduction of the two modal statements at $Tn(o11)$ results in the building of a new pair of nodes by Prediction after the requirement at the current node has been fulfilled; the predicate *andika* will then turn out to be (minimally) ternary. Whether or not the introduction of the second object is registered at the unfixed node depends on whether e^* Partial Resolution is operative, but since this rule has been introduced mainly for the discussion of the semantics of e^* in Chapter 5, I assume here that e^* is resolved by Merge. Note that I have not introduced any thematic information, nor any other requirement on the kind or order of $Ty(e)$ expressions, for the reasons given earlier.

The lexical entry for *-IL-* defined in this section follows the analyses discussed in section 6.3 in assuming that the applicative morpheme introduces a new $Ty(e)$ expression, and that it encodes a syntactic operation. Although in the solution sketched here there is a lexical entry for *-IL-*, the contribution of the morpheme is analysed as being purely syntactic. This follows from the fact that the building of tree structure in DS is to a large extent lexically driven. The crucial point is that *-IL-* is analysed as a separate morpheme with its own particular lexical actions. In contrast, I will develop an analysis below where *-IL-* does not have its own lexical entry, but is found under the entry of the verb with which it is associated.

6.4.3 Phonological evidence against a lexical entry for *-IL-*

The syntactic analysis of applied verbs sketched in the preceding section was based on the assumption that *-IL-* has a separate lexical entry. However, this assumption is disconfirmed by phonological evidence regarding the domain-hood of *-IL-*.

With respect to the overall perspective of the model of utterance interpretation outlined in Chapter 2, the assumption that the applicative morpheme has a separate lexical entry is doubtful. Recall that it was claimed that the role of phonology in utterance interpretation is to divide a continuous input stream into phonological domains to provide lexical access. For the analysis developed here so far, which has been illustrated mainly with examples from English, phonological evidence was not needed. In the case of applied verbs discussed here, however, phonological domains are important, since the phonological evidence indicates that *-IL-* is not a separate domain. The relevant evidence comes from vowel harmony; the quality of the vowel of the applicative morpheme is determined by the vowel in the verbal root:

(12a)   *ham-a* 'move from'   *ham-i-a* 'move to'

(12b)   *fik-a* 'arrive'   *fik-i-a* 'reach, stay'

(12c)   *nuk-a* 'stink'   *nuk-i-a* 'smell nice'

(12d)   *sem-a* 'speak'   *sem-e-a* 'speak about'

(12e)   *omb-a* 'beg'   *omb-e-a* 'ask on behalf'

As can be seen from the data in (12), the applicative morpheme surfaces as /i/ after the stem vowels /a/, /i/, and /u/, while after /e/ and /o/ the applicative morpheme surfaces as /e/. The underlying phonological structure of applied verbs can be represented as follows:

(13)   *Schematic Representation of Swahili Applied Verbs*

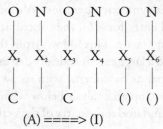

The first three skeletal positions (X_1 to X_3) correspond to the verbal root, which consists of one nuclear (N) and two onset (O) constituents, corresponding to two consonants (C) with an intervening vowel. The applicative morpheme corresponds to the skeletal positions X_4 and X_5, and is lexically associated with a phonological element (I) as nucleus, and an empty expression as onset. The vowel harmony can be analysed as the spreading of the element (A), if present, from the nucleus of the root to the nucleus of the suffix.[8] From the perspective of lexical access, the structure in (13) provides evidence for assuming a representation such as the following phonological domains for applied verbs:[9]

(14)   [[CVC] IL]

A structure like (14) can be seen as an instance of analytic morphology where both the verbal root [CVC] and the complex form as a whole, i.e. the applied verb, are phonological domains, and thus provide lexical access, but where crucially the suffix is not a separate phonological domain. The phonological evidence thus disconfirms the syntactic analysis sketched above; the applicative morpheme does not provide lexical access because it does not constitute a phonological domain. Rather, from the phonological evidence it follows that information from the applicative is accessed under the entry of the verb with which it is found.

In view of the apparently general and uniform syntactic function of the applicative morpheme, the view that it can only be accessed from the entry of the verb with which it combines seems to be surprising. However, given the function of lexical rules in the DS model, an analysis which incorporates the phonological evidence can be modelled, since, as pointed out previously, structure building is largely driven from the lexicon. In fact, an analysis could be developed in which schematic lexical entries for transitive and intransitive verbs are defined which include optionally one of the two clauses given in the entry for -*IL*-, above. While I think that this approach is basically correct, so that I will develop an analysis along these lines in what follows, the perspective that the applicative morpheme is lexically associated with its verb provides a good starting point from which to consider more data.

6.4.4 Lexicalized forms

There are in Swahili, and in most Bantu languages, a number of lexicalized applied verbs. Although these data have been mentioned, they have not been included in analyses of applicative constructions in Bantu. In fact, Port (1981) argues that analyses of applicative constructions should not include lexical

---

[8] A fuller discussion of Swahili vowel harmony is provided in Marten (1997).
[9] The sketch of the relation between phonological domains and lexical access here follows Kaye (1995).

forms, since a generalization would be lost. I believe the opposite is true. For a full understanding of the function of applied verbs, lexicalized forms provide very good evidence, especially in view of the fact that a lexical analysis of applied verbs is supported by independent evidence.

Lexicalized applied verbs are verbs marked with an applicative morpheme, but which fail to necessarily introduce a Ty(e) expression.

For example, there are a number of word pairs, often expressing movement or motion, where the apparent base verb and the applied verb are not clearly distinguished with respect to their valency:

(15a)	*kimbia*	'run from'	*kimbilia*	'run to'
(15b)	*geuka*	'turn, turn to'	*geukia*	'turn to'
(15c)	*hama*	'move from'	*hamia*	'move to'
(15d)	*nuka*	'stink'	*nukia*	'smell sweet, nice'

The pairs in (15a) to (15c) are transitive, while the pair in (15d) is intransitive. The semantic relation appears to be one of opposition.

Another group of applied verbs has a lexicalized or idiomatic reading under which the difference in valency between base form and applied form is unpredictable:

(16a)	*fika*	'arrive'	*fikia*	'stay'
(16b)	*tembea*	'walk'	*tembelea*	'walk about, promenade'
(16c)	*toka*	'come from'	*tokea*	'come from'
(16d)	*vua*	'take off (clothes)'	*vulia*	'take off clothes'

Thus, for example, the difference between *fika*, 'arrive', which can be used intransitively or with a location object, and *fikia*, 'stay', which tends to have a location object, can be partly analysed as related to a change in valency. However, in the case of *tembea*, 'walk' and the intransitive use of *tembelea*, 'walk about', or *toka*, 'come from' and *tokea*, 'come from, appear', this is no longer possible. Lexicalized forms such as in (16) thus illustrate that applied forms do not always encode a change in valency, and seem again to favour a lexical over a syntactic analysis. While in a syntactic analysis, both a general rule and the blocking of the rule for particular lexical items in particular contexts have to be stated, in a lexical analysis all information relevant for the interpretation of applied verbs is found in the lexicon.

6.4.5 Sample lexical entry for *vaa*

A more complex case is illustrated by the verb *vaa*, 'wear (clothes)':

(17)   *vaa* 'wear (clothes)'   *valia* 'dress up (in clothes)'

The unextended verb can be found in transitive structures, while the applied form is found with one object or two objects:[10]

(17a)   *Juma   a-me-va-a   kanzu*
          Juma   SCDI-PERF-wear-FV   kanzu
          'Juma was wearing a Kanzu'

(17b)   *Juma   a-me-m-val-i-a   mtoto   kanzu*
          Juma   SCD-PERF-OCCLI-wear-APPL-FV   child   kanzu
          'Juma was dressing the child in a Kanzu'

(17c)   *?Juma   a-me-val-i-a   kanzu*
          Juma   SCDI-PERF-wear-APPL-FV   kanzu
          Int.: Juma was wearing a Kanzu

(17d)   *Juma   a-me-val-i-a   nguo   za   rasmi*
          Juma   SCDI-PERF-wear-APPL-FV   clothes GEN   official
          'Juma was dressed up in official/formal clothes'

The sentences in (17) show the difference between non-idiomatic and idiomatic readings of *vaa*, 'wear'. In (17a), the transitive base form is used with one object, *kanzu*, a piece of clothing, while in (17b), the applied form is used with the additional benefactive object *mtoto*, 'child'. The sentence in (17c), with the applied form and only one object is unacceptable in the non-idiomatic reading. In contrast, in (17d) the applied form is acceptable under the idiomatic reading with only one object, *nguo za rasmi*, which here reinforces the idiomatic reading.

---

[10] The following attested example shows the applied form even without any object (from the Zanzibari author Muhammad Said Abdulla's *Mwana wa Yungi Hulewa* (1976: 52)):

(i)   *kijana wa   Kihindi,   ka-val-i-a   vizuri*
        youth of   Indian   SCDI.PERF-wear-APPL-FV   well
        'an Indian youth, dressed (up) well . . .'

Here the applied verb encodes concept strengthening and allows object-drop. In the light of examples like this, the lexical entry in (18) could be modified to include an intransitive use of *valia*.

The examples with *vaa* in this section show that some applied verbs can be regarded as fully or partly lexicalized, because they express a specific lexical or idiomatic meaning. In addition, the examples considered here appear to be lexicalized because they do not increase the valency of the base form. The rather unanalysed notion of 'idiomatic reading' with which I have characterized some applied forms here will be analysed as an instruction for concept formation in more detail below. Before that, however, the following provides a lexical entry for the various forms of *vaa*. The lexical entry for *vaa* has to specify a rule for three different cases; the transitive use of the base form, the ditransitive use of the applied form, and the idiomatic transitive use of the applied form. A lexical entry for *vaa* can thus be defined as follows:

(18) *Lexical entry for* va

IF $?Ty(e \rightarrow t)$

THEN $make(\langle \downarrow^* \rangle)$, $put(Fo(va'), Ty(e \rightarrow (e \rightarrow (e^* \rightarrow t))))$,
$go(\langle \uparrow^* \rangle ?Ty(e \rightarrow t))$,
$put(?\langle \downarrow_1 \rangle Ty(e \rightarrow (e \rightarrow t)))$,
$make(\langle \downarrow_o \rangle)$, $put(?Ty(e))$

OR $make(\langle \downarrow^* \rangle)$,
$put(Fo(vali''), Ty(e \rightarrow (e \rightarrow (e \rightarrow (e^* \rightarrow t)))))$,
$go(\langle \uparrow^* \rangle ?Ty(e \rightarrow t))$,
$make(\langle \downarrow_1 \rangle)$,
$put(?\langle \downarrow_1 \rangle Ty(e \rightarrow (e \rightarrow (e \rightarrow t)))), ?\langle \downarrow_o \rangle Ty(e))$,
$go(\langle \uparrow_1 \rangle)$,
$make(\langle \downarrow_o \rangle)$ $put(?Ty(e))$

OR $make(\langle \downarrow^* \rangle)$, $put(Fo(vali^{2'}), Ty(e \rightarrow (e \rightarrow (e^* \rightarrow t))))$,
$go(\langle \uparrow^* \rangle ?Ty(e \rightarrow t))$,
$put(?\langle \downarrow_1 \rangle Ty(e \rightarrow (e \rightarrow t)))$,
$make(\langle \downarrow_o \rangle)$, $put(?Ty(e))$

ELSE abort

The complex lexical entry in (18) licenses three different sets of lexical actions. The first set comprises the *vaa* actions needed for the transitive use, the second set is the process performed for the applied form in the non-idiomatic reading. The third set of actions expresses the idiomatic meaning of the applied form with one object. The two formula values of Fo(vali') distinguish between the two different readings by means of a numerical superscript. Although the entry looks rather long, all three cases have to be covered, which is achieved by the entry. What this entry implies—and I think this is correct—is that three different tree continuations are developed in parallel, one for each set of actions. Recall that the phonological parsing results in two domains, one for the base verb and one for the applied verb, so that both forms are accessed lexically. However, at the time when the lexical entries are scanned, it is not clear which one will eventually be used. In a situation like this it follows, from basic DS assumptions about incrementality as discussed in Chapter 4, that all possible continuations should be represented. I discuss this point further below.

6.4.6 Lexicalization of relevance

As pointed out above, lexicalized applied verbs like the ones discussed here have not received much attention in the literature, on the grounds that these forms are not productive. But that argument does not quite work. While it is correct that lexicalized forms are not productive, it still needs to be explained, at least in outline, what the underlying pattern of the lexicalization process is. Note that the lexicalized forms are not simple lexical forms, characterized by an arbitrary relation between sound and meaning. Rather, the term 'lexicalization' implies that lexicalized applied verbs are frozen forms which took part in a productive process at some time in the past. This means that one can sensibly ask which productive process has been lexicalized. The problem for an analysis of applicative constructions as valency-changing operation is that it predicts that applied verbs should be lexicalized with their appropriate increased valency. But this prediction is not, at least on the face of it, borne out by the data presented here. The problem for valency-changing analyses of applied verbs is thus not that lexicalized applied verbs are not productive, but rather that it is not the postulated productive process which appears to have been lexicalized. Proponents of the valency-changing analysis are thus forced either to ignore lexicalized applied verbs or to assume that in the process of lexicalization the main characteristic of the productive process, the additional object, somehow disappeared.

Here I try to develop an alternative hypothesis, which builds on the notion of concept formation. In particular, I explore the idea that applied verbs encode an explicit instruction for concept formation. Under this hypothesis, applied verbs instruct the hearer to construct a concept which is sufficiently different from the concept that would be constructed from the base form in the given circumstances. This does not mean that two concepts are constructed and then compared. Rather, this is a process of strengthening the concept addressed by the base verb plus the instruction that more contextual implications have to be derived. Note that both the base form and the applied form are lexically accessed, so that the set of contextual assumptions addressed by the base form is tentatively entertained also when the applied form is scanned—which, however, adds the instruction to construct a different, 'stronger' concept.

From this perspective, the idiomatic sense of the applied form *valia* can be characterized as follows. Consider again the contrast between the base form and the idiomatic applied form:

(19a) *Juma   a-me-va-a   nguo   za   rasmi*
       Juma   SCDI-PERF-wear-FV   clothes GEN   official
       'Juma was wearing official clothes'

(19b) *Juma   a-me-val-i-a   nguo   za   rasmi*
       Juma   SCDI-PERF-wear-APPL-FV   clothes GEN   official
       'Juma was dressed up (wearing official clothes)'

The applied form in (19b) does not differ in valency from the base form in (19a). Rather, two different concepts are addressed. The difference between (19a) and (19b) can be described as follows: in (19a) the hearer is instructed to entertain the proposition that Juma was wearing official clothes, while in (19b) the hearer is instructed not only to entertain the proposition that Juma was wearing official clothes, but to derive additional contextual effects—for example, that he had dressed with great care and effort, possibly had spent a lot of money on the clothes, or maybe had a reason for wearing the particular official clothes he was wearing. Note that typical uses of the lexicalized applied form *valia* have an object which denotes special clothes, rather than everyday garments, which facilitate the derivation of inferences such as those mentioned above. The difference between (19a) and (19b) is that in (19b) a stronger concept is addressed.

On the assumption that the characterization of the difference between (19a) and (19b) offered here is correct, it appears that the lexicalized form *valia* encodes a particular process of conceptual enrichment vis-à-vis the base form. This means for lexicalized uses of *valia* that before its idiomatic sense was lexicalized, the form encoded an instruction for concept formation. In the following section, I develop the hypothesis that this is also the function of applied verbs in present-day Swahili.

6.5 APPLIED VERBS AS AN INSTRUCTION FOR CONCEPT FORMATION

In this section, I develop the ideas introduced in the preceding section, and formulate the hypothesis that applied verbs instruct the hearer to strengthen the concept addressed by the base verb so as to derive more inferential effects. I show that it is this instruction which is the basic unifying meaning of applied verbs, and that the syntactic facts can be regarded as following from this basic meaning. At the end of the section I propose a formalization of this hypothesis by defining a disjunctive lexical entry, which, however, reflects only partly the conceptual claim. The following section provides an evaluation of the argument presented.

6.5.1 Pragmatic licensing

In the discussion of lexicalized applied verbs above, I have noted that the lexicalized form *valia* is prototypically used with an object denoting 'special', rather than ordinary clothes, which, I have proposed, facilitates the derivation of additional contextual effects. A similar observation can be made with respect to the productive use of applied verbs. Consider the following examples:

(20a) *Salma   a-li-ka-a   kiti-ni*
       Salma   SCDI-PAST-sit-FV   chair-LOC
       'Salma was sitting on a chair'

(20b) *#Salma a-li-kal-i-a   kiti*
       Salma   SCDI-PAST-sit-APPL-FV chair
       'Salma was sitting on a chair'

(20c) *Salma   a-li-kal-i-a   kiti   cha   uvivu*
       Salma   SCDI-PAST-sit-APPL-FV chair   GEN   laziness
       'S/he was sitting on (in) a comfortable chair'

The example in (20a) shows the intransitive use of *kaa*, 'sit', with a locative marked adjunct. In (20b) the applied form *kalia* is used, which does indeed license the introduction of the unmarked object *kiti*. In the present context, however, the contrast between (20b) and (20c) is the relevant one. Both sentences are grammatical, but (20b) is, in a 'neutral' context, infelicitous, in contrast to (20c), which differs from (20b) in that a more specific object is used. In view of the hypothesis developed here, the interpretation of these data is that an object like chair gives just too little contextual information to construct, in the absence of any other contextual information, a concept which is sufficiently stronger than the one constructed from *kaa* in (20a), since there is nothing particular about sitting on a chair; it is what one normally does. In contrast, the object in (20c) provides enough information to build a strengthened concept which may license additional contextual effects such as, for example, that

Salma was sitting lazily, slumped back, eyes half-closed, that she didn't intend to get up in the near future, that she wasn't nervous. The (weakest) conclusion to be drawn from the example discussed here is not only that applied verbs introduce objects, but also that the use of applied verbs is subject to 'pragmatic licensing'; they need enough contextual information so that a strengthened concept can be constructed.

A similar example is given below:

(21a) *Bi Sauda*   *a-li-kat-a*   *mkate*   *kwa*   *kisu*
       Ms Sauda   SCDI-PAST-cut-FV   bread   with   knife
       'Ms Sauda cut bread with a knife'

(21b) #*Bi Sauda*   *a-li-kat-i-a*   *mkate*   *kisu*
       Ms Sauda   SCDI-PAST-cut-APPL-FV   bread   knife
       'Ms Sauda cut bread with a knife'

The example in (21a) shows the transitive verb *kata*, 'cut' with the object *mkate*, 'bread' and the PP *kwa kisu*, 'with a knife'. The corresponding applied verb in (21b) licenses the introduction of *kisu* as an object, but the sentence is infelicitous in a neutral context. The applied verb can be used, for example, in a situation where the bread is in some way unsuitable for being cut with knives (e.g. the sort of bread which is broken, not cut, or perhaps dried, hard bread), or when the state of the sliced bread gives reason to wonder how it was cut. In (21c), proper contextualization is, imperfectly, expressed by adding a demonstrative pronoun to the first object:

(21c) *Bi Sauda*   *a-li-kat-i-a*   *mkate*   *huo*   *kisu*
       Ms Sauda   SCDI-PAST-cut-APPL-FV b   bread   this   knife
       'Ms Sauda cut this bread with a knife'

Relevant contextual effects might include that Bi Sauda doesn't know how to cut bread properly, or that the kitchen is now full of crumbs, or that the knife is now probably blunt. Given the appropriate context, all those inferences could also be derived from (21a), but the use of the applied verb indicates that some occasion-specific contextual effects need to be derived, so that the use of the applied form in (21b) without sufficient context is inappropriate.

The examples in this section have shown that the use of applied verbs requires the derivation of additional contextual effects, i.e. that the concept constructed from the applied verb should be stronger than the concept addressed by the base verb. Since in the examples considered here the applied verb also licenses the introduction of an additional object, the examples only provide evidence for the conclusion that applied verbs require pragmatic licensing, in addition to their syntactic quality as increasing the valency of the base verb. From the perspective adopted in this study, however, this conclusion is suspicious, since it implies that syntax and pragmatics operate independently of each other. Rather, as discussed in the preceding chapter, the introduction of Ty(e) expressions contributes to the process of concept formation. It is thus natural that applied verbs license the introduction of Ty(e) expressions, since they carry an explicit requirement to construct a specific (i.e. strengthened vis-à-vis the base verb) concept, for which additional information from additional Ty(e) expressions might be provided. On the other hand, if a sufficiently strong concept can be constructed without information from additional Ty(e) expressions, they should not be licensed. In other words, applied verbs, in the analysis developed here, should license an additional Ty(e) expression, but they should not require more Ty(e) expressions than (independently) required by the base verb. That is, applied verbs may change the valency of the base verb, but they do not do so necessarily.

6.5.2 Concept formation and valency

In order to show that the hypothesis developed in the last section is plausible, it needs to be shown that productive, non-lexicalized applied verbs do not necessarily require one more object than the corresponding base verb, in particular in contexts where a sufficiently strengthened concept is constructed without the licensing of an additional Ty(e) expression. In this section, I discuss examples which show that this prediction is borne out.[11]

Consider the following data:

(22a)   *Bi Asha a-li-andik-a*   *barua*   *kwa*   *kalamu*
        Bi Asha SCDI-PAST-write-FV   letter   with   pen
        'S/he wrote a letter with a pen'

(22b)   *Bi Asha a-li-andik-i-a*   *barua*   *kalamu*
        Bi Asha SCDI-PAST-write-APPL-FV   letter   pen
        'S/he wrote (in) a letter with a pen'

(22c)   *Bi Asha a-li-andik-i-a*   *barua*   *kwa*   *kalamu*
        Bi Asha SCDI-PAST-write-APPL-FV   letter   with   pen
        'S/he wrote (in) a letter with a pen'

---

[11] Here and in the following examples, the description of inferential effects is rather impressionistic, as reconstructed from field notes and with the provision that contextual effects are more occasion-specific than indicated here. A more formalized analysis of these and similar data with respect to contextual appropriateness remains to be done.

The example in (22a) shows the transitive base form *andika*, 'write', with one object and the PP *kwa kalamu*, 'with a pen', while (22b) shows the applied form *andikia* with two objects, so that this sentence is subject to contextual requirements, discussed below. However, the interesting example in the present context is (22c), where the applied form is used as a transitive verb, namely with one object and one PP. It is example (22c) which shows the dependency of valency changing on concept construction; under a syntactic analysis of applied verbs, (22c) should be ungrammatical. Both examples of the applied verb carry a specific instruction for concept formation; if, in a given context, the necessary additional contextual effects can be derived without the information from additional Ty(e) expressions, no change of valency is necessary, as in the case of (22c). If, on the other hand, contextual effects are derived by including information from another Ty(e) expression, its introduction is licensed, as in (22b). Thus, all examples in (22) instruct the hearer to entertain the proposition that Bi Asha wrote a letter with a pen, but (22b) and (22c) require the derivation of additional contextual effects. In (22b), these might include that Bi Asha did not use a typewriter, or that, given her handwriting, the letter is illegible, while in (22c) possible contextual effects are that the letter is personal, or that, if it is a long letter, her hand must be painful now. Thus, these examples show that, rather than syntactically encoding a change in valency, applied verbs encode an instruction for concept formation, in particular the instruction to strengthen the concept addressed so as to derive more contextual effects than licensed by the base form.

While the example discussed above involves an 'instrumental' Ty(e) expression, the following examples show the same paradigm with an optional 'locative' expression:[12]

(23a) *Bw Msa   a-li-andik-a*   *barua   meza-ni*
       Mr Msa   SCDI-PAST-write-FV   letter   table-LOC
       'Mr Msa wrote a letter on the table'

(23b) *?Bw Msa   a-li-andik-i-a*   *barua   meza*
       Mr Msa   SCDI-PAST-write-APPL-FV   letter   table
       'Mr Msa wrote a letter on the table'

(23c) *Bw Msa   a-li-andik-i-a*   *barua   meza-ni*
       Mr Msa   SCDI-PAST-write-APPL-FV   letter   table-LOC
       'Mr Msa wrote a letter on the table'

---

[12] In general, ditransitive applied verbs are better with instruments than with locatives. Of the examples shown here, (23c), i.e. the transitive use of the applied, is strongly preferred to (23b). As discussed here, the acceptability of applied form depends on an appropriate context. In addition, the locative suffix *-ni* might well be bleached, so that its syntactic function is indeterminate. For the present discussion, it is the acceptability of (23c) that is the important point.

As in the preceding example, (23a) shows the transitive use of *andika*, here with a locative-marked optional Ty(e) expression, *mezani*, 'on the table'. The applied form is used with two objects in (23b); note that the second object, *meza*, is not marked with the locative suffix *-ni*. Again, the last sentence (23c) is the most interesting one, since the applied verb is used, as the transitive verb, with one object only, and thus provides evidence against a syntactic analysis of applied verbs as encoding a change in valency. The additional inferential effects required by (23b) and (23c) can be characterized analogously to the preceding example; for (23b) they might include that the family had lunch on the floor, or that the tablecloth needs changing, while for (23c), they might include that Bw Msa did not, this time, write his dissertation on the table, or that he was writing very concentratedly, or for a long time.

Note that this analysis requires both underspecified verbs and parallel parses, since all Ty(e) expressions are integrated into the verb, and since adjuncts may precede objects:[13]

(23d)   *Bw Msa*   *a-li-andik-i-a*   *meza-ni*   *barua*
       Mr Msa   SCDI-PAST-write-APPL-FV   table-LOC   letter
       'Mr Msa wrote a letter on the table'

The example in (23d) is identical to (23c) except for the order of locative adjunct and object. In order to derive the relevant contextual effects, all Ty(e) expressions have to be considered.

As a final example of the relation between concept formation and valency, consider the following examples involving the verb *pika*, 'cook':

(24a)   *Mpishi a-li-pik-a*   *jiko-ni*
       cook   SCDI-PAST-cook-FV   kitchen-LOC
       'The cook was cooking in the kitchen'

(24b)   *Mpishi a-li-pik-i-a*   *jiko-ni*
       cook   SCDI-PAST-cook-APPL-FV   kitchen-LOC
       'The cook was cooking in the kitchen'

In (24a), *pika* is used intransitively with the locative adjunct *jiko-ni*, 'in the kitchen', in the same way as in (24b), where, however, the applied form *pikia* is used. As in the previous examples, the concept constructed from *pikia* has to be stronger than the one constructable from the base form, thus

---

[13] The word order facts are not clear, though. In addition, the corresponding example with an instrumental is unacceptable.

including for example that the cook was cooking extensively, or habitually in the kitchen.

The examples discussed in this section show that concept formation may, but does not necessarily, involve an increase in valency. The syntactic effect of applied verbs thus follows from the fact that they encode an instruction for concept strengthening. The data thus also provide evidence against proposals which analyse applied verbs as syntactically increasing the valency of the base verb. Before considering the formal aspects of the analysis developed so far, I discuss applied verbs used with human objects.

6.5.3 Human objects

The majority of examples discussed in the preceding sections involve applied verbs with locative and instrumental Ty(e) expressions, but not with benefactives. In contrast, most previous analyses have mainly been concerned with applied verbs with an additional benefactive object. This is, I believe, one of the reasons why the hypothesis developed here departs from the common assumption that applicative constructions involve an increase in valency, since it is examples like the ones discussed so far which show clearly that applied verbs encode an instruction for concept strengthening, and that syntactic facts follow from that. However, applied verbs with benefactive objects do indeed imply a change in valency, as shown by the following examples (from the beginning of this chapter, repeated here):

(25a)   *A-li-andik-a*   *barua*
        SCDI-PAST-write-FV   letter
        'S/he wrote a letter'

(25b)   *A-li-mw-andik-i-a*   *shangazi   barua*
        SCDI-PAST-OCDI-write-APPL-FV   aunt   letter
        'S/he wrote a letter to the aunt'

(25c)   **A-li-andik-i-a*   *barua   kwa   shangazi*
        SCDI-PAST-write-APPL-FV   letter   to   aunt
        'S/he wrote a letter to the aunt'

As illustrated in (25), with a benefactive object, applied verbs invariably show an increase in valency with respect to the base form.

For the present analysis the question is then why benefactives should differ from instrumentals and locatives. The first point to be raised in order to explain this fact is the objection to thematic roles, already discussed earlier in this study. I have used the notions of locative and instrumental in this chapter as useful descriptive terms, but they did not play a role in the analysis. The contrast can thus not be phrased with reference to the thematic role benefactive. Rather, I believe it is more correct to construe a contrast between human and non-human referents, so that the question really is: why do applied verbs with a human object invariably show an increase in valency? This question can be answered with two statements, further discussed below. First, human objects are invariably morphologically marked on the verb in Swahili; and second, constructing a concept which involves an additional human referent is sufficiently stronger than the concept constructable from the base verb.

Syntactic objects can be morphologically marked by means of a morpheme prefixed to the verb:

(26a) *A-li-on-a*   *kisima*
       SCDI-PAST-see-FV   well
       'S/he saw a well'

(26b) *A-li-ki-on-a*   *kisima*
       SCDI-PAST-OCD7-see-FV   well
       'S/he saw the well'

The example in (26a) shows the transitive verb *ona*, 'see', with object, but without object marker. In (26b) the object marker is found in the verbal template; *-ki-* agrees in class with the object. The characterization of the difference between (26a) and (26b) as involving definiteness, as implied in the glosses, is at best an oversimplification. However, the point here is that the object marker in examples such as in (26) is generally optional, in contrast to human objects:

(27a) *A-li-mw-on-a*   *Sudi*
       SCDI-PAST-OCCLI-see-FV   Sudi
       'S/he saw Sudi'

(27b) **Aliona Sudi*

(27c) *A-li-mw-on-a*
       SCDI-PAST-OCCLI-see-FV
       'S/he saw her/him'

As can be seen from the contrast between (27a) and (27b), with objects denoting human referents, the object marker is required.[14] As can also be seen, the object marker precedes the verb, in contrast to the full NP. Finally, object

---

[14] See Wald (1993) for an analysis of the role of human and non-human object markers in Swahili.

markers can be used as incorporated pronouns, since the sentence in (27c) is fine.[15] I assume here that the (human) object marker fulfils a requirement $?Ty(e)$, in the same way as the subject marker discussed above. I also assume that Swahili inflectional morphology does provide lexical access, in contrast to derivational morphology, i.e. that the object prefix does have a lexical entry, in contrast to the derivational suffix *-IL-*.

Thus a sample derivation of the sentence in (27a) proceeds as follows:

(28a)   *Tree for* "A-li-

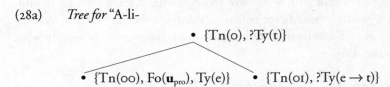

This parse stage is achieved after subject marker and tense morpheme have been scanned. The next step is the introduction of the object marker:

(28b)   *Tree for* "A-li-mw

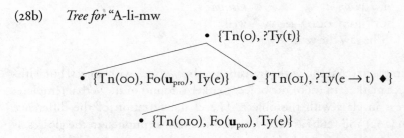

As can seen in (24b), the object marker builds a new argument node which is annotated with a pronominal formula value of $Ty(e)$, and moves the pointer back to the VP node. At this stage, the verb is scanned and introduced at an unfixed node:

(28c)   *Tree for* "A-li-mw-on-a

$$\bullet \ \{Tn(0), ?Ty(t)\}$$

$$\bullet \ \{Tn(00), Fo(\mathbf{u}_{pro}), Ty(e)\} \quad \bullet \ \{Tn(01), ?Ty(e \rightarrow t)\}$$

$$\bullet \ \{Tn(010), Fo(\mathbf{u}_{pro}), Ty(e)\} \quad \bullet \ \{Tn(011), ?Ty(e \rightarrow (e \rightarrow t))\}$$
$$\{Tn(01^*), Fo(on'), Ty(e \rightarrow (e \rightarrow (e^* \rightarrow t)))\}$$

At this stage, the derivation could end (cf. (27c), above), but there is further input, namely *Sudi*. Given the characterization of the (human) object marker

---

[15]   See again Bresnan and Mchombo (1986, 1987).

as building a Ty(e) node, the corresponding analysis of (human) NPs is that they are lexically introduced at unfixed nodes with the weak requirement that they be fixed in the tree, i.e. below Tn(o):

(28d)   *Tree for* "A-li-mw-on-a Sudi

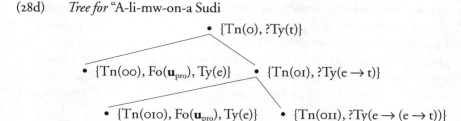

$\bullet$ {Tn(o), ?Ty(t)}

$\bullet$ {Tn(oo), Fo($\mathbf{u}_{pro}$), Ty(e)} $\bullet$ {Tn(o1), ?Ty(e $\rightarrow$ t)}

$\bullet$ {Tn(o1o), Fo($\mathbf{u}_{pro}$), Ty(e)} $\bullet$ {Tn(o11), ?Ty(e $\rightarrow$ (e $\rightarrow$ t))}

{Tn(o1*), Fo(on'), Ty(e $\rightarrow$ (e $\rightarrow$ (e* $\rightarrow$ t)))}
{Tn(o*), Fo(sudi'), Ty(e)}

The unfixed node Tn(o*) can be fixed at Tn(o1o) by Merge under the further assumption that meta-variables such as Fo($\mathbf{u}_{pro}$) are defined such that they can be replaced by conceptual formula values such as Fo(sudi').[16] With two applications of Merge, the derivation is thus completed.

The difference between human and non-human objects can thus be characterized by the fact that human objects are introduced into the derivation before the verb, whereas non-human objects are in general introduced after the verb.

From the point of view of concept formation as encoded in applied verbs, this means that at the time the instruction is registered, there is already one potentially optional Ty(e) expression in the tree; all that is required is to check whether a suitably strong concept can be constructed by including an additional human entity into the concept, which is, as I have assumed earlier, generally the case. Thus the implicational relation between applied verbs with human objects can be explained by independent syntactic facts of Swahili, without recourse to thematic roles, and while maintaining the general analysis of applied verbs as encoding an instruction for concept formation.

In the next section I turn to the question of how this hypothesis can be more formally expressed.

6.5.4 Lexical entry and sample derivations

In this section, I develop lexical entries for applied verbs and show the relevant tree transitions. However, the formalization does not fully express the

---

[16] For an analysis of pro-drop language along the lines sketched here, see Kempson et al. (1998). I do not go into full details of such an analysis here.

hypothesis developed here. Ideally, following what has been said so far, the valency of a given applied verb would in an obvious way result from the process of concept strengthening. But the way I have defined verbal under-specification and the contribution of verbs to tree building does not offer a way to state this elegantly. In addition, there is no easy way to state the process of concept formation more precisely.[17] As already indicated, I thus assume that lexical entries specify parallel parses, so that conceptual enrichment effectively results in disambiguation. On the other hand, the advantages of a lexical as opposed to a syntactic approach still hold, so that the formalization proposed in this section is still to be preferred over the syntactic analysis of *-IL-* sketched above.

The lexical entry for *andika* can thus tentatively be defined as follows:

(29)   *Lexical Entry for* andik *(first version)*

IF	?$Ty(e \rightarrow t)$	
THEN		make($\langle \downarrow * \rangle$), put($Fo(andik')$, $Ty(e \rightarrow (e \rightarrow (e^* \rightarrow t)))$),
		go($\langle \uparrow * \rangle$?$Ty(e \rightarrow t)$),
		put(?$\langle \downarrow_1 \rangle Ty(e \rightarrow (e \rightarrow t))$),
		make($\langle \downarrow_0 \rangle$), put(?$Ty(e)$)
OR		make($\langle \downarrow * \rangle$),
		put($Fo(andikIL'')$, $Ty(e \rightarrow (e \rightarrow (e \rightarrow (e^* \rightarrow t))))$),
		go($\langle \uparrow * \rangle$?$Ty(e \rightarrow t)$),
		make($\langle \downarrow_1 \rangle$),
		put(?$Ty(e \rightarrow (e \rightarrow t))$, ?$\langle \downarrow_1 \rangle Ty(e \rightarrow (e \rightarrow (e \rightarrow t)))$),
		make($\langle \downarrow_0 \rangle$) put(?$Ty(e)$)
ELSE	abort	

The entry specifies actions for the base form, which are the actions for transitive verbs. The second set of actions is relevant for applied forms with human objects. Since the argument node of the VP node has already been built and filled, the lexical actions from *andikIL'* need to build the corresponding functor node, and the argument node of that node.

With the lexical specifications given, I consider now a sample derivation of (30) (= (21b), above):

(30)   *A-li-mw-andik-i-a*   *shangazi   barua*
       SCDI-PAST-OCCLI-write-APPL-FV   aunt   letter
       'S/he wrote a letter to the aunt'

---

[17] Preliminary work towards this goal is reported in Hunter and Marten (1999).

In (30), the applied form of *andika*, 'write', is used with a human object in addition to the object of the base form. I assume that the derivation proceeds as in the preceding derivation of *alimwona* up to the introduction of the verb:

(31a)   *Tree for* "A-li-mw-

$$\bullet\ \{Tn(o),\ ?Ty(t)\}$$

$$\bullet\ \{Tn(oo),\ Fo(\mathbf{u}_{pro}),\ Ty(e)\}\quad \bullet\ \{Tn(or),\ ?Ty(e \rightarrow t)\}$$

$$\bullet\ \{Tn(oro),\ Fo(\mathbf{u}_{pro}),\ Ty(e)\}$$

At this stage, the object marker has built the argument node $Tn(oro)$. Scanning triggers the lexical statements of the applied form, and the following tree results:

(31b)   *Tree for* "A-li-mw-andik-i

$$\bullet\ \{Tn(o),\ ?Ty(t)\}$$

$$\bullet\ \{Tn(oo),\ Fo(\mathbf{u}_{pro}),\ Ty(e)\}\quad \bullet\ \{Tn(or),\ ?Ty(e \rightarrow t)\}$$

$$\bullet\ \{Tn(oro),\ Fo(\mathbf{u}_{pro}),\ Ty(e)\}\quad \bullet\ \{Tn(orr),\ ?Ty(e \rightarrow (e \rightarrow t))\}$$

$$\bullet\ \{Tn(orro),\ ?Ty(e)\ \blacklozenge\}$$

$$\{Tn(or^*),\ Fo(andikIL'),\ Ty(e \rightarrow (e \rightarrow (e \rightarrow (e^* \rightarrow t))))\}$$

The next word, *shangazi*, 'aunt', is assigned to an unfixed node, following the analysis outlined above, and the final word, *barua*, 'letter', fulfils the requirement $?Ty(e)$:

(31c)   *Tree for* "A-li-mw-andik-i-a shangazi barua

$$\bullet\ \{Tn(o),\ ?Ty(t)\}$$

$$\bullet\ \{Tn(oo),\ Fo(\mathbf{u}_{pro}),\ Ty(e)\}\quad \bullet\ \{Tn(or),\ ?Ty(e \rightarrow t)\}$$

$$\bullet\ \{Tn(oro),\ Fo(\mathbf{u}_{pro}),\ Ty(e)\}\quad \bullet\ \{Tn(orr),\ ?Ty(e \rightarrow (e \rightarrow t))\}$$

$$\bullet\ \{Tn(orro),\ Fo(barua'),\quad \bullet\ \{Tn(orrr),$$
$$Ty(e)\}\qquad\qquad ?Ty(e \rightarrow (e \rightarrow (e \rightarrow t)))\}$$

$$\{Tn(or^*),\ Fo(andikIL'),\ Ty(e \rightarrow (e \rightarrow (e \rightarrow (e^* \rightarrow t))))\}$$
$$\{Tn(o^*),\ Fo(shangazi'),\ Ty(e)\}$$

As before, two applications of Merge complete the tree.

Next, consider the example in (32) (= (18b), above):

(32) *Bi Asha a-li-andik-i-a*   *barua*   *kalamu*
      SCDI-PAST-write-APPL-FV   letter   pen
      'Bi Asha wrote a letter with a pen'

The first difference is that there is a lexically overt subject in (32). I assume that the subject is assigned to an unfixed node and merged with the pronominal formula in a similar way as lexically overt objects. With this in mind, the tree at the introduction of the verb looks as follows:

(33a) *Tree for* "Bi Asha a-li-

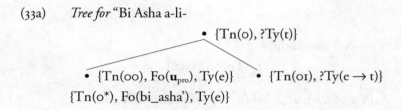

The lexical actions necessary at this step are not yet defined in the lexical entry above, but I assume that actions from the lexicon result in the following tree:

(33b) *Tree for* "Bi Asha a-li-andik-i-

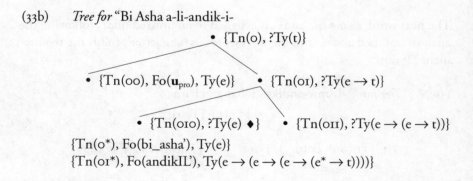

The introduction of *barua*, 'letter', results in the fulfilment of the requirement at $Tn(010)$, and by applications of Completion and Prediction in the pointer movement to the new functor node. All of these latter actions result ultimately from modal statements introduced from the lexicon. This can be seen when the lexical rules are defined below.

(33c)　*Tree for* "Bi Asha a-li-andik-i-a barua

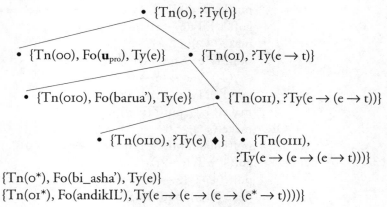

$$\{Tn(o), ?Ty(t)\}$$

$$\{Tn(oo), Fo(\mathbf{u}_{pro}), Ty(e)\} \quad \{Tn(oi), ?Ty(e \rightarrow t)\}$$

$$\{Tn(oio), Fo(barua'), Ty(e)\} \quad \{Tn(oii), ?Ty(e \rightarrow (e \rightarrow t))\}$$

$$\{Tn(oiio), ?Ty(e) \blacklozenge\} \quad \{Tn(oiii),$$
$$?Ty(e \rightarrow (e \rightarrow (e \rightarrow t)))\}$$

$$\{Tn(o^*), Fo(bi\_asha'), Ty(e)\}$$
$$\{Tn(oi^*), Fo(andikIL'), Ty(e \rightarrow (e \rightarrow (e \rightarrow (e^* \rightarrow t))))\}$$

The final word scanned is then *kalamu*, 'pen', which duly fulfils the requirement holding at Tn(oiii), so that the tree can be completed.

As a final example, consider the transitive use of *andikia*, 'write', in (34) (= (18c), above):

(34)　*Bi Asha a-li-andik-i-a*　　*barua*　*kwa*　*kalamu*
　　　 SCDI-PAST-write-APPL-FV　letter　with　pen
　　　 'S/he wrote (in) a letter with a pen'

I do not give a tree here, since the derivation parallels the derivation of a normal transitive verb. However, the form has to be represented in the lexical entry.

The final lexical entry for *andika* is given below:

(35)　*Lexical Entry for* andik *(final version)*
　　　 IF　　　?Ty(e → t)
　　　 THEN　　make($\langle\downarrow^*\rangle$),
　　　　　　　 put(Fo(andik'), Ty(e → (e → (e* → t)))),
　　　　　　　 go($\langle\uparrow^*\rangle$?Ty(e → t)),
　　　　　　　 put(?$\langle\downarrow_1\rangle$Ty(e → (e → t))),
　　　　　　　 make($\langle\downarrow_o\rangle$), put(?Ty(e))
　　　　　 OR　make($\langle\downarrow^*\rangle$),
　　　　　　　 put(Fo(andikIL''), Ty(e → (e → (e → (e* → t))))),
　　　　　　　 go($\langle\uparrow^*\rangle$?Tsy(e → t)),
　　　　　　　 make($\langle\downarrow_1\rangle$),
　　　　　　　 put(?Ty(e → (e → t)), ?$\langle\downarrow_1\rangle$Ty(e → (e → (e → t)))),
　　　　　　　 make($\langle\downarrow_o\rangle$) put(?Ty(e))

OR $make(\langle\downarrow*\rangle)$,

put($Fo(andikIL^2)$, $Ty(e \to (e \to (e \to (e^* \to t))))$),

$go(\langle\uparrow*\rangle?Ty(e \to t))$,

$make(\langle\downarrow_1\rangle)$,

put($?Ty(e \to (e \to t))$, $?\langle\downarrow_0\rangle Ty(e)$,

$?\langle\downarrow_1\rangle Ty(e \to (e \to (e \to t)))$),

$go(\langle\uparrow*\rangle?Ty(e \to t))$

$make(\langle\downarrow_0\rangle)$, put($?Ty(e)$)

OR $make(\langle\downarrow*\rangle)$,

put($Fo(andikIL^3)$, $Ty(e \to (e \to (e^* \to t)))$),

$go(\langle\uparrow*\rangle?Ty(e \to t))$,

put($?\langle\downarrow_1\rangle Ty(e \to (e \to t))$),

$make(\langle\downarrow_0\rangle)$, put($?Ty(e)$)

ELSE   abort

The final version of the lexical entry thus specifies four different sets of actions: for the transitive use of the base form, for the applied form with human object, for the applied form with two non-human objects, and for the transitive use of the applied form, in that order.[18] Note that the first and the last set of actions are identical except for the formula value.

The formulation of the lexical entry in (35) provides rules for all four readings of *andika* discussed in this section. The first sub-entry can be accessed separately, when the base form of *andika* is introduced into the tree. However, if an applied form is scanned, all four sub-entries are activated. Since the entries specify different tree continuations, four different trees are built. However, this analysis, which involves families of lexical sub-entries, runs close to reducing the role of pragmatic inferencing to disambiguation, in a context where there is in fact very little evidence that applied verbs are ambiguous. I have nevertheless chosen to present a descriptively adequate analysis of applied verbs in Swahili, rather than proposing a conceptually more interesting, but probably less explicit, analysis which relies heavily on the notion of concept formation without a clear link between this process and the formal model provided by DS.

---

[18] There is in addition an intransitive use of the base form:

(i)   *ni-li-mw-on-a*   *a-ki-andik-a*
      1.SG.-PAST-OCDI-see-FV   SCDI-SITU-write-FV
      'I saw her/him reading'

I have ignored this use in the lexical entry above, but it might easily be added.

6.6 SUMMARY AND CONCLUSION

In this chapter, I have developed the argument that applied verbs in Swahili encode an explicit instruction to construct an occasion-specific concept which is stronger than a concept constructed from the base form in that more contextual effects need to be derived. Both the process of strengthening and the derivation of additional contextual effects are quite general pragmatic processes and interact freely with contextual information. In order to show that this hypothesis is plausible, I have adduced phonological evidence indicating that the applied verb provides lexical access both to the base form and to the applied form, but not to the applicative morpheme. Further evidence was presented from lexicalized senses of applied verbs which show that applied verbs are not necessarily of a higher arity than their corresponding base form. The next step was to show that productive uses of applied verbs which do change the valency of the base verb are in need of pragmatic licensing, which provides a sufficiently rich context in which to derive additional contextual effects. The final step in the argument was to show that applied verbs can be used without any change in valency provided that an appropriately strong concept can be constructed from the context without the information provided by optional Ty(e) expressions. The evidence considered shows that the instruction for concept formation is the basic unified meaning of applied verbs, and that an increase in valency is a possible but not a necessary syntactic reflex of concept formation. I then have turned to potential counter-evidence in the form of applied verbs used with human objects, which always display a change in valency. I have argued that this fact results from independent syntactic properties of Swahili, namely that human objects are obligatorily marked by an object marker prefixed to the verb. This means that human objects precede rather than follow the verb, so that they are naturally incorporated into the process of concept formation. The introduction of a representation of a person into a constructed concept provides enough contextual effects for this process reliably to happen. Finally, I have proposed a formalization of this hypothesis in the form of a complex disjunctive lexical entry, but I have noted that the formalization does not express the generalizations captured adequately.

Several conclusions can be drawn from the discussion in this chapter. First, the analysis of the relation between concept formation and valency proposed in this study has been supported. Swahili applied verbs constitute evidence for the importance of this relation, since the process of concept formation has been shown to have an effect on complementation. Concept formation may, but does not necessarily, imply a change in complementation, although it does always imply that the eventual arity of a given concept is fixed. The formalization of this relation as underspecified type values for verbs has proved to be correct, although matters of implementation remain outstanding.

The analysis proposed in this section also contributes to the study of Swahili and Bantu languages more generally. The argument developed provides an alternative to the view that applicative constructions are sufficiently analysed as encoding a change in valency, which has been proposed on various occasions in the literature. More specifically, the analysis shows that contextual factors need to be addressed even when analysing apparently purely syntactic data. The role of pragmatic licensing, and more generally of contextual assumptions, is an area where more research is needed, and in more than one respect the hypothesis developed here needs to be tested against more and more detailed data.

Finally, the analysis shows the need to provide a more explicit link between the DS system and pragmatic processes relevant for the construction of meaning in context. The case of Swahili applied verbs illustrates clearly that the process of structure building as modelled in DS is thoroughly intertwined with the process of concept formation explored in relevance theory. Yet there is currently no explicit interface to state this relation. While, on the one hand, the model of utterance interpretation developed in DS appears too structural to incorporate non-demonstrative inference, the analysis of concept formation in relevance theory is not structural enough to be incorporated into DS trees. From the point of view adopted here, it would be useful if the relation could be stated more explicitly. However, this has to remain a goal for future work.

7

Conclusion

7.1 SUMMARY

In this study I have argued that subcategorization information provided by verbs is underspecified. Verbs may specify how many Ty(e) expressions, including NPs and PPs, they minimally require in order to derive an expression of Ty(t), but they are in general flexible with respect to how many Ty(e) expressions can optionally be introduced into the verb phrase. This view is supported by linguistic evidence which shows that arguments and adjuncts behave alike in a number of respects, where the only difference between the two is the obligatoriness of arguments as opposed to the optionality of adjuncts. Of two possible ways to analyse adjuncts, I have argued that an analysis of VP adjunction which treats the adjunct as a functor taking the verb or the VP as argument does not adequately explain this fact, and that furthermore an analysis involving an Adjunction rule implies the restructuring of trees, which goes against the overall aim of the DS system to model utterance interpretation on-line. In contrast, an analysis which assumes that verbs are lexically underspecified, and thus permits adjuncts to be integrated into the VP under the same structural relation as arguments, provides an incremental parse of adjuncts which accounts for the parallelism of arguments and adjuncts, as well as for the optionality of adjuncts. The formal statement of verbal underspecification involves the underspecified type value e^*, which is defined as follows:

(1) Definition of $(e^* \rightarrow t)$
     $(e^* \rightarrow t)$ = def $\{(t) \vee (e \rightarrow (e^* \rightarrow t))\}$

The definition states that verbs with such a type can be used with any number of Ty(e) expressions, since the underspecified type can be recursively resolved by introducing additional Ty(e) expressions. The introduction of the notion of underspecification into the type specification of verbs is motivated also by the fact that structural underspecification is already employed in the DS system for values of the tree node and formula predicates. The definition of e* for verbs thus extends the notion of underspecification, which is used in the DS system mainly for the analysis of preposed constituents, to the analysis of predicate–argument structure. The e* analysis entails that PPs are Ty(e) expressions, and that the function of prepositions is mainly to license the building of additional Ty(e) nodes. In English, underspecified verbs are also unfixed, since they are lexically projected onto an unfixed node. However, the combination of these two types of underspecification is not a necessary feature of the analysis, since in verb-final structures, underspecified verbs are projected onto fixed nodes.

The analysis of adjunction as involving verbal underspecification is motivated empirically by the parallelism of arguments and adjuncts in several respects, and from considerations of the overall DS model. However, as shown in Chapter 5, there is no clear analysis of the interpretation of underspecified verbs in the traditional semantic sense. This results from the fact that underspecified verbs are essentially dynamic, and only interpreted in context, with recourse to the utterance situation, while model-theoretic approaches to verb meaning assume that predicates are static, have a fixed arity, and are diectly related to natural language verbs, without the mediation of intermediate representational structure. After considering two possible semantic analyses of underspecified verbs, I have turned to providing a novel, pragmatic approach to verb meaning in context with recourse to the notion of enrichment developed in relevance theory.

The relevance-theoretic notions of pragmatic enrichment and concept formation help to show that natural language expressions quite generally do not address fully specified concepts, i.e. expressions of the language of thought, but rather provide an instruction for the hearer to construct an occasion-specific ad hoc concept which serves to derive particular occasion-specific inferential effects. Concepts addressed by verbs, in particular, are interpreted with the aid of their complements in the verb phrase, and the propositional structure expressed by an utterance can only be established when the concept addressed by the verb has been fixed in a way appropriate to the utterance situation. Part of this process of fixing the conceptual contribution of the verb is to determine its occasion specific arity, which may vary from one use to another. The syntactic reflex of the indirect way in which lexical verbs address the concepts they eventually stand for is their underspecified subcategorization information.

Verbal underspecification can be seen as the overt encoding of the need for conceptual enrichment of verb denotations. As further shown in Chapter 5, the resolution of verbal underspecification is thoroughly pragmatic, and involves both the strengthening of the concept addressed and the selection of the hypotheses entertained as a result from the activation of concepts. The analysis thus shows how instructions from words, structural syntactic processes, and pragmatic inference interact in the process of utterance interpretation.

In Chapter 6, I have developed a novel analysis of applied verbs in Swahili as encoding an instruction for concept formation. Applied verbs have often been analysed as involving a process of valency changing, in that an additional Ty(e) expression is introduced. The argument developed in this study is that applied verbs instruct the hearer to build a stronger concept than a possible concept built from the base verb, so that additional inferential effects can be derived. This instruction for concept formation may, but does not necessarily, result in the introduction of an additional Ty(e) expression. From this perspective, the syntactic facts follow from the underlying meaning of applied verbs, which is essentially pragmatic. I have presented evidence for this view, and have argued that it provides a better explanation of the facts than syntactic analyses, which view applied verbs as only encoding a change in valency.

7.2 CONCLUDING REMARKS

This study has aimed at providing a comprehensive theory of verb phrase adjunction within a hearer-based, formal model of syntax, which takes account of the facts that adjunction processes are free and general, and that arguments and adjuncts often behave alike, and which at the same time provides a model of adjunction in which structures are built incrementally, on-line. In order to make the overall perspective explicit, the argument developed is embedded in a model of utterance interpretation according to which utterance interpretation involves different aspects of cognitive activity: the ability to relate a physical signal to lexical units, the ability to build structured representations from lexical instructions, and the ability to construct mental concepts from the information provided by words and contextual assumptions. One of the central conclusions of this study is that these different abilities interact freely, and that for the analysis of verb phrase interpretation, all aspects have to be taken into account. More specifically, the analysis of verb phrase adjunction and the interpretation of underspecified verbs shows that there is no well-defined level of an interface between syntactic and pragmatic processes. The two processes can be distinguished, since the former are either computational rules or lexical instructions, which interact to result in increasingly complex structures representing the semantic content of the utterance they are modelling, while the latter involve non-demonstrative inference and access to world and contextual knowledge. However, the eventual tree representation of the proposition communicated by the utterance does not result from syntactic knowledge alone. In order to derive a well-formed output tree with all requirements fulfilled and all underspecification resolved, i.e. in order to complete the syntactic part of the parse, the hearer has to engage in relevance-based reasoning about the appropriate construction of the concept meant to be communicated by the speaker, which, as a process of enrichment, involves pragmatic knowledge. The interpretation of underspecified verbs thus shows exactly how these two types of knowledge interact, and in that sense provide a sketch of the syntax–pragmatics interface.

A number of comments are in order regarding the implementation of the basic ideas presented here. The most obvious way, maybe, to think about verbal underspecification is that the verb is lexically underspecified and that Ty(e) expressions are just added if and when pragmatically licensed. However, the approach taken here is more cautious, putting more weight of the explanation on the syntax, in that prepositions are lexically defined as building Ty(e) nodes and no general rules for introduction of Ty(e) expressions are available. The more daring alternative would be, of course, to allow a general introduction rule and invoke pragmatic infelicity for examples such as (2):

(2)   John met Bill Sally Donovan.

Under the current proposal, the string in (2) is ungrammatical because the NPs *Sally* and *Donovan* cannot be introduced into the parse. While this alternative is less radical, it has the advantage that it gives a structural reason for the ungrammaticality of strings like (2), and it also provides an analysis of prepositions—and, by extension, case marking—as licensing VP adjuncts. On the other hand, both NPs and PPs are analysed uniformly as Ty(e) expressions, and thus their parallel behaviour finds its formal reflex.

Another aspect of this implementation is that optional arguments have to be analysed as lexically licensed by the verb, as have the various complementation patterns for applied verbs in Swahili. This is, on the one hand, not problematic for a strongly lexically based framework as DS, but, on the other hand, it remains to be seen whether or not a more general formulation of optional arguments can be found. The case of applied verbs points to another area for further research, namely other processes of valency-changing operations. While for applied verbs, it turned out that their valency changing aspects could be related to a more general explanation, a similar argument has still to be developed for verb forms such as passives and causatives.

There is more room for enlarging the empirical coverage of the analysis presented. For example, little has been said about the representation of verbs taking a sentential or adjectival complement. Outside the domain of verbs, there is scope for inquiry as to whether other word forms incorporate a similar aspect of underspecification in their lexical information, in particular, of course, those words which have been argued to have argument structure, such as nouns. All these aspects remain for the time being challenges for future research.

However, the ideas developed in this study are relevant for work outside of DS, or logic-based frameworks. Head-Driven Phrase Structure Grammar (HPSG), as discussed in Chapter 5, has mechanisms for introducing adjuncts as syntactic arguments, and the idea has been discussed more generally, as pointed out in Chapter 1. Abstracting away from matters of implementation, the key issue raised in this work is the role and function of verb phrase adjuncts, and the structure of the verb phrase beyond semantically or thematically licensed nominal expressions. A full understanding of this matter, I have argued, takes us beyond the domain of syntax, and leads to questions of how language can be used to convey an unlimited set of meanings, by employing the same structural resources on different occasions. The two complementary notions of underspecification on the one hand and contextual enrichment on the other, independent of their particular detailed characterization, provide powerful theoretical tools which make the interplay between structure and context more explicit. Both notions have been explored independently of each other, and independently of verb phrase interpretation, and one result of this study is that their combination may shed new light on seemingly unrelated problems. It remains to be seen if by continuing research along these lines, more phenomena can be characterized as resulting from the particular interface explored here.

Notwithstanding issues which have to be developed further, the main points and findings of the study can then be summarized as follows. Verbs are lexically underspecified with respect to their subcategorization information. This means that Ty(e) expressions can be introduced into the verb phrase either as obligatorily required arguments or as optional adjuncts. However, every Ty(e) expression is assigned to a position with the same structural relation to the verb, so that once an expression is introduced, there is no longer any difference between adjuncts and arguments. In addition, this analysis entails that verbs are found with different complementation patterns and varying arity on different occasions of their use. The interpretation of verb phrases, which includes the resolution of their type underspecification, is subject to pragmatic enrichment, employing background and contextual knowledge. The main consequence of this analysis is that, since the eventual syntactic structure of the verb phrase can only be established with recourse to pragmatic knowledge, verb phrase underspecification provides a strong argument for the free interaction between syntax and pragmatics in the process of utterance interpretation. From this perspective, there is no syntactically defined output level which feeds into a general reasoning module; rather, hearers employ their relevance-based inferential abilities not only for the interpretation but also for the establishment of logico-syntactic structure in context. The syntactic structure of human language thus reflects in a fundamental way our cognitive propensity for communication.

References

Alsina, Alex, and Sam A. Mchombo. 1993. Object asymmetries and the Chichewa applicative construction. In *Theoretical Aspects of Bantu Grammar*, ed. Sam A. Mchombo, 17–45. Stanford, Calif.: CSLI.

Ashton, Ethel O. 1947. *Swahili Grammar*. 2nd edn. Harlow: Longman.

Baker, Mark C. 1988. *Incorporation: A Theory of Grammatical Function Changing*. Chicago: University of Chicago Press.

Barwise, Jon, and Robin Cooper. 1984. Generalized quantifiers and natural language. *Linguistics and Philosophy* 4: 159–219.

——and John Perry. 1983. *Situations and Attitudes*. Cambridge, Mass.: MIT Press.

Bennett, David C. 1975. *Spatial and Temporal Uses of English Prepositions*. London: Longman.

Berwick, Robert, and Amy Weinberg. 1984. *The Grammatical Basis of Linguistic Performance*. Cambridge, Mass.: MIT Press.

Biloa, Edmond. 1993. Clitic climbing in Bantu. In *Topics in African Linguistics*, ed. Salikoko Mufwene and Lioba Moshi, 67–77. Amsterdam: Benjamins.

Blackburn, Patrick, and Wilfried Meyer-Viol. 1994. Linguistics, logic and finite trees. *Bulletin of the Interest Group for Pure and Applied Logic* 2: 3–29.

Bouma, Gosse, Rob Malouf, and Ivan A. Sag. 1997. Satisfying constraints on extraction and adjunction. MS, Groningen and Stanford Universities.

——and Gertjan van Noord. 1994. Constraint-based categorial grammar. *Association for Computational Linguistics* 32: 147–54.

Bresnan, Joan. 1978. A realistic transformational grammar. In *Linguistic Theory and Psychological Reality*, ed. Moris Halle, Joan Bresnan, and George Miller, 1–59. Cambridge, Mass.: MIT Press.

——and Sam A. Mchombo. 1986. Grammatical and anaphoric agreement. *Proceedings of the Chicago Linguistic Society* 22: 278–97.

————1987. Topic, pronoun, and agreement in Chichewa. *Language* 63: 741–82.

——and Lioba Moshi. 1993. Object asymmetries in comparative Bantu syntax. In *Theoretical Aspects of Bantu Grammar*, ed. Sam A. Mchombo, 47–91. Stanford, Calif.: CSLI.

Brody, Michael. 1995. *Logico-Lexical Form: A Radically Minimalist Theory*. Cambridge, Mass.: MIT Press.

Butt, Miriam, and Wilhelm Geuder, eds. 1998. *The Projection of Arguments*. Stanford, Calif.: CSLI.

Campe, Petra. 1994. *Case, Semantic Roles, and Grammatical Relations: A Comprehensive Bibliography*. Amsterdam: Benjamins.

Cann, Ronnie. 1993. *Formal Semantics: An Introduction*. Cambridge: Cambridge University Press.

Carston, Robyn. 1988. Implicature, explicature and truth-theoretic semantics. In *Mental Representations*, ed. Ruth M. Kempson, 155–81. Cambridge: Cambridge University Press.

——1996. Enrichment and loosening: complementary processes in deriving the proposition expressed. In *UCL Working Papers in Linguistics* 8, 61–88. Department of Phonetics and Linguistics, University College London.

——2000. Explicature and semantics. MS, University College London.

Charette, Monik. 1991. *Conditions on Phonological Government*. Cambridge: Cambridge University Press.

Chierchia, Gennaro. 1989. Structured meanings, thematic roles and control. In *Properties, Types and Meaning*, ii: *Semantic Issues*, ed. Gennaro Chierchia, Barbara H. Partee, and Raymond Turner, 131–66. Dordrecht: Kluwer.

——1995. *Dynamics of Meaning*. Chicago: University of Chicago Press.

Chomsky, Noam. 1957. *Syntactic Structures*. The Hague: Mouton.

——1964. Current issues in linguistic theory. In *The Structure of Language: Readings in the Philosophy of Language*, ed. Jerry A. Fodor and Jerrold J. Katz, 50–118. Englewood Cliffs, NJ: Prentice-Hall.

——1981. *Lectures on Government and Binding*. Dordrecht: Foris.

——1995. *The Minimalist Program*. Cambridge, Mass.: MIT Press.

Chung, Sandra. 1982. Unbounded dependencies in Chamorro grammar. *Linguistic Inquiry* 13: 39–77.

——and Carol Georgopoulos. 1988. Agreement with gaps in Chamorro and Palauan. In *Agreement in Natural Language: Approaches, Theories, Descriptions*, ed. Michael Barlow and Charles A. Ferguson, 251–67. Stanford, Calif.: CSLI.

Clements, George N., James McCloskey, Joan Maling, and Annie Zaenen. 1983. String vacuous rule application. *Linguistic Inquiry* 14: 1–17.

Copestake, Ann. 1996. Underspecification and defaults in lexical semantic representation. Paper presented to the Max Planck Research Group, Berlin.

——Dan Flickinger, and Ivan A. Sag. 1997. Minimal Recursion Semantics: an introduction. MS, CSLI, Stanford University, Stanford, Calif.

Dowty, David R. 1979. *Word Meaning and Montague Grammar*. Dordrecht: Reidel.

Fillmore, Charles. 1988. The mechanisms of 'Construction Grammar'. *Proceedings of the Berkeley Linguistic Society* 14: 35–55.

——1994. Under the circumstances (place, time, manner, etc.). *Proceedings of the Berkeley Linguistic Society* 20: 158–72.

Fodor, Janet D. 1995. Comprehending sentence structure. In *An Invitation to Cognitive*

Science, i: *Language*, ed. Lila R. Gleitman and Mark Liberman, 209–46. Cambridge, Mass.: MIT Press.

Fodor, Jerry A. 1973. Three reasons for not deriving 'kill' from 'cause to die'. *Linguistic Inquiry* 1: 429–38.

—— 1975. *The Language of Thought*. New York: Crowell.

—— 1981. *Representations*. Cambridge, Mass.: MIT Press.

—— 1998. *Concepts: Where Cognitive Science Went Wrong*. Oxford: Clarendon.

Frazier, Lynn, and Janet D. Fodor. 1978. The sausage machine: a new two stage parsing model. *Cognition* 6: 291–325.

Gawron, Jean Mark. 1985. A parsimonious semantics for prepositions and CAUSE. *Proceedings of the Chicago Linguistic Society* 21, 2: 32–47.

Georgopoulos, Carol. 1985. Variables in Palauan syntax. *Natural Language and Linguistic Theory* 3: 59–94.

Gorrell, Paul. 1995. *Syntax and Parsing*. Cambridge: Cambridge University Press.

Grice, Paul. 1967. *Logic and Conversation*. William James Lectures, repr. in Grice (1989: 1–143).

—— 1989. *Studies in the Way of Words*. Cambridge, Mass.: Harvard University Press.

Grimshaw, Jane. 1990. *Argument Structure*. Cambridge, Mass.: MIT Press.

Groenendijk, Jeroen, and Martin Stokhof. 1991. Dynamic Predicate Logic. *Linguistics and Philosophy* 14: 39–100.

Heine, Bernd, Ulrike Claudi, and Friedrike Hünnemeyer. 1991. *Grammaticalization: A Conceptual Framework*. Chicago: University of Chicago Press.

Hinrichs, Erhard, and Tsuneko Nakazawa. 1994. Linearizing AUXs in German verbal complexes. In *German in Head-Driven Phrase Structure Grammar*, ed. John Nerbonne, Klaus Netter, and Carl Pollard, 11–37. Stanford, Calif.: CSLI.

Hopper, Paul J., and Elizabeth Closs Traugott. 1993. *Grammaticalization*. Cambridge: Cambridge University Press.

Horrocks, Geoffrey. 1987. *Generative Grammar*. London: Longman.

Hukari, Thomas E., and Robert D. Levine. 1994. Adjunct extraction. In *Proceedings of the Twelfth West Coast Conference on Formal Linguistics*, 283–98. Stanford, Calif.: CSLI.

—— —— 1995. Adjunct extraction. *Journal of Linguistics* 31: 195–226.

Hunter, Anthony, and Lutz Marten. 1999. Context sensitive reasoning with lexical and world knowledge. In *SOAS Working Papers in Linguistics and Phonetics* 9, 373–86. Department of Linguistics, School of Oriental and African Studies, London.

Jackendoff, Ray. 1983. *Semantics and Cognition*. Cambridge, Mass.: MIT Press.

—— 1998. *The Architecture of the Language Faculty*. Cambridge, Mass.: MIT Press.

Kamp, Hans, and Uwe Reyle. 1993. *From Discourse to Logic*. Dordrecht: Kluwer.

Kay, Paul. 1995. Construction Grammar. In *Handbook of Pragmatics*, ed. Jef Verscheuren, Jan-Ola Ostman, and Jan Blommaert. Amsterdam: Benjamins. Repr. in Kay, *Words and the Grammar of Context*, 123–31. Stanford, Calif.: CSLI, 1997.

Kaye, Jonathan. 1989. *Phonology: A Cognitive View*. Hillsdale, NJ: Erlbaum.

—— 1995. Derivations and interfaces. In *Frontiers of Phonology: Atoms, Structures, Derivations*, ed. Jacques Durand and Francis Katamba, 289–332. Harlow: Longman.

Kaye, Jonathan, Jean Lowenstamm, and Jean-Roger Vergnaud. 1990. Constituent structure and government in phonology. *Phonology* 7: 193–231.

Kayne, Richard, and Jean-Yves Pollock. 1978. Stylistic inversion, successive cyclicity, and Move NP. *Linguistic Inquiry* 9: 595–621.

Keenan, Edward L. 1996. The semantics of determiners. In *The Handbook of Contemporary Semantic Theory*, ed. Shalom Lappin, 41–63. Oxford: Blackwell.

—— and Leonard M. Faltz. 1985. *Boolean Semantics for Natural Language*. Dordrecht: Reidel.

Kempson, Ruth M. 1988. The relation between language, mind, and reality. In *Mental Representations*, ed. Ruth M. Kempson, 3–25. Cambridge: Cambridge University Press.

——1996. Semantics, pragmatics, and natural language interpretation. In *The Handbook of Contemporary Semantic Theory*, ed. Shalom Lappin, 561–98. Oxford: Blackwell.

—— Malcolm Edwards, and Wilfried Meyer-Viol. 1998. Resumptive pronouns in English and Arabic. In *SOAS Working Papers in Linguistics and Phonetics* 8, 35–57. Department of Linguistics, School of Oriental and African Studies, London.

—— Wilfried Meyer-Viol, and Dov Gabbay. 1999. VP ellipsis: toward a dynamic, structural account. In *Fragments: Studies in Ellipsis and Gapping*, ed. Shalom Lappin and Elabbas Benmamoun, 227–89. Oxford: Oxford University Press.

——————2001. *Dynamic Syntax: The Flow of Language Understanding*. Oxford: Blackwell.

Kibble, Rodger, Lutz Marten, and Wilfried Meyer-Viol. 1997. Incremental interpretation using a tree description language. In *Proceedings of the 11th Amsterdam Colloquium*, 199–204. Institute for Logic, Language and Computation, University of Amsterdam.

Kimenyi, Alexandre. 1980. *A Relational Grammar of Kinyarwanda*. Berkeley, Calif.: University of California Press.

Ladusaw, William A., and David R. Dowty. 1988. Toward a nongrammatical account of thematic roles. In *Syntax and Semantics* 21: *Thematic Relations*, ed. Wendy Wilkins, 61–73. New York: Academic Press.

Lakoff, George. 1971. On generative semantics. In *Semantics: An Interdisciplinary Reader in Philosophy, Linguistics and Psychology*, ed. Danny D. Steinberg and Leon A. Jakobovitz, 232–96. Cambridge: Cambridge University Press.

Lambek, Joachim. 1958. The mathematics of sentence structure. *American Mathematical Monthly* 65: 154–70.

Lappin, Shalom, and David E. Johnson. 1999. *Local Constraints vs. Economy*. Stanford, Calif.: CSLI.

Levine, Robert D., and Georgia M. Green, eds. 1999. *Studies in Contemporary Phrase Structure Grammar*. Cambridge: Cambridge University Press.

Lyons, John. 1977. *Semantics*. 2 vols. Cambridge: Cambridge University Press.

Mabugu, Patricia, and Ronnie Cann. 2001. Polysemy and the applicative verb construction in Chishona. Paper presented at the 32nd Annual Conference of African Linguistics, University of California, Berkeley.

McCloskey, James. 1979. *Transformational Syntax and Model Theoretic Semantics: A Case Study in Modern Irish*. Dordrecht: Reidel.

McConnell-Ginet, Sally. 1982. Adverbs and logical form: a linguistically realistic theory. *Language* 58: 144–84.

McGee Wood, Mary. 1993. *Categorial Grammars*. London: Routledge.

Maling, Joan. 1993. On nominative and accusative: the hierarchical assignment of grammatical case in Finnish. In *Case and Other Functional Categories in Finnish Syntax*, ed. Anders Holmberg and Urpo Nikanne, 51–76. Dordrecht: Mouton de Gruyter.

Marantz, Alec. 1993. Implications of asymmetries in double object constructions. In *Theoretical Aspects of Bantu Grammar*, ed. Sam A. Mchombo, 113–50. Stanford, Calif.: CSLI.

Marten, Lutz. 1997. Licensing constraints for Swahili vowel harmony. In *Proceedings of the Sixth Manchester Postgraduate Linguistics Conference*, 239–55. Department of Linguistics, University of Manchester.

Matsinhe, Sozinho. 1994. The status of verbal affixes in Bantu languages with special reference to Tsonga: problems and possibilities. *South African Journal of African Languages* 14: 163–76.

Montague, Richard. 1974. *Formal Philosophy: Selected Papers of Richard Montague*, ed. Richmond Thomason. New Haven, Conn.: Yale University Press.

Morrill, Glyn V. 1994. *Type Logical Grammar*. Dordrecht: Kluwer.

Muhammad Said Abdulla. 1976. *Mwana wa Yungi Hulewa*. Dar es Salaam: East African Publishing House.

Nakamura, Masanori. 1997. Object extraction in Bantu applicatives: some implications for minimalism. *Linguistic Inquiry* 28: 252–80.

Perrett, Denise. 2000. The Dynamics of Tense Construal in Hadiyya. Doctoral dissertation, School of Oriental and African Studies, University of London.

Pollard, Carl, and Ivan A. Sag. 1994. *Head-Driven Phrase Structure Grammar*. Chicago: Chicago University Press.

Port, Robert F. 1981. The applied suffix in Swahili. *Studies in African Linguistics* 12: 71–82.

Pratt, Ian, and Nissim Francez. 1997. *Temporal Prepositions*. Technical Report UMCS 97-4-2, Department of Computer Science, University of Manchester.

Przepiórkowski, Adam. 1999. On case assignment and 'adjuncts as complements'. In *Lexical and Constructional Aspects of Linguistic Explanation*, ed. Gert Webelhuth, Jean-Pierre König, and Andreas Kathol, 231–45. Stanford, Calif.: CSLI.

Rapold, Christian. 1997. The applicative construction in Lingala. MS, Rijksuniversiteit Leiden.

Ravin, Yael. 1990. *Lexical Semantics without Thematic Roles*. Oxford: Clarendon.

Sacleux, P. Ch. 1909. *Grammaire swahili*. Paris: Procure des PP. du Saint-Esprit.

Sag, Ivan A. 1998. Criteria for evaluating analyses of unbounded dependencies. Paper presented at the School of Oriental and African Studies, London.

——and Thomas Wasow. 1999. *Syntactic Theory: A Formal Introduction*. Stanford, Calif.: CSLI.

Samsom, Ridder, and Thilo C. Schadeberg. 1994. Kiinimacho cha mahali: kiambishi tamati cha mahali -ni. *Afrikanistische Arbeitspapiere* 37: 127–38.

Schadeberg, Thilo C. 1992. *A Sketch of Swahili Morphology.* 3rd edn. Cologne: Köppe.

Shibatani, Masayoshi. 1996. Applicatives and benefactives: a cognitive account. In *Grammatical Constructions: Their Form and Meaning,* ed. Masayoshi Shibatani and Sandra A. Thompson, 157–94. Oxford: Clarendon.

Sperber, Dan, and Deirdre Wilson. 1986. *Relevance: Communication and Cognition.* Oxford: Blackwell.

————1995. *Relevance: Communication and Cognition.* 2nd edn. Oxford: Blackwell.

————1997. The mapping between the mental and the public lexicon. In *UCL Working Papers in Linguistics* 9, 107–25. Department of Phonetics and Linguistics, University College London.

Swinburne, David. 1999. ⟨LINK⟩ and the Dynamics of Utterance Interpretation. Doctoral dissertation, School of Oriental and African Studies, University of London.

Tenny, Carol L. 1994. *Aspectual Roles and the Syntax–Semantics Interface.* Dordrecht: Kluwer.

Tomaselli, Allessandra. 1997. Commentary on part 1: aspect, argument structure and case selection. In *Parameters of Morphosyntactic Change,* ed. Ans van Kemenade and Nigel Vincent, 134–46. Cambridge: Cambridge University Press.

Wald, Benji. 1993. Longterm evolution of the syntax of discourse and the Swahili person markers. In *Historical Linguistics 1991: Papers from the 10th ICHL, Amsterdam,* ed. Jaap van Marle, 325–41. Amsterdam: Benjamins.

Wilson, Deirdre, and Dan Sperber. 1999. Truthfulness and relevance. MS, University College London.

Zaenen, Annie. 1983. On syntactic binding. *Linguistic Inquiry* 14: 469–504.

Zwarts, Joost. 1997. Vectors as relative positions: a compositional semantics for modified PPs. *Journal of Semantics* 14: 57–86.

Index